KT-476-127

Jean Vanier and l'Arche

A Communion of Love

KATHRYN SPINK

Darton, Longman and Todd
London

First published in 1990 by
Darton, Longman and Todd Ltd
89 Lillie Road, London SW6 1UD

© 1990 Kathryn Spink

British Library Cataloguing in Publication Data

Spink, Kathryn, *1953–*
    Jean Vanier and l'Arche: a communion of love
    1. Residential institutions for mentally handicapped
persons: Arches (Association)
    I. Title
    362.385

ISBN 0–232–51801–7

Phototypeset by Input Typesetting Ltd, London SW19 8DR
Printed and bound in Great Britain by
Courier International Ltd, Tiptree, Essex

Jean Vanier and l'Arche

WINCHESTER SCHOOL OF MISSION

04164

C44/05

Contents

List of Illustrations   vii

Acknowledgements   ix

1 The Voice of the Poor   1

2 The Initial Grace   10

3 The Hidden Grounding   20

4 A School of the Heart   38

5 Sharing the Word   58

6 Between Two Worlds   79

7 Towards Communion   98

8 Servants of Communion   124

9 More Earthy and More Heavenly   137

10 Part of our Broken World   155

11 Opening the Door to Lazarus   181

Books by Jean Vanier   203

Addresses of l'Arche Communities   205

Illustrations

(between pages 86 and 87)

Jean Vanier in naval uniform

Père Thomas Philippe

Jean and members of his family

Jean with Raphael, one of the first members of the Trosly
community

Père Thomas gives the Host to a member of the community
in Trosly

The founder members of the Daybreak community in
Canada

Sharing a meal in the Erie community, USA

Robert Larouche (top) and Nadine Tokar with the
community in Tegucigalpa, Honduras

Praying together in Ouagadougou, Burkina Faso

Bill and Jan from the community in Kent, England

Faith and Light: the pilgrimage to Rome, 1975

Robert Runcie, Archbishop of Canterbury, during an
ecumenical retreat in 1983

Thierry and Paul at the Lambeth workshop in South London

Kashi from Asha Niketan, Calcutta

Michelle from the Lambeth community

Jean, Père Thomas and Pope John Paul II

Celebrating at 'La Forestière', Trosly

Acknowledgements

It would be impossible to do justice individually to all those people who have contributed directly and indirectly to the writing of this book, but I would like to express my particular thanks to the l'Arche communities in Trosly-Breuil, Toronto, Erie, Tegucigalpa, Choluteca and London for the warmth of their welcome and the generosity with which they gave of their time and their experience. I would also like to acknowledge a special debt of gratitude to the purveyor of cups of tea and a multitude of other things, whose desire to remain hidden I have respected but whose support kept me 'hanging on in there'.

November 1989   *Kathryn Spink*

1

The Voice of the Poor

On the edge of the Compiègne forest just north of Paris lies the often cloud-hung village of Trosly-Breuil. It was here that in 1964 l'Arche began. Jean Vanier had bought one of the unassuming stone-built houses which line the narrow, winding streets and, in response to a call which he could scarcely have defined but which he knew to be 'irreversible', invited three mentally handicapped people to leave the institution where they had been living and to make their home with him. It was an invitation issued, by Jean Vanier's own admission, naively but unquestioningly in the knowledge that 'Jesus wanted it'. It was also one which would enable him and the community which would grow out of it to touch in a special way upon the mystery of the handicapped person; for what began as an act of compassion toward the suffering that had moved him so profoundly was to lead to the very concrete discovery of the riches of the biblically poor.

The desire simply to live together, not as 'educators' and handicapped people, but as sharers in a life of communion was to highlight by contrast the great gulf that is more often fixed in our divided world between the strong and the weak, the powerful and the vulnerable, the clever and the handicapped. There are, Jean Vanier has not hesitated to point out, the poor, the oppressed – those who feel themselves useless and without power, who have no voice in human affairs yet who cry out for recognition and appreciation – and there are the rich, the powerful and the effective, whose tendency is to crush others apparently less capable than themselves. They have work, possessions, status, but often they lack the essential: the capacity to love, to live relationships of communion without fear, without hiding behind the many trappings of success, power and defence. Between these two worlds there exist terrible tensions and barriers that are founded upon fear. The rich regard the poor and weak as problems and seek to resolve those problems according to their own vision, theories and personal plans, refusing to enter into a dialogue of trust with those who are oppressed and in distress. They will not listen to them. Sometimes they even want to prevent their very existence. To them it is inconceivable that the despised and the pitied might hold in the depths of their hearts the solutions to the very problems they allegedly represent. In each one of us there is a strong resistance to change and that, Jean Vanier asserts, is why the rich can not enter into dialogue with the poor: for such a dialogue inevitably calls upon the rich man to change. The cry of the person in need inconveniences those who are comfortable and satisfied with themselves and their lot. The anguish of people with a handicap reveals our own anguish, their shadows are our shadows, and so we turn away.

Yet the small community in Trosly-Breuil would soon increase in number, not only of handicapped people but also of 'assistants' who were prepared not to turn away but who sought instead to share their lives. Twenty-five years of 'living together' with mentally handicapped people, with those afflicted with a very particular form of poverty, have served to bring home to Jean Vanier and the many others who have become members of the more than eighty-five l'Arche communities now scattered across the continents, the fact that God has chosen the weak, the 'crazy' and the despised of our world to confound the strong, the clever and the respected.

The communities which grew so rapidly out of the small house in Trosly-Breuil and the desire to create homes – not institutions but 'foyers' with all the associations of family life gathered about a shared hearth that the French word conveys – where handicapped people and assistants could experience together all the joy and the difficulties of a community life inspired by the Beatitudes, would inevitably vary in their outer expression. Some four hundred people now live together in the original community made up of more than twenty houses scattered throughout Trosly-Breuil and its neighbouring villages: more recent communities may be composed of no more than six people. As in France, l'Arche in India, North America, Britain, the Ivory Coast, Honduras, Burkina Faso, Australia and in the many other countries where it now exists seeks to integrate with and so express itself in terms of the local culture. Some communities are set in the heart of capital cities; others in rural areas. Some have their own workshops; in others the handicapped people go out to work elsewhere. Some welcome severely mentally handicapped people; some welcome children; some have not felt called or are not equipped to do so.

Religious belief is not an obligatory part of life in l'Arche. L'Arche in Trosly-Breuil has an oratory and two chapels, one of which is a converted barn the stone walls and beams of which are still exposed. Chapels in communities elsewhere may be even simpler and more improvised: a tiny room with rush matting on the floor, a candle, an icon, a tabernacle where the blessed sacrament is reserved, an unoccupied bedroom or the corner of an attic. Some do not set aside a specific place in which to pray. In countries where the local people are not Christian the communities are not necessarily Christian. Where people are Christian they may be of different denominations. There are also those in l'Arche who would not lay claim to any particular belief, though most assistants who stay for any length of time, because of the very quality of relationship the life entails, acknowledge the call to some form of prayer. So it is that attempts at tidy definition tend to crumble, but at the heart of every community, be it in London or Haiti, the aim to constitute a family in which handicapped people can find security and peace in which to grow remains the same, as does the spirit – that of a special sensitivity to both the needs and the prophetic role of the poor. Furthermore, it would be difficult to refute that in that sensitivity and in its own poverty, whatever form that poverty might take, each community is close to God, hidden in some way in the heart of God.

L'Arche is lived on many levels, on a level so inexpressible that even to attempt to put the experience into words is, as one assistant put it, in some way to set fire to it; but on a level also which is very tangible and physical. Those levels are intimately linked. There is a stillness about the chapels and the oratory at Trosly which is yet not separated from the reality of brokenness that is so much a part of our world. During the daily Mass which is celebrated there, there is somehow a profound message in the relationship between the broken bread upon the altar and the broken but life-giving presence of the handicapped people who may shuffle their feet, comb their hair or yawn uninhibitedly, but whom no one could judge to be irreverent.

L'Arche, as distinct from many other communities, is founded not on the word but in a very particular way on the body. Mentally handicapped people tend to be people of few words but people for whom the body with its pains, its pleasures and its capacity for expression and relationship features prominently. 'God reveals himself to people first of all by the word which is very close to the spirit, filled with light and touches us in our intelligence and our hearts,' claims Jean Vanier. 'And then there is the revelation of God through the body which seems to be the opposite to the creativity, the power, the beauty, and the wisdom of the word: the littleness of the body, the fragility of the body, the ugliness, the dirt, the smell as it dies. With our people here there are little words and a lot of body.' In some extraordinary way perhaps it is the mysterious relationship between the two that lies at the heart of l'Arche and perhaps it is a mystery which can only really be understood in that experience of 'living with'.

It is not difficult to appreciate that to recognise the presence of Jesus in the poor and to talk about it is one thing; actually to be confronted by the poor man salivating, sometimes violent, uninhibited, intuitive, disconcertingly discerning and craving real attention is quite another. As one l'Arche assistant put it, 'You have to find out what it is to share a bathroom with these people'. For me one of the most memorable experiences of l'Arche was that of watching two young men eating a meal together. They were both in their early twenties, both dark-haired and bearded, but one was bright-eyed and in this world's terms good-looking. The other, with wasted limbs and a body that did not hide his suffering, was physically a distorted reflection of the first. Severely handicapped, he could not so much as swallow without a guiding hand to close his mouth and tilt his head backwards. Throughout that long and difficult meal what passed between those two was very much more than the small spoonfuls of food so gently delivered and so silently but appreciatively received. For me it brought a new and potent actuality to the word 'communion'.

Nevertheless, before a humanly speaking deformed face can be seen as extraordinarily beautiful there are often many barriers to be surmounted, there is a great deal of 'living with' to be done; for there is a rich man in all of us who will find every possible excuse not to go to the wedding feast. The poor man cries out for love, but to commit oneself to him means in some way dying to oneself: to one's comforts, wealth, leisure, reputation, success, and possibly even one's family and friends. It means becoming poor oneself, not externally but internally. It means feeling oneself poor in the presence of the poor and so being 'reduced', in the deepest meaning of the word, to prayer. It is Jean Vanier's belief that God has a way of calling people to go forward into the double world of the poverty outside and the poverty inside: 'For me the macrocosm and the microcosm are intimately connected, so that the whole vision of Jesus is the gradual discovery that the poor are not people whom we have to change from our pedestal and make them like us but people from whom we can drink. That means that the outside poverty and the inside poverty is the same reality to drink from. The presence of God is in our own littleness and poverty, in our need for love and recognition.' So it is that the parable of Lazarus and the rich man, between whom there is a great gulf fixed (Luke 16: 20–31), applies to both the outer and the inner world. 'There is a gulf between the rich and the poor and there is the gulf of our own consciousness and everything in life is the passage through that divide.'

My own invitation to go to l'Arche in Trosly-Breuil was accepted with what I would subsequently discover was a far from uncommon sense of being mysteriously drawn and yet afraid. I had little previous experience of mentally handicapped people and was acutely aware of my own overdeveloped if unwarranted sensibilities when it came to such superficial considerations as table manners and hygiene. I was given a gentle introduction. At table in the various houses to which I was invited I was tactfully placed next to people who were not too likely to deposit their food in my lap, who were frequently gifted with the ability to allay all my apprehension with the most beguiling of smiles, who accepted my silences and who, because of their own speech difficulties, would listen with exceptional patience and understanding to my halting French. I had gone there to gather material for a biography of the founder of the l'Arche communities, but having experienced something of the life he shared, watched the horseplay and the quieter moments he enjoyed with other members of

the community and sensed a little of the delicacy and the
mutuality of their shared relationship, it came as no surprise
that Jean Vanier disclaimed that title. Growth in community
meant the progression from 'my work' to 'our work' to 'God's
work'. More specifically, the role of founder belonged as much
to Père Thomas Philippe – the Dominican priest who had
been the younger man's spiritual inspiration and whose sometimes unrecognised but prayerful presence was still very much
at the heart of the community – and to the handicapped
people who despite, or rather because of their physical and
psychic wounds, were the source of the community's life. As
to the assistants, they were aware that they were there because
Jean Vanier had chosen this life but, as one of them expressed
it without in any way wishing to detract from Jean Vanier's
inspiration, 'L'Arche is not just something Jean Vanier
dreamed up. It was a grace announced to Jean by God, but
also to us all. If we are here it is because we too have
received that grace and it is a source of comfort to me that
l'Arche is something larger than all of us, something which
I do not always understand and which does not belong to us.'

Jean Vanier is a tall, slim man with a charismatic presence
and a gift for putting the word on an experience. Words came
quietly but with great fluency, delivered in a compelling voice
and often emphasised with gestures of both hands, but he
spoke most readily of spiritual truths that touched one upon
another in a network of relationships which became ever
more subtle with deepening understanding, and of others,
preferring to reveal himself only in terms of the struggle within
each one of us between the voice of the poor man calling to
smallness and the call of the rich man to strength, power,
achievement and the ladder of ambition. The only justification he could see for writing anything about him was for
people to see that in his errors, weakness and brokenness,
Jesus had used him to be part of the 'folly' of the plan of
God, that they might discover that they too were called to do a
work of love. A childlike and, to use his own word, 'nonsense'
quality about him took great delight in water fights over the
washing up, feigning exclusive possession of a box of chocolates or manoeuvring his 6ft 4ins angular frame to the front
of queues, but his distinctive laugh, ready trust and easy
manner went hand in hand with an unpressing ability to

engineer the receptivity of others to the voice of Jesus and the poor.

Sadly, it was as impossible to see all of the l'Arche communities throughout the world as it would be to do justice to them all on paper, but almost without realising what was happening I found myself visiting not only l'Arche in England but also the communities of Daybreak in Canada, Erie in the United States and Tegucigalpa and Choluteca in Honduras. I journeyed from the snow of Toronto to the dusty heat of a Honduran barrio in an attempt to see how the initial vision of Trosly-Breuil expressed itself in different cultures, and in the course of those travels, the voice of the poor gained, as Jean Vanier had doubtless known it would, a special resonance.

I saw something of what it meant to welcome the poor in the relative material affluence of Canada and the United States, where government funding could not only provide but actually require a certain standard of living but where the struggle for a sense of community and simplicity of life was possibly all the harder for it. I saw a little of the many faces of poverty, of what it meant to be poor in Honduras, for example, where handicapped children may be an intolerable burden on mothers with large families and no husbands to help care for them but where the spirit of materially impoverished people spontaneously recognises the tiny symbols of hope that the l'Arche communities are. I lived moments gentle and not so gentle but often stripped of the barriers which the attempts to cover vulnerability more usually erect, and I learned something of the maturity and the understanding of the handicapped. Beyond the cultural differences it became possible to discern what it was that Randy with his television set, his readily available shower water at a prescribed temperature, his lunch box and his exercise bike had in common with Felipe who had been left to fend for himself on the dirt tracks of the barrio, whose only means of getting about was an improvised wooden cart which someone else must pull for him, and whose poverty had brought him close to death. I discovered, not for the first time, what it was to be touched by the poor and to be sustained by them. It was not that the assistants were not welcoming. Far from it – they were extraordinary in their gifts, their acceptance of their own and others' handicaps and their generosity of heart, but in each community I learned to trust that it would be the 'handi-capped' people who would most astutely sense my weariness, feelings of strangeness or inadequacy, my own poverty and, in an intuitive, subtle way, effect some healing. For two days in Choluteca I found myself 'handicapped' by my very limited knowledge of Spanish and of the Honduran way of carrying out the simplest of daily tasks. I struggled ineptly to make tortillas and cook them over a wood fire and stammered inappropriate responses to well intentioned questions only to find myself tacitly supported by Vilma, a Honduran girl, herself only rarely able to speak. She could not know that I, like her, was virtually blind in my left eye – my handicap was less visible than hers – but she took me by the hand in moments of confusion and showed me where to go and what to do.

Overwhelmed with gratitude for the very people I had feared, for Johnny whose twisted smile was so infectious, for Lita whose uncontrollable dribbling I no longer noticed, for Dave who with his pipe between his lips would solemnly entertain me with stories of his early life that were so flagrant-ly but absorbingly untrue, for Peggy who concealed her disappointment so graciously when I and not, as she had expected, Princess Diana arrived for dinner, and for the multi-tude of others I met along the way, I was left with a very strong sense of there being many 'founders' of l'Arche, in the sense that so many had laid the foundations for its essential life. Borne along by the spirit of celebration which invariably greeted my presence as a guest, by the messages of welcome, the crayoned pictures on my bed, the flowers pressed into my hand on arrival, the prayers for my journey, it was only in Miami airport on the way back to England that the profound suffering of those rejected for the strangeness of their bodies and disregarded for having something missing from their minds really struck me, and with this came a fuller appreci-ation of the extent to which the mysterious potency of poverty and weakness was the source of life in l'Arche. Despite its many communities scattered throughout the world, l'Arche was something small and fragile, as fragile as the relationship of communion for which it strove and as the wounded people it endeavoured to hold at its heart. It had begun as a response to the cry of the poor, had brought with it increased under-standing of poverty, a sense of personal poverty on the part of those who set out to 'help' the poor and ultimately the recognition that the cry was not only the expression of the need of the world but also of its hope. There was the poverty which Jean Vanier was quick to point out: his own. There was the poverty of Père Thomas, of the assistants, of the community, of those who did not know how to respond to the handicapped person's call for love and relationship; and through all this poverty there was extraordinary grace and growth.

2

The Initial Grace

Part of the fragility of the beginnings of l'Arche derived, Jean Vanier insists, from the fact that he himself was hardly equipped for life with handicapped people. He was born on 10th September 1928, a French Canadian and the fourth of five children of Pauline Archer Vanier and Georges Philias Vanier, who would subsequently become the nineteenth Governor-General of Canada. At the time of Jean's birth his father was serving as military adviser to the League of Nations in Geneva, Switzerland, but Jean or 'Jock' – as his Scottish nanny would christen him and as he would thereafter be known by his family and many personal friends – was to receive a largely English education. The Vaniers spent most of the 1930s in London where Georges Vanier, then a Lieutenant-Colonel, was Secretary at the office of the Canadian High Commissioner, Vincent Massey. During that time Jock was sent to St John's, the preparatory school for Beaumont College in Old Windsor until impending war in 1939 made Georges Vanier (by that time Canadian Minister in Paris) abandon the initial decision to educate his children in England and gather his family about him, if not in Paris, at least in France. At a time when families who could afford to do so were fleeing Paris and the threat of bomb attack for the safer villages to the south of the capital, Madame Vanier and her children found themselves living in a very large chateau in Baillou, la Sarthe, with a number of other people in a similar position. Jean and his three brothers were despatched to a French school in the nearby town. Life in the chateau was possibly, according to their sister Thérèse, their first unfortunate experience of community.

In May 1940 Madame Vanier, the children and their grandmother began gradually retreating with the rest of the population. In Bordeaux they waited to see what the next step was to be but, by June, Georges Vanier had joined them and the decision was made that they should return to Britain. The women and children of the family, together with others related to British and Commonwealth representatives, were put on board an English merchantman that had been diverted from transporting meat from the Argentine to pick up refugees in Bordeaux. The journey to Milford Haven in Wales took five days. It was a memorable experience, not so much from the point of view of the possible threat of submarine attack as from that of the contact with human distress it brought. As they were about to set sail a tug containing more refugees came alongside the already heavily overloaded boat. The captain, who would later commit suicide, was obliged to refuse to take them in the interests of the safety of those already on board. The scene which ensued would carve itself indelibly on the memory of Thérèse Vanier and doubtless also on that of her younger brother. The boat's crew was under considerable strain. Their passengers were fed on tinned salmon, bread which the ship's baker seemed to be baking twenty-four hours a day and tea made with one-third salt water. It was Jock who went round with a bell calling out 'premier service' to signal meal times. Georges Vanier, who left Bordeaux after the rest of his family with the British Ambassador and others, was packed into a sardine boat and from there on to a British naval destroyer which landed him in England within twenty-four hours. 'Women and children first' was a principle which his family would thereafter view with a certain ambivalence.

From England the Vaniers returned to Canada. In 1942 Georges Vanier, distinguished and courageous soldier that he was, was posted as General in charge of M.D.5, the Military District of Quebec. His age and the loss of one of his legs prevented him from more active service. His third son, however, seemed destined from an early age to follow his father into a military career. At the age of thirteen, while still being educated by the Canadian Jesuits, Jock took it upon himself to apply for entry into the Royal Naval College at Dartmouth. Armed with all the necessary paperwork, he requested an interview with his father in his office and asked him to sign his permission to proceed with the venture. In an exchange which constitutes one of the few incidents of his early life which Jean Vanier is prepared to talk about as relevant to what was to follow, the General responded simply, 'I trust you.' The fact that, despite all the obvious dangers of one so young crossing the Atlantic in wartime to join the British Navy, his father was prepared to trust his intuition was 'probably one of the two most important things that happened, because if he trusted me then I could trust myself, and if my own intuitions were true then I could work with them'. Madame Vanier, by her own account, was in less ready agreement: '1942 was the time of the worst torpedoing. The bombing was still going on in England and I just cried.' But her husband remarked, with what she now recalls with a certain pleasure because of the vision the comment displayed: 'You know, we mustn't clip that child's wings. We don't know what he may become in later life.'

What was it that attracted a young French Canadian to Dartmouth and a naval life during the Second World War? Apart from his father's military example, there was the pull of a life of travel for one who had already travelled extensively. There was the challenge of actually being accepted for Dartmouth, the training ground for officers for what was then, as Jean was quick to point out to his father, 'the best navy in the world'. Wartime had increased the excitement of this challenge. The escape from France had undoubtedly left its impression. Thérèse Vanier had been horrified by what she had seen of wartime Europe and shocked at the apparent lack of interest she encountered in Canada. Part of her seemed to have been left in Europe. She returned to England with the Mechanised Transport Corp at the age of eighteen and before Jean, who – although much younger and unlikely to have expressed himself in the same way – possibly shared something of her feelings. The adult Jean Vanier is reluctant to attempt analysis: 'What attracts when one is thirteen? I've no idea. Why I actually made the passage from the childish attitude to heroism and warfare, and then more deeply between the dream and the actual walking, the going steadily towards it, I've no means of knowing.'

Communication between Canada and England at the time Jean Vanier crossed the Atlantic was almost impossible, but somehow Thérèse, who was staying with friends of friends in London, received a message to expect him some time within the next fortnight or so. She and her friends worked out a roster so that somebody would be in the flat most of the time to receive him, but on the night he actually arrived everyone was out. They arrived home at nine in the evening to find 'this pathetic little form sound asleep on the doorstep with all his belongings scattered about him'.

Because of problems with the Atlantic crossing, which he had eventually made by troop ship, Jock Vanier was late joining his term of forty-eight young cadets aged thirteen years at Dartmouth. He missed the official train at Paddington and, when he did finally arrive, distinguished himself from the other newcomers wearing uniforms for the first time in their lives by the fact that he was much taller than the rest and dressed in grey flannels and a trilby hat; he had not yet had the opportunity to visit the uniform suppliers. In many ways Dartmouth was just like many other public schools of the day, except that in addition to the usual academic subjects and sporting activities cadets were also instructed in seamanship and sailing. It took time before they moved on to navigation and the more complex aspects of the Service, and the introduction to gunnery and torpedos came only after they had left the naval college. Academically, Jock specialised in French and Spanish and was put in the Alphas, the top dozen of his term, but his contemporaries remember him not so much for any outstanding academic achievement as for his performance on the tennis courts, where his height contributed to a powerful serve, and on the rugby field as a prop forward in the first fifteen. They also recall the occasional presence of General and Madame Vanier supporting their son from the touch line.

The Sunday before the cadets were due back at Dartmouth for their second term, two Messerschmidt light bombers attacked the front of the college building and more or less put it out of action for the remainder of the war. The bombing took place at 11 a.m. Had it occurred only one week later the whole college would have been on parade and provided an even more vulnerable target. As it was, the remainder of Jean Vanier's naval-college time had to be spent first near Bristol and then at Eaton Hall, just outside Chester. The college occupied not only the main Victorian building of the Duke of Westminster's home but also a number of nissen huts, and instead of the superb facilities of the River Dart, students had to make do with the River Dee.

It was an existence not devoid of pressures for boys between the ages of fourteen and seventeen. Until the third term cadets had to move at the double everywhere in public throughout the day. It was entirely single-sex, very service-orientated and potentially in some ways a lonely experience, but Jock 'had resources'. He was a Canadian with a strange accent who had entered an unfamiliar world, and circumstances cannot have allowed him to return very often to Canada during college holidays, but his parents' diplomatic time in London had left them with a network of friends in Britain. He also then, as now, had a gift for finding the amusing aspects of life. He was not a seeker after high visibility but a very 'likeable sort of chap' possessed of an authority for which he did not have to strive and capable of finding the potential for humour, even in practising flag signals by writing on his partner's back in the damp cold of an English winter's morning. His own memories of naval college focus on one daily event in particular. Each morning there was a formal parade at which the order was given: 'Roman Catholics fall out'. The handful of Roman Catholics present would then have to take a step forward, turn right and double away smartly. 'We would then go behind a hedge,' he remembers with full appreciation of the ridiculousness of the image, 'and say the "Hail Mary" because the others would all be saying the "Our Father" so it wouldn't have made any sense for us to say that too!'

He came from a practising Roman Catholic family. His mother went daily to Mass and his father, though for many years not quite such a frequent Mass goer, was a man whose scale of priorities gave primacy to the spiritual, whose spiritual life was – as Jean Vanier would later write in his account of his father's spiritual journey, 'the source of his success in public matters'. In the same book there is a description of the General by one who had known him well:

He was in many ways a living example of him whom the Bible and the ancients called the 'just man', the man of duty: duty to his family, to his country, to his God. His motto might well have been: 'I seek but to serve.' But these qualities of justice and honesty do not by themselves explain the warmth of goodness that radiated from him. Many who wrote about him at the moment of his death

spoke of another, even more impressive characteristic. They
used the term 'love'.

As parents General and Madame Vanier paid a great deal
of attention to religious instruction with considerable importance attached to the sacraments, to first communion and
confirmation, and great respect for people of God, for priests
and religious. There were too, all the intangibles that went
with the fact that both parents were practising Christians.
They tried to lead good lives in the sense of caring for each
other and their children and the people with whom they came
into contact. *In Weakness Strength* highlights the small details
which others might have considered nonsensical but which
were important to Georges Vanier, even as Governor-General
of Canada, in his relationships with other people. Such shortcomings as his failure to enquire after someone's mother-in-
law would be a source of considerable concern to General
Vanier, possibly more so than his absence from Mass,
although clearly in his case the two were very closely linked.
To come from such a background, having had little if any
contact with other denominations, to an environment where
Roman Catholics were required to 'fall out'; cannot have been
easy; but the faith which in some sense separated undoubtedly
also sustained. Although not one to talk about his religious
convictions to his naval friends, he was remembered by one
of them, who would himself become an Anglican priest and
General Secretary for l'Arche in the United Kingdom, as
'pretty plainly Catholic, and firmly so.' At the same time he
was manifestly 'quite touched and interested by the Anglican
Church and by the college chaplain'. Some time after he had
left the navy, Jean Vanier would in fact write enquiring after
the Reverend Geoffrey Tiarks, who had been an outstandingly
good college chaplain and who later became assistant to the
Archbishop of Canterbury.

By the time Jock and his contemporaries had completed
their prescribed eleven terms, it was 1945 and the Second
World War was drawing to an end. They were sent to H.M.S.
Frobisher, a training cruiser which the working cadets, despite
their limited knowledge, manned virtually from top to bottom.
Jean Vanier, who had been made a cadet captain in his ninth
term and who had spent the last months at naval college
dressed in butterfly collars with a gold chevron on his arm,

found himself scrubbing decks barefoot at 5 a.m. *Frobisher* put to sea, for the first time after suspension during the war, in January 1946. In the course of eight months and two cruises the ship toured all the West Indian islands, including Jamaica and Montego Bay, and the coasts of Sweden, Denmark and Norway. Its cadets worked the engines, fired the guns, dropped the anchor, took their turn on the bridge. Having completed their training at sea, they then became midshipmen and were allocated in groups of three or four to different ships as required.

Jean Vanier's had been in some ways an exceptional term: three of its number would later become admirals; one, William Stavely, would become a First Sea Lord. They went into the fleet at an exceptional time when there was considerable tension between naval men who had seen and were in many cases tired of the action of war and those concerned with the return to all the spit and polish of peace time. Many ships' companies were made up of hostilities-only ratings who did not take kindly to young 'straight-ringed snotties', and in many instances the fresh young midshipmen did not take kindly to the loss of responsibility and range of activity which the return of more experienced officers meant to them. This did not initially, however, affect Jean Vanier unduly. He and a fellow midshipman, Geoffrey Upfill-Brown, who had both been in the same house and become cadet captains together, were among others to be appointed to H.M.S. *Vanguard* which was to take King George VI and the Royal Family on a cruise to South Africa. Part of their implied duties during the cruise was to provide companionship for the royal princesses Elizabeth and Margaret who were about the same age. There were teas with the princesses and deck games, and officers took it in turn to dine with the King and Queen. A midshipman's log for the cruise contains accounts not only of such exercises as oiling at sea or instruction in radar jamming but also of careful rehearsals and rigorous snow clearing for their Majesties' embarkation at Portsmouth, the celebrations aboard when the ship 'crossed the line' and of subsequent ports of call in Cape Town, East London, Port Elizabeth and Durban. It may be surmised that the gunroom was fairly carefully chosen. Geoffrey Upfill-Brown doubts that there was any special method of selection: 'In my case I'm sure it was because I was quite good at cricket and they wanted a good cricket team.' A naval report on Jean Vanier commented at the time that he showed good qualities as an officer but lacked respect for his senior officers. His father's response was characteristic: 'As long as he shows respect for those under him, he'll be all right.' Ill at ease at cocktail parties and similar social gatherings and not one for joining in the naval term reunions, Jean Vanier only speaks of his time in the navy now in relation to the ways in which it did or did not equip him for l'Arche. Certainly it was not without value to him in his future life: 'I needed to have been in the navy. It formed my body physically. When I compare myself to adolescents who come here, boys of 16 to 19 are really fragile. I had an adolescence which was completely geared without the slightest wavering to one thing and that thing was not at all materialistic. I see so many young people wavering now, not knowing what to do with themselves, dissipating their energies. In the navy there was a utilisation of energies and forces in a very constructive way.'

H.M.S. *Vanguard* arrived in Portsmouth from Cape Town in May 1947, and shortly afterwards Jean Vanier transferred from the British to the Canadian navy. Somewhere inside him he was still a Canadian. There had been a number of Canadian midshipmen aboard *Vanguard* and possibly they had awakened in him some sense of his national identity. He scarcely remembers now. The fact remains that by the time he was twenty he was an officer on Canada's only aircraft carrier. It was becoming increasingly apparent to him, however, that naval life was not for him in the long term. When the *Magnificent* put into New York he found himself visiting Friendship House which Catherine Doherty had founded for the city's down-and-outs and to which young people from a number of different countries gravitated. Jean Vanier's explanation of the conviction that he was to leave the navy amounts simply to the reflection that when he found himself reciting the Divine Office instead of attending to the night watch it was obvious that he was not in the right place. A letter written in 1951, one year after he had resigned his commission with the navy, sheds a little further light:

I think that I might have felt that the naval officer's life and the life of a Christian were in opposition – if I did think that I was wrong – granted it is much harder to live

completely the message of Christ for people will persecute
you, think you are mad . . . It takes courage but is not
impossible – the temptations are much greater.

The same letter provides an insight into Jean Vanier's understanding of the officer's role as one for which he has the
greatest regard, that of one responsible for a great number of
men not only from 'a service point of view' but also 'morally
and in education' in a way which 'touches the very roots of
life for it is a bit eternal':

The officer in some ways has the responsibility of their
souls. It is quite easy relatively speaking to die for one's
men in time of action or emergency but to die by 'pin
pricks' throughout one's life is a lot harder – I mean by
that – devoting all one's energy to their welfare. The officer
must love his men with a real love.

The writer did not feel that he had made a mistake at the
age of thirteen and a half. The eight years he had spent in
uniform had been invaluable to him. Nor did he leave the
service because of the service – its many defects were far
surpassed by all the good points. Rather he left because:

I felt that my place in the world was somewhere
else . . . During courses I began to realise that my life has
to develop along other lines – if not I would be stifling all
my natural and supernatural inclinations – 'Thy will be
done on earth as it is in heaven' – we all have our place,
our vocation – my vocation wasn't in the navy.

His departure from the service came as no surprise to those
who had been close to him in the navy. There had always
been a feeling, though one without any really definable foundation, that he would go into the Church. Of his parents, this
time it was his mother who most readily understood his course
of action. On leave with them in Paris, where his father was
by then Canadian ambassador, Jean had previously expressed
the desire to consult a priest about his possible future. So it
was that Madame Vanier had introduced him to the French
Dominican priest Père Thomas Philippe who had become her
spiritual director. The meeting between the two men was, to
quote Jean Vanier, 'very, very deep'. It was in fact 'the second
great thing' in his life. On his return to the navy the young

man had corresponded with three priests, one of whom was Père Thomas, and when finally he handed in his resignation in the conviction that his vocation was to the priesthood but uncertain as yet where he was being called to serve, he embarked upon 'at least a year of study, peace and prayer' under the spiritual direction of Père Thomas, a holy priest at whose feet he would, to use his own expression, 'receive the gift of prayer'.

3

The Hidden Grounding

In his room at the 'Farm' – the collection of converted farm buildings in Trosly-Breuil where now Père Thomas is available six days a week to welcome people, to guide them and often to suggest to them truths which they will carry with them for the remainder of their lives – he spoke a little of his own life. Twenty-three years older than Jean Vanier, he is conscious of having entered the later of what he regards as the two golden ages of the heart: early childhood and old age. Despite the constant demands made upon his theological and spiritual resources, Père Thomas is somehow a priest with time. He speaks in a distinctive high-pitched voice, his sentences punctuated with the often repeated question, 'Vous voyez?', his body craning forward for further confirmation that he has been understood and in compensation for the deafness that has grown more acute with his advancing years. He is a philosopher who is fundamentally Thomist, with a particular interest in Marian theology, a priest who has striven to live a life rooted in the Beatitudes and a man who is manifestly a witness to an 'open religion', which moves towards mystical experience and is ultimately an experience of God irrespective of whether one is Buddhist, Hindu, Roman Catholic or Anglican. In the words of Jean Vanier, 'He cares about the law and can put it in its place, but he is continually directing people to come back to their consciences, to their experience of God.'

Born on 18th March 1905 into a northern French family, some fifteen kilometres from Lille, Thomas Philippe was the son of a notary and one of twelve children, an extraordinary number of whom were destined for the religious life. His mother's brother was a Dominican priest, a man of great spirituality and intelligence who undoubtedly exerted an influence and watched over the raising of his nephews. Père

Thomas was aware of his vocation from a very young age. The local village priest remarked to his mother, when the boy was only five years old, that he was more sure of her little son's vocation than of that of most of the seminarists to whom he gave instruction at Lille. During the First World War his father spent four years in the army and the family went through hard times. Barefoot or in rough shoes the numerous children learned something of what it was to go short of many things. Afterwards Père Thomas went to study with the Jesuits in Lille. In the absence of public transport during that postwar period he rode the fifteen kilometres by bicycle each morning and evening, but not without a struggle. He was only thirteen, and it took him an hour and a half each way. He was also already having problems with his ears. Deafness was a family weakness, as a result of which he had some difficulty in hearing during lessons and became a subject of mockery among his classmates. In 1923, at the age of eighteen, he decided to enter the diocesan seminary of Issy-les-Moulineaux, but shortly before doing so sensed that his vocation was more specifically to be a Dominican. Not daring, however, to change course so swiftly, he followed the advice of his Dominican uncle that he should join the seminary for which he had already applied. If he was meant to change direction it would happen of its own accord. At the seminary Père Thomas felt his call to be a Dominican ever more strongly, a call to a more religious and apostolic life than that of a parish priest. After only two months he left to join the Dominicans and continued his studies at Kain in Belgium since, on the separation of the Church and the State in 1905, all the Dominican monasteries had been compelled to leave France. He was ordained in July 1929 at the unusually young age of 24. In his family two elder sisters had already joined the Benedictines. Another younger one would follow them. His younger brother, Père Marie Dominique, would become a priest shortly after him. Another sister became a Dominican and two other brothers started their Dominican novitiate. Of these one died during the war; the other left the order. Only three of the children married.

In 1936 Père Thomas went on to the Dominican university in Rome but during the Second World War he served as a military chaplain and afterwards became Master of Studies at the Dominican Priory and house of studies on the outskirts of Paris, the Saulchoir. Shortly afterwards, in response to the expressed needs of a number of his students, he founded a small community close by in three houses, one of which became known as the Pavillon Maritain because Jacques Maritain came there for a number of years to give summer courses. The study of theology and philosophy at the Saulchoir necessarily implied a commitment to enter the Dominican novitiate, but Père Thomas had recognised that there were those who were potentially interested in the study of philosophy and theology who were not necessarily ready to commit themselves to the priesthood. A vocation might well reveal itself in the course of those studies. If it did not, Père Thomas was still able to perceive the value of the knowledge acquired for a layman in a world wanting to build peace and in which countries long dominated by colonialism were being liberated.

He had identified the need in that postwar period for what he describes as 'international work of the heart' and his community 'Eau Vive' would become a 'small international centre for students who wanted to come and get to know something of the theology and spirituality of the Church, for lay people who wanted to know more and who would afterwards take that knowledge back to their respective countries and use it to help shape future development'. It began with ten students, but their numbers very soon multiplied. The centre attracted all kinds of people. It was in fact the first place of study in France to take in a German student after the war, an act of reconciliation which was a very concrete expression of what the community was already trying to live. An extract from the diary of a friend from Jean Vanier's naval days who visited him at Eau Vive in 1951 also notes the presence of 'Arabic philosophers, a Persian merchant, several Germans, a woman who went into a concentration camp for being a key worker in the "underground" during the war'. Père Thomas himself would refer to the presence of Syrians, Lebanese, Egyptians and Moroccans. In all, there were some twenty countries represented among the eighty or so students. It was a highly diverse assembly with a strong intellectual element, but in its community life Eau Vive tried to live as the early Christian communities lived, particularly from the point of view of 'unity' based on the directive, 'that you may be one', a unity that was founded on love and charity. It became known as a place of peace and of great grace. Eau Vive was also very poor. Accommodation was often provided in huts or stables and food was very simple, of the kind which would enable even the poorest to participate in and listen to the new thinking that was going on amongst the Dominicans at the time, much of which would lead to or be fed into the Second Vatican Council.

Père Thomas admits in the pursuit of this spiritual and intellectual life to having paid scant regard to the financial running of the community. There came a point, however, where Eau Vive had run into such financial difficulties that he had to attempt to raise funds. Having heard of the Canadian ambassadress's charitable work with the Canadian Red Cross it was to Madame Vanier that he turned with a request to help him organise a bazaar. She claims to have been really very rude to this unknown and somewhat importunate priest: 'Firstly, I'm not a good organiser and secondly I was far too busy. I got up and made him understand that the conversation had ended; but he was a very persevering man – still is.' Two or three weeks later he appealed to her again, this time with a suggestion that if she was not prepared to organise a bazaar, she might at least be willing to contact the wives of ambassadors who would be interested in the work that was going on at Eau Vive and give it support? Despite herself, Madame Vanier found herself agreeing to do so, but what was of greater significance to her was the fact that in the course of conversation Père Thomas, who was still very much a stranger to her, informed her that he felt that she was searching which way to turn in her spiritual life. She had indeed been feeling that she lacked direction in her spiritual journey and was looking for a Carmelite convent where she could go and pray. Père Thomas's next unprompted suggestion was that she might like to come to some talks on spirituality he was giving in a Carmelite convent near Paris. His intuition shocked her, but it was the beginning of a profound friendship and the basis for her suggestion to her son, when he too was 'searching', that he should talk to Père Thomas.

There is much about Père Thomas and about his relationship with Jean Vanier that defies words. 'Père Thomas is there, a rock, and you get to a point where you can say no more,' Jean Vanier has said. Speaking of the nature of true friendship in general he would draw attention to the fact that

St Thomas Aquinas, writing of friendship, posed the question as to whether friendship was 'mutually living inside one another' and adds that it was a 'very hidden reality'. Henri Nouwen, the Dutch priest and writer, now at the Daybreak l'Arche community in Canada, describes how, having talked with Père Thomas four or five times during a year he spent at Trosly-Breuil, he had found his vision immensely stimulating and learnt some good ideas about which he could write sermons, but how it was only later, when Henri was going through a deep spiritual crisis, that he really met the French priest. In a state of anguish Henri Nouwen attended a retreat for the priests of l'Arche:

> Père Thomas spoke for a week and every day he wanted me to come to be with him, and suddenly I knew that in his presence some healing took place that had very little to do with any of these great ideas. I suddenly knew that he knew anguish as nobody else did and that he was no longer talking about how to deal with certain things but that he became the source himself, the place where grace was given; that he was so empty that when you were in his presence you were in the presence of God. I was in the presence of a holy man, a man who radiated the presence of Jesus in a way that, whether you were a believer or not, you knew you were there.

One of the founders of L'Arche in Erie, Father George Strohmeyer, would describe how his meeting with Père Thomas was instrumental in those beginnings. During a visit to Trosly-Breuil, the elderly priest had told him and the Sister who had accompanied him there to 'go back home and change something'.

> We had two interviews with him through an interpreter. It was a week or two later that I realised he had talked only in scholastic terms, in terms of Thomistic, scholastic philosophy and theology, in terms of what I had learned half-heartedly as a student of philosophy and theology. I had learnt it, but I hadn't appreciated it. Suddenly Père Thomas spoke in the same terms but gave it all heart. For the first time I understood, because Père Thomas was living it.

To Father George Strohmeyer Père Thomas is possibly

best understood as a person who is 'enlightened', as one who is capable of passing on that enlightenment which is a spiritual and not a mental, cognitive formation. There are others who do not see, or seek to see, beyond the lengthy homilies which Père Thomas still delivers in his unusual voice in the chapel at Trosly, or beyond the Thomist theology and the speculations about the Virgin Mary which the contemporary theological world might well not easily appreciate. Because of the depth and intimacy of his spiritual life, Père Thomas feels so comfortable with Jesus and Mary that he speaks of them almost as if they were part of his family. There are doubtless those who find such an approach a little too uncritical, but there are also those who love to listen because they know that underneath, or beyond, or in it, there is a spirit of purity, and there are those who seek, as Jean Vanier has done at times, simply to be silently in his presence because he is in some mysterious way a powerful reflection of the presence and the love of God.

Père Thomas recalls recognising, when Jean Vanier left the navy, that the young man was seeking primarily 'to know God better'. Père Thomas's response to the young man's request to come to Eau Vive was typed by a former art student in Paris, Jacqueline d'Halluin. She had been invited initially by the first German student at Eau Vive to spend a day there, had fallen in love with the trees that surrounded the community houses, had later returned for a week knowing that she was in some way taking a definitive step, and remained for seven years. Meeting Père Thomas, she had agreed to help him and, thinking it impolite to say 'No' to a priest, had not admitted when he asked her to do some typing that she had never used a typewriter before. In those days she believed not so much in the will of God as in inspiration and intuition. Not for the last time, for she would later follow Père Thomas and Jean Vanier to l'Arche, the priest's intuition with regard to the young naval officer surprised her:

It took me three days to type that letter because I had never typed anything in my life before. People were impressed by my industry because they could hear the typewriter going constantly, but in fact I was typing the same thing over and over again with one finger and filling up the waste-paper basket. I said to myself, 'This young man is crazy.

He has everything going for him at sea.' But, at the same time, what Père Thomas said to Jean Vanier in his letter about the Holy Spirit made me enter into something different. I didn't keep a copy of that letter, but not surprisingly I know it off by heart.

Jean Vanier refers to being attracted to Père Thomas's person and what he was saying about prayer and silence, to his incredible abilities as a theologian. He recalls knowing that Père Thomas was 'an instrument of God' for him and 'realising somehow that there was a covenant between us'. Much later he would advocate for others in community what he describes as 'filiation' as opposed to the structured acquisition of knowledge based on clear principles which 'formation' implies, as the only means by which certain knowledge at a spiritual level can be transmitted. He would write in 1976 in *Community and Growth*:

Today, many ministers and priests are formed in universities or seminaries, by professional teachers. In India, if you want to become a guru, you live with a guru until he confirms you and sends you out to be a guru who forms disciples in his turn. These days, we tend to believe that everything can be learned from books. We forget that there is another way to learn: by living with a master.

In Père Thomas, it may be inferred, he had identified such a master. Père Thomas, for his part, describes Jean as being attracted to the Christian religious formation at Eau Vive as something which went beyond both the naval training he had received and the education a French university might offer him. There remains the impression that Jean Vanier's subsequent yearning to help the poor and search for community was firmly anchored in the search for God, and that his appreciation of Père Thomas was of a man who had a deep knowledge of God's communication with people, a man who really knew the ways of God.

At Eau Vive Jean Vanier began his studies of theology and philosophy and Latin with ordination in mind. It was a life far removed from torpedos, gunnery, rifles, sports, uniforms and the need to do well on naval courses. But in his small room in a hut, the wide windows of which gave out on to trees and grass and birdsong, he seems to have found peace

and an excited enthusiasm for the spiritual writings of St
Francis of Sales and the primacy of love as revealed in the
New Testament. In a letter to a friend he wrote at that time:

> Alas, Christians everywhere – and Catholics are no excep-
> tion – have lost faith in the truths of the New Testament.
> We have lost the sense of prayer, forgotten that 'without
> me you can do nothing', forgotten that all is *love*: *Deus caritas
> est*, that God is love – he is the way, the truth and the life
> – that the meaning of the cross is love – Christ died out of
> an excess of love. 'God so loved the world.' Read in St
> John at the Last Supper how many times the word 'love'
> is used.

Sadly, in 1952, not very long after Jean Vanier's arrival in
Eau Vive, the man who had drawn him there was recalled
to Rome, but it is an indication of Père Thomas's perception
of his relatively new student that he nominated him as his
successor in the direction of the community. Relations with
the nearby Saulchoir had been strained for some time,
although hitherto students at Eau Vive had been permitted
to study and use the library there. In some way the new
spirituality which Eau Vive had been exploring seems to have
posed a threat in terms of orthodoxy and raised questions
around the issue of authority. The Dominicans at the Saulchoir had considered Eau Vive to be under their jurisdiction
and were not satisfied that it should be directed by a layman.
'I knew nothing,' Jean Vanier would recall, 'only that Père
Thomas had asked me, and if he had asked me to stay on,
I was going to stay on.' The doors of the Saulchoir were
subsequently closed to members of EauVive, and the majority
of the students left. Those who remained continued their
studies at the Institut Catholique in Paris, and Eau Vive
survived for another six years.

The period at Eau Vive had brought with it an experience
of conflict which Jean Vanier prefers now to pass over. Yet
it was one in which, in the years after the closure of the centre
in 1956, he was able to discern both the cross and grace.
From Paris in 1963 he wrote to a friend who was going
through a not dissimilar period of trial:

> I have always felt that for all of us who were there [at Eau
> Vive] it was a very great grace, for it made us live effectively

what we had always been wanting to live – the mystery of the cross, and the primacy of suffering and prayer over purely external works and activities. And as the years go by, the more I realise how grace springs from these sufferings, which render fruitful our activities which without the sufferings would be sterile.

The same letter provides an intimation of the cause of the suffering:

One of the great graces that Jesus gave me in '56 and since, is to realise that in the Church there must be two sorts of men – there must be those who know how to *conserve* those traditions that have come down to us through the ages, but there must also be those who, like Jesus, have primarily at heart *the salvation of their fellows* and are always trying to find new ways – human and divine – to make the message of Jesus more living. Without those who have at heart the conservation of tradition, the eager and merciful apostles (unless they are really possessed in all the details of their lives by the Holy Spirit) will risk to abandon certain essential aspects of tradition – not necessary, perhaps, for them, but necessary for the Church and souls in general: on the other hand without these apostles, those who have at heart the conservation of tradition will tend to forge a sterile religion of rites, without love, without mercy. And in the designs of Jesus these two groups will always make each other suffer.

The requirement to leave Eau Vive, accepted though it was, left Jean Vanier in a state of uncertainty. He had, by his own account, experienced no adolescent crisis. Everything in the navy had been very clear for him. He had come to Eau Vive with a very open mind, without any previous knowledge of philosophy, and had 'just walked into the metaphysics and the spirituality of Père Thomas'. A whole world of the intelligence and of prayer had been opened up, and through Père Thomas he had lived interiorly very deep experiences. From there he would progress to a 'period of waiting'. Deciding against entering a seminary as planned, but not knowing quite where he was to go, he spent a year in the guest house of the Trappist monastery at Bellefontaine. His elder brother Benedict had become a Trappist and Jean Vanier too at that time seems to have felt the call to greater solitude and silence. He went on, first to live on a small farm and then to Fatima in Portugal to 'a very blessed spot'. Dr Thompson, a British psychiatrist attached to UNESCO in Paris who had been close to Eau Vive, had been very touched by Fatima, and as early as 1953 had suggested buying some land there. It was a time when land at Fatima was cheap and with Jean Vanier's parents' financial backing it had been possible to purchase a plot with the vague possibility of creating another Eau Vive in mind. The decision to buy land had not, however, been separate from the reality of Fatima, and so when, on leaving Eau Vive, Jean Vanier was looking for intimations as to which way to turn, the possibility of living in a small cottage in a place of prayerfulness and pilgrimage seemed like a small sign.

The years between 1956 and 1962 were years lived very much alone but for what he described then as 'a slight apostolic activity' with those who wished to go and see him. They were years during which he felt he was brought back more and more to the reality of the Gospels, particularly to St John's account of the Last Supper and St Matthew's Sermon on the Mount, to discover the mystery of the Christian life, the spiritual life, the life of love that Jesus proposed through the evangelists. Intellectually, he continued his studies in philosophy and theology. There was a period during those years which he spent in Rome with Père Thomas, and it was under his influence and under that of his brother Père Marie Dominique that Jean Vanier began a doctoral thesis on the ethics of Aristotle. Now he explains the choice of Aristotle in terms of being drawn to the realistic vision of the world which Aristotle offered:

> He's a very realistic guy. The intuition of Plato stems from his inner experience whereas Aristotle is something about outer experience. Somewhere in Christianity is the harmonisation of the two, but from a philosophical point of view just to love reality and to touch, to look at things, to listen to people is very Aristotelian.

He would not, however, have been able to offer that kind of reason at the time he made his choice. It was one which seemed then to arise quite spontaneously from conversations with the two Thomist Fathers, Marie Dominique and Thomas

Philippe. As to why he chose the ethics of Aristotle, at the Institut Catholique in Paris he had a very good teacher: 'A fearful man like an eagle but clear in his thinking. He certainly helped.' In 1962 Jean Vanier successfully defended his thesis at the institute, still, however with no very distinct idea of what the next step was to be.

In his eighties, Père Thomas would be able to trace quite clearly a path which led almost inexorably to l'Arche. He would recall the same Dr Thompson who had felt drawn to Fatima as one who exercised a significant influence along the way and who had, above all else, opened up for him the dimension of the heart. Dr Thompson was not only an eminent and discerning psychiatrist, a disciple first of Freud and subsequently of Jung, but also a man capable of integrating the place of the human heart into the philosophical vision of Père Thomas. Père Thomas was moved by the fact that Thompson had adopted a German Nazi boy he had found lying in the street and by the fact that so respected a man had been converted to Catholicism because he had been 'touched in a very particular way by the papacy'. It was at a time when Pius XII was Pope and Monsignor Roncalli, the future Pope John XXIII was papal nuncio in Paris. In fact Angelo Roncalli had visited the community at Eau Vive, and Père Thomas recalls with pleasure an exchange with the papal nuncio in which he had given his whole-hearted approval to Père Thomas's recipe for a life in which Muslims, members of the Orthodox Church, Catholics and Protestants could pray harmoniously together. Père Thomas advocated praying together but the avoidance of contradictory discussion. If people wished to talk they could do so privately with him. It was, the future pope agreed, 'a good method'.

What had moved Dr Thompson to the point of conversion to the Roman Catholic Church was the fact that Jesus had appointed to the head of his Church a servant of the servants of God, not a doctor or a prestigious man but Peter, a simple fisherman. Based on his experiences at international meetings for UNESCO, Dr Thompson also drew Père Thomas's attention to the fact that councils could be prudent, they could also be reasonable, but they could not be compassionate. Only the human heart, he maintained, could be that. He was a sensitive advocate of St Augustine's emphasis on the richness of the human heart and simultaneously an extraordinary thinker well equipped to help Père Thomas to discover a new dimension in psychology. The Dominican priest had been familiar with the work of Freud but less so with that of Jung. Through Thompson he discovered the whole concept of the communion of mother and child and the anguish which arises out of the rupture of that communion, a concept now widely recognised but which then came as a more radical revelation. It would form the basis of much of both Père Thomas's subsequent thinking and that of Jean Vanier. Years later Jean Vanier would comment:

> I find that we've been clouded by Freud in the understanding of the mother/child relationship. I find he's lost some sort of simplicity in the bonding between mother and child. The child is not an egotistical creature but very fragile. There is this incredible relationship between the mother and child in which the child is filled with love and peace, with communion.

What he and Père Thomas together would discover at l'Arche they would see as the particular wound of the person with a handicap stemming from this experience of 'broken communion'.

It was Dr Thompson also who introduced Père Thomas to Dr Preaut. Dr Preaut was a man with many years of professional experience with mentally handicapped people, who in 1960 – together with a M. Prat – had begun in the village of Trosly-Breuil a home and workshop for mentally handicapped young men known as the Val Fleuri. M. Prat was himself the father of a mentally handicapped boy. Reluctant to put his son into a mental institution and concerned for his future, he had been persuaded by Dr Preaut to use the legacy intended for his child to open a home to help not only his own boy but others too. A condition had been built into the agreement that his son would have a place there for life.

In 1962, in his capacity as chairman of the Board of Directors, Dr Preaut invited Père Thomas to come as chaplain to the old village chateau and stables that were now the Val Fleuri and its protected workshops. The ageing priest was by this time working at a school for young delinquents, also founded by Dr Preaut, about ten kilometres from Trosly-Breuil. He had long been attracted to the poor, sensing in them the special action of the Holy Spirit, but his vision of the poor had focused first on the worker or the docker with his 'simple working life'. His years at Eau Vive had brought him into contact with another Dominican priest who worked amongst the dockers and who had impressed upon Père Thomas his own discovery 'that though they were in many respects coarse and rough, they often had extraordinary hearts'. Progressively Père Thomas had discovered what it meant to be a delinquent or marginal. Dr Preaut's intimation that there was special work to be done among the mentally handicapped, that they were people who were poor and weak in the extreme, and that they needed teaching not by force but through trust, touched a chord of recognition.

He accepted the invitation, arriving in Trosly-Breuil shortly before Christmas 1963 as one of the poorest of the poor. He was poor in the material sense, for he had many years previously chosen a way of poverty. He was poor also in the sense that, in the recollection of one who had known him from Eau Vive, since leaving there he had been 'put a little to one side'. The interior vision directed so exclusively towards God from such an early age had inevitably brought him suffering. He was poor to the extent that in the very place where he had been invited to stay he found there were those who did not want him. Among the educators at the Val Fleuri were a number of former seminarists who had been rejected for the priesthood or who had opted to leave the seminary before ordination. Strong feelings of anti-clericism prevailed, and Père Thomas was quick to sense that they would prefer that he did not live with them in the building which is now the place of welcome for l'Arche at Trosly-Breuil. A priest did not impose his presence nor that of the sacraments. Instead, he sought a place to live in the village where those who wanted the Eucharist could have ready access to it. He found two rooms off the village square, the Place des Fêtes, one of which was to become a chapel. In the other which is now a sacristy, he had a bed, a desk and the few possessions he needed to live. There was no electricity. When it was cold Dr Preaut's son would bring him wood from the forest to burn, and when it rained the water poured through the leaking ceilings of his dilapidated rooms.

This poverty made him all the more readily accepted by the local villagers, many of whom were themselves elderly and poor, and he felt at once drawn both to them and, in a very particular way, to the mentally handicapped people in his pastoral care at the Val Fleuri.

> They had been born poor and the aim was not so much to help them out of their poverty – as in the case of delinquents – but to help them accept their poverty and enable them to see in it the grace granted by God, to show them that their handicap was not necessarily a curse but could be a mark of God's special love for them.

Dr Preaut had begun a programme of research into the mentality of handicapped people, an attempt to identify the principal characteristics of the mentally handicapped people with whom Père Thomas found himself involved. The enquiry was to reveal to him the fact that,

> mentally handicapped people in psychiatric institutions were considered to be gregarious in the sense that they flocked together and appeared to need to be led. They were regarded as having an intelligence far inferior to that of the rest of humanity and more on a par with that of animals. But it was society and its overbearing attitude of superiority that made mentally handicapped people 'gregarious'. By nature they were the most spontaneous of beings, who actually found living crowded together difficult, who when approached roughly withdrew into themselves, but who when approached with love, responded with extraordinary warmth and generosity.

Their intellectual knowledge was limited. It was frequently hardly worth teaching them to read. Yet one of the first revelations to surprise the psychiatric profession was that they could make the most beautiful mosaics and that with encouragement they would display quite extraordinary artistic gifts. Though the qualities of their intellects were limited, they were rich in qualities of the heart, and those qualities of the heart called directly to people. They had a profound need for relationship, and in relationships of trust, love and freedom their particular gifts would flourish.

Characteristically, Père Thomas would relate the journey of discovery he made with Dr Preaut to what Thompson had already shown him with regard to human consciousness and its operation not only on the level of reason and the mind but at the level of the heart. Thompson had cited the example of the human baby, born in a state of such dependency on its mother that it is incapable even of turning itself over to avoid suffocation without assistance, as an illustration of how the human child is obliged to put its trust in its mother and is thus made to be a religious being. If man were a purely rational being, Thompson had argued, this would constitute premature birth. Philosopher and skilled theologian that he was, Père Thomas aligned himself with Teilhard de Chardin whose writings he knew well: 'With all the discoveries that clever men had made about life, our world and the universe, Teilhard de Chardin had not been able to find any single philosophy capable of assuming them all in a synthesis, other than the teachings of Jesus.' Those teachings emphasised the importance of, indeed found their most potent expression in, the little people of this world. There can be little doubt that Père Thomas, despite his scholastic language and intellectual abilities, was a man in whom the heart consciousness was already well developed. By his own account, however, his ministry among mentally handicapped people brought home to him more powerfully than ever the need to 'rediscover all my theology under the sign of the heart'.

Anxious to refurbish, not so much the room where he was living, but the small chapel that was to house the sacraments, Père Thomas set about doing it himself. He borrowed tools and enlisted the help of some good friends. Among those who came to his aid was Jean Vanier. He helped the older man set himself up in his simple lodgings, and Père Thomas – feeling that there was a vocation there for the ex-naval officer who in his mid-thirties was still uncertain of what he was to do with his life – suggested in his gentle way that there was 'something special to be done among handicapped people'. Jean Vanier, for his part, recalls feeling that Père Thomas had 'discovered something'. He was deeply impressed by what the priest had learnt of the spiritual openness of handi-capped people and of their place in the heart of God. His first encounters with the Val Fleuri left him both touched and fearful at the same time. In those days there were men in the Val Fleuri who were violent and noisy. In December 1963, he was present at a theatrical production put on in the large hall. He enjoyed the production but, by his own admission, did not feel fully at ease.

In January of the following year Jean Vanier took up a

post at St Michael's College of the University of Toronto to teach ethics. It came as an extraordinary revelation to him to discover there the 'power of teaching'. He had had no previous idea that he had the capacity to teach. He had studied but, compared with others in his position, he had read less than most. He had, however, listened to Père Thomas, and so intently that without taking notes he had found that he could give the priest's words back as if recorded on a tape in a way which he recognised to have formed him very deeply and which he saw as an experience of God. At St Michael's College, without his fully understanding why, the fruits of all that had gone before began to come out with great force. He was asked to give talks to the whole college and the hall would be packed to bursting point. It was an experience that would have great relevance to his agreement a few years later to take a retreat in Toronto and to the many other retreats that would develop out of it. 'It is one of the advantages of getting older', he would confide much later in his journey, 'that you can see how everything had meaning. You think everything is your choice but it's not. Gradually there is the discovery of being chosen, of being shaped in order to be an instrument.' At the time, he knew only that he did not see teaching as something permanent and that, though not exactly seeking, he was in a state of waiting.

Some months later, on his next visit to France and Père Thomas, there was the same gentle hint, the same question: was there something special to be done among the people with handicaps? Encouraged by Père Thomas and by Dr Preaut, he went to see the person in charge of institutions for people with a handicap in the area, who confirmed what by this time was shaping itself into the resolve 'to do something'. In the late spring of 1964 he began visiting different centres for people with a mental handicap. He was overwhelmed by what he found, especially in the asylum of St Jean des Deux Jumeaux south of Paris, where some eighty mentally handicapped men lived together in two dormitories and a chaotic atmosphere of violence and uproar. Solid concrete walls surrounded buildings constructed of cement blocks. The occupants had no work. They went round in circles all day long. From 2 p.m. to 4 p.m. there was an obligatory siesta and then a walk. One man, Dany had lived all his life in a collar and spat at anyone who approached him. 'There was something terrifying about it, but at the same time something difficult to touch, something profoundly of God. I have found the same thing in prisons and places for leprosy sufferers,' Jean Vanier would reflect years later. 'In places of horror there is a kind of presence of God. Peace and chaos – one is frightened yet captivated.'

Gradually the conviction that 'Jesus wanted something to be done' was becoming more concrete. With hindsight he would claim that he knew nothing then except about warships and Aristotle, but he was and is, someone who lives the present moment with a certain naivety and trust. Jesus wanted it, so there were no real questions to be asked.

It was a conviction which not everyone shared so readily. Madame Vanier admits to having rebelled completely against the idea of what her son was proposing to do. It was Tony Walsh, of Benedict Labre House in Montreal, who helped her and her husband to accept the decision. An Irishman by origin, he had gone out to Canada to teach Indian children in the North-West Territories and to help them rediscover their roots and their identity at a time when the Indian culture in Canada had been strongly repressed. He had then gone on to found a house in a very poor part of Montreal which provided accommodation for a number of 'gentlemen of the road' and was a centre to which people could come for a meal and have a chat. Both the General and Madame Vanier used to help there. Madame Vanier, who had a special regard for Tony Walsh because he had identified the fact that, 'for all my apparent wealth, I too was poor', waited at tables and served meals, especially at Christmas, and kept the men amused with her talents as a raconteur and a clown. Benedict, her eldest son who would subsequently become a Trappist monk, Jean and Thérèse, all knew Tony Walsh.

Thérèse Vanier acknowledges that he influenced her in the direction of l'Arche and that he probably influenced her brother in a similar way: 'For someone of his generation he was extremely radical as far as the Church was concerned and yet extremely anchored, very sure of his place in the Church, very challenging of its attitudes, but acting out his challenge in what he was doing.' He was a layman who had voluntarily adopted a life of smallness, simplicity and poverty, one who in a quiet unobtrusive way reflected the love of God to his fellow man, and who conveyed a message to the Church and to the world about the place and the power of the poor not merely by words but through his very life. 'Jock', Tony Walsh told Madame Vanier, 'has to go to the end of his ideal, that of poverty.'

4

A School of the Heart

Jean Vanier had heard what today he would call 'the primal cry of people with handicaps', a cry which expresses in their very flesh a yearning for friendship combined with a sense of being unworthy and the doubt that anyone could ever want them. In some ways afraid but also deeply moved, he embarked upon a programme of action. He was after all a man schooled in efficacy and efficiency. Before he had so much as found a house in which to live, he informed Père Thomas that he would open a small *foyer* on the 4th/5th August, two saints' days which represented for him fidelity to the Holy Spirit: that of St Dominic (because Père Thomas was a Dominican) and that of Notre Dame de la Merci. Thereafter, with the help of Louis Pretty, a Canadian architect who had come to France to visit Taizé and see something of the new Christian communities that were developing, the plan evolved very rapidly. A small house in Trosly-Breuil, only a few minutes walk away from both the Val Fleuri and the tiny chapel behind which Père Thomas was living, seemed a suitable property. The owner had had no intention of selling it but obligingly agreed to its sale. A legal structure had to be created to carry responsibility for what was to come into being. Dr Preaut suggested that it should become part of an already established charitable organisation, S.I.P.S.A. (Societé pour l'instruction des enfants sourds, muets ou arriérés) and that this society should undertake the administration for l'Arche. Jean Vanier agreed subject to two conditions: that he become the chairman and that he appoint half the members of the board. It was agreed with the appropriate government health authority that the house should be considered a 'placement familiale' linked to the Val Fleuri and that he should receive 21 francs a day for each person he welcomed.

It was a time when the general climate was conducive to

such undertakings. The policy of French legislation was to facilitate and encourage the creation of homes for mentally handicapped people. In other respects also 'everything was given' in such a way that it became very quickly apparent to Jean Vanier that he was embarking on something definitive. Mme Martin, the directress of St Jean des Deux Jumeaux was an extraordinary woman. She had created a very closed and disturbed institution. At the time Jean Vanier felt himself too naive to be unduly critical but now he would describe it as repulsive on the grounds that it was devoid of any real attempt to achieve the well-being of its residents. Yet Mme Martin was also possessed of a certain generosity of spirit. She gave the young man advice which, despite the fact that she herself was a woman in a house full of men, included the directive never to have women assistants to live with handicapped men. She also supported him in his venture. Eventually it was she who suggested which three men he should invite to live with him from amongst the many whom Jean Vanier had identified as crying out for love, affection and relationship. It was decided that on the 4th August she would bring these three, Raphael, Philippe and Dany to the small *foyer* in time for lunch. The initial invitation was for a month's holiday, and if all went well they would be asked at the end of the month whether they would like to remain permanently.

With their limited funds Jean Vanier and Louis Pretty had hired a small truck and bought some second-hand furniture from Abbé Pierre's Emmaus Community. Other necessities had been lent or given. By the time the day of welcome arrived the furnishings in the little house included a small statue of the Virgin Mary (which is still there in what would become known as the 'Foyer de l'Arche') and a dining table. Mme Martin brought with her a celebratory meal for the newcomers and the welcoming party which included Père Thomas, Dr and Mme Preaut and others, for Jean Vanier had recognised early that he would need to gather a few people about him in order to be able to begin the project. Afterwards, however, the guests all left and he found himself alone with his three new companions.

'I was completely lost,' he would recall, 'especially with Dany. He couldn't hear and he couldn't speak. It was crazy taking him. I should never have been asked to remove him from his highly closed institution to a free situation.' In a state of total insecurity, Dany began to hallucinate. He ran out into the quiet streets of Trosly-Breuil and made menacing gestures at the uncomprehending passers-by. The night of the 4th/5th August was a memorable one for Jean Vanier. As an illustration of his own incompetence he tells of how he had thought there was no electricity in the house. In fact, as he would discover a few days later, there was electricity and he simply had not found the meter; but that first night was spent in darkness and turmoil with Dany constantly on the move and Jean Vanier unable to find any rest in his bed up in the loft. The walls of the little house were sound but the interior left much to be desired. There was no lavatory, only a bucket.

Next morning, the practical side of his character recognised that it was impossible for Dany to stay. From the telephone in the village café he called Mme Martin and with great sadness asked her to come and collect him. So it was that from the very first night of the founding of l'Arche Jean Vanier was to experience the need to make choices and to know suffering; his own suffering and sense of failure and the suffering of the men who had come to live with him.

Both Raphael and Philippe were to some degree physically as well as mentally handicapped. Raphael had a vocabulary of only about twenty words and some limited understanding. He communicated by grunts and had the real appearance and eyes of a handicapped person. In Philippe's case the physical handicap was more obvious in that he could only walk with a crutch. He talked a lot but frequently about the same things and lived to a large extent in his own dream world. Both had been placed in the asylum in Seine-et-Marne on the death of their parents. Yet Philippe, not realising that his mother was dead, constantly asked after her. Mme Martin had told Jean Vanier of the woman's death but no one in the family had thought to inform Philippe. In response to Philippe's persistent questions Jean Vanier set about finding a member of his family to tell him the truth. An uncle came to Trosly-Breuil and Jean Vanier asked him to take Philippe to his mother's grave and so help him to accept the reality of her death.

He threw himself on his mother's grave and howled and howled in a way that you could hear for miles around, and

I think those howls were not only because his mother, the only person he had ever loved, was dead but also because no one had treated him as her son. I began to discover a world of immense suffering.

It was being plunged into this world of suffering that was to bring about a gentle revolution. Like Père Thomas, Jean Vanier was poor when he arrived in Trosly-Breuil. To wait until his mid-thirties to find his true vocation had been an impoverishing experience. By the time he took up residence in Trosly-Breuil he had, as one friend of his would put it, 'lost a lot of his baggage'. The life he led with Raphael and Philippe in their little home with one tap and one wood-burning stove was simple in the extreme. They went shopping together, prepared meals, cleaned the house, did the washing. Raphael and Philippe helped as best they could with the different chores in the house and garden. In the morning they went to Mass and in the evening they said part of the rosary together.

Jean Vanier was conscious of a bond of commitment, a covenant between himself and Raphael and Philippe which in some mysterious way reflected and flowed from the covenant that existed between God and the suffering poor of this world (Exodus 3:7–8). He wanted to create a family around them, a place where they could grow in all the dimensions of their being. They began to get to know each other, to learn how to live together, to care for one another, to have fun and to pray together. Theirs was a life which was poor and simple in a way which Jean Vanier would look back on as being open to the action of the Holy Spirit and which would enable him to see those initial months as a period that was 'prophetic'. Precisely because of that poverty, he was to share Père Thomas's experience of the generosity of the poor, particularly in the guise of the local village women who brought apples and soup and whatever gifts they had to offer – parcels of food even arrived through the post – but also in the form of the men with a handicap and all that they had to show him, for in their shared life he was to learn the value of really listening to them. With hindsight Jean Vanier would reflect that

the idea of living together was there from day one, the idea of living happily together, of celebrating and laughing a lot, came very quickly and spontaneously. When the idea of the poor educating us came, I don't know exactly. The words of St Vincent de Paul, 'The poor are our masters,' were always there, but when they became a reality I'm uncertain.

The change of attitude from that of 'wanting to do things for' to that of 'listening to' was one which would take some time, but it was a revolution which was no doubt made possible by his own openness and readiness to be shaped by experience and events. During those first months he learned a great deal. He discovered the immense pain hidden in Raphael and Philippe's hearts, but also their beauty and their gentleness, their capacity for communion and for tenderness. Dimly he began to sense how living with them could transform him, not by developing his intelligence or qualities of leadership but by awakening the qualities of his heart, the child that was within him.

He had taken it for granted that he and his companions would go to Mass each morning, until one day Philippe asked him why he should. It was only then that he would recognise that in order to remain there and not return to the institution Philippe would have been prepared to make virtually any concession, even that of going to Mass when he did not want to. Yet the Holy Spirit could only express itself in freedom. There came the realisation that the more fragile a person's liberty was, the more it must be respected and protected. Such was the pedagogy, not of force but of freedom, which Dr Preaut and Père Thomas had recognised handicapped people so specifically needed. It was a principle which would become absolutely fundamental to the communities that would follow.

Jean Vanier lays claim to being conscious of only two things at the beginning of l'Arche, two things which he would not have been able to put into words at the time: one was that what he was doing was irreversible; the other was a somewhat ambivalent feeling about possible growth – 'If nobody came we would remain the size of a car so that we could still travel together, but there was also a desire to start building little barrack huts right from the beginning.' Somewhere in his heart and in his head there was a model of community which consciously or unconsciously he was following.

In 1954 he had come to know the Little Sisters of Jesus in Montreal. L'Arche would share a similar spirituality to that of the Little Sisters and Brothers to whom over the years it would come to feel very close. They would discover a common basis in the spirituality of Nazareth, in the discovery of the presence of Jesus in the poor, and in the simplicity of their daily life. Eau Vive also undoubtedly had an influence, although there for Jean Vanier it had been more a question of discovering the ways of the Spirit. He had been influenced by Dorothy Day's paper, the *Catholic Worker* in New York. Catherine Doherty's Friendship House, Tony Walsh and Benedict Labre House had also touched him profoundly as communities based very much on pain, on mercy and welcoming people. They were communities in which lay people lived a life of simplicity and poverty with the very poor. He had also visited the Foyer de Charité which Cardinal Leger had begun in Montreal. There people with physical and mental handicaps were welcomed in a spirit of prayer. Elements of all these would find their way into l'Arche.

Jean Vanier professes not to be a man of much vision, yet from the very earliest days there does seem to have been a vision in operation. In September 1964 Dr Preaut asked him to welcome another man with a handicap, Jacques Duduit. At the beginning of November, a Sister Marie Benoit who was living in the village with two other sisters, asked to come and work on a regular basis in the house. Meals improved dramatically. Then, in December a social worker asked them to welcome Jean-Pierre Crépieux. The little family was gradually growing.

Jacqueline d'Halluin was by this time dividing her time between Paris where she was looking after three invalids and the little house with a garden, which was in those days overgrown and so seemed to her very much part of the forest. Drawn once again to the trees and to the new life which she sensed somehow to be being born there, it had been she who was called upon to write a prayer which the tiny community could say as they gathered together around the flickering light of a candle. The l'Arche prayer was compiled on the basis of some suggestions made by Jean Vanier even before the arrival of Raphael and Philippe. It was addressed to Mary in whose life was contained the mystery of the relationship between the Word and the body; 'Mary who lived off and was nourished

by the prophetic Word as a young girl, filled with grace until
the incarnation when it's no longer the Word but that silent
body, first of all inside her and then in her arms.' The prayer
centred upon three invocations of Saint Vincent de Paul:
'Lord, bless us through the hands of your poor, Lord smile
at us through the faces of your poor, Lord receive us one day
into the happy company of your poor.' It would be modified
over the years to enable non-Christians and Christians of
different denominations to join together in worship all over
the world. I would hear it sung to the accompaniment of
guitars, murmured softly against the roar of traffic beyond
thin wooden walls, uttered falteringly by those able only to
say the first line over and over again, in Spanish, English,
French . . . and in its essential it would not change, for it
reflected the special relationship of reciprocity which remains
at the very heart of l'Arche and which has altered only in its
deepening:

O Mary,
We ask you to bless our house,
Keep it in your immaculate heart,
Make l'Arche a true home,
A refuge for the poor, the little ones,
So that here they may find the source of all life,
A refuge for those who are deeply tried,
So that they may find your infinite consolation.

O Mary,
Give us hearts that are attentive,
Humble and gentle,
So that we may welcome with tenderness and compassion
All the poor you send us.
Give us hearts full of compassion
So that we can love, serve,
Dissolve all discord
And see in our suffering and broken brothers the humble
    presence of
Jesus.

Lord,
Bless us with the hands of your poor.

Lord,
Smile at us through the eyes of your poor.

Lord,
Receive us one day
into the blessed company of your poor.

Amen

When it came to choosing a name for the small community, Jacqueline d'Halluin was asked to make up a list of biblical names. When Jean Vanier read it he chose 'l'Arche', the French word for both ark and arch, without a moment's hesitation. Now he can give a rational answer as to why it seemed so obviously appropriate but he insists that it is not the real explanation: 'I'm one of those people, I think, that discovers reasons afterwards but I think we're in a domain which is symbolic, not rational. It goes very, very deep.'

His room in Trosly-Breuil contains a bed, a book case with a modest collection of books and a desk covered with letters and papers. In the middle of the room two chairs face each other before a fire place. The mantelpiece is packed with photographs and small ornaments from all over the world, many painstakingly made by people with a handicap. The floor is strewn with more books and papers; one corner is set aside for prayer. In the momentary quiet between phone calls and laughter, knocks on the door and the sounds of exterior decorating being enthusiastically carried out by two of 'our people' he would delve into the depths to produce a series of reasons which failed still to satisfy him completely:

The passages in Genesis which tell the story of Noah are rich and meaningful. The Ark is the first covenant between God and humanity even before the birth of the Jewish people. So it's the whole vision of a boat where we welcome people who are in pain. It's the place where we are saved. It's the place of the covenant, and that's very important to us. Also Mary, who carried the saviour in her womb, has been referred to by the Fathers of the Church as the 'Ark of the Covenant'. Then there is the whole idea of the arch as a bridge, the bridge between two worlds. Then the ark of the covenant as the inner sanctuary, and then, something which is possibly deeper, the idea that we're looking at humanity somewhere before today's Christianity and we welcome people because they are people and not because they are baptised.

He was also a naval man, and to one who when speaking English will break frequently into French, not always in an attempt to find the *mot juste* but sometimes simply for the sake of euphony, there was also the attraction of the very sound of the word 'l'Arche': 'It's not a hard "k"; it's something soft, gentle and holding.'

Somewhere in the early vision, of which both Jean Vanier and Père Thomas were a part, was the idea of welcoming anyone who wished to come, be they the very elderly, drug addicts or simply 'gentlemen of the road'. At Christmas 1964 Jean Vanier went to collect his sister Thérèse who was arriving at Compiègne station from England. On the way there he noticed a man walking along the road and, seeing him again on the return journey, he invited him for Christmas lunch. Showered and refreshed, Gabriel presided over the Christmas festivities, smoked cigarettes and regaled the assembled company with stories. He had previously tried his vocation as a Dominican but had remained for only a few months. He was now a traveller and after a couple of days was back on the road with an open invitation to return. This he did in January 1965 but, as soon as he decided to install himself on a more permanent basis, it became quickly apparent that he was not suited to living long in community. He was very jealous of Raphael and Philippe. The two archangels in particular did not get on and, when finally Jean Vanier walked into the dining room one day to find plates flying through the air, it was decided that for the sake of Raphael and Philippe, Gabriel must leave. To Jean Vanier it became increasingly apparent that the vision was gradually focusing to suggest that l'Arche could not take in all who were in need but was to be for those suffering from a particular form of poverty, the mentally handicapped.

Brother Andrew, co-founder with Mother Teresa of the Missionary Brothers of Charity and one with whom l'Arche feels a close affinity, would recall the question of the nature and focus of community arising during his very first meeting with Jean Vanier in Calcutta in the early 1970s. As Superior of the Missionary of Charity Brothers, Brother Andrew had just had to ask two much loved men with very good qualities to leave the congregation:

One had done much good work with the poor but was

moving more and more towards a political approach to their problems, and felt strongly that this was the only way. He was keen to move the whole emphasis to this, but it would have involved a big change in purpose and style from those for which our congregation was established. The other was a very likeable and popular man who had a taste for drinking and who was drawing younger brothers along with him. When Jean arrived I had just gone through this painful business and I told him about it. Everyone knows Jean's great love for the human person, and I was surprised by the promptness of the response. He said that he believed that one of the prime roles of the superior or leader of any group was to discern who had the spirit of the group and who had not. And if there was a destructive influence he had to send away the person from whom it came. No matter how loving and kind one wanted to be the greater good of others was a vital consideration.

The special call to people with mental handicaps was to be powerfully endorsed when, at the end of 1964, a crisis occurred at the Val Fleuri as a result of which all the staff handed in their notice. In the following March Jean Vanier was asked to take over as its director. The precise nature of the crisis remains unclear. Relations between l'Arche and the much larger residence which housed thirty-two handicapped men had been a little strained. The director there, a Monsieur Wattier, had been a good man but not one who was very creative or rich in ideas. Conscious of Jean Vanier's friendship both with Dr Preaut and Père Thomas he appears to have seen the French Canadian's presence in the village as a threat. He had allowed Raphael and Philippe and subsequently Jacques and Jean Pierre to go to the Val Fleuri for showers but otherwise there was little contact between the two houses. In those days the residents of the Val Fleuri were kept firmly under lock and key except during a daily walk which was taken in a line with one member of staff in front and another bringing up the rear. The atmosphere inside the building was disrupted by violence and screaming. It was not without a certain apprehension that Jean Vanier responded to Dr Preaut's request to pick up the pieces following the departure of all but two of the staff. There was a reluctance too to take a step which would radically alter the prophetic little family in the Foyer de l'Arche. As one of the earliest assistants would put it: 'The community there was poor in every way except in its prayer which was magnificent, but it got poorer because we couldn't even have the kind of community we wanted.'

At the 'Farm' Père Thomas would recall how Jean Vanier loved his little *foyer* and the family life he led there, where he did the cooking himself and was dependent on the villagers for help, and how the assumption of the directorship of the Val Fleuri and consequent uniting of his little family with a much larger state-supported structure was not a transition easily made: 'Jean did it only because he felt it was the will of God.' Jean Vanier for his part would remember: 'I had told Père Thomas that I wasn't capable of running it, but he thought it would be right. In many respects it was madness. I had just no idea how to look after thirty-two people with a lot of violence and screaming.' As at previous significant junctures in his life, however, he took the circumstances as they arose without excessive questioning or introspection.

I suppose there has always been something in me. There's naivety, but there's also risk and trust in self which is both good and bad. You just keep going. I think those are strengths that carry weaknesses also. You make mistakes, but I think also, as you look at the story, there is the presence of Jesus, of one who is using me with all my defects, fragilities and qualities, and bringing something to birth.

There was also obedience to the will of God and to Père Thomas.

On Sunday, 22nd March 1965, Jean Vanier took over the Val Fleuri. The outgoing director had no great desire to become involved in showing him how the place functioned. He pointed out some of the books and handed him a heavy bundle of keys to cupboards, offices and files. The younger man set up his office without knowing so much as the names of the people who lived in the building. Within an hour someone had stolen his bunch of keys. With only two staff members remaining to help him, the house, the workshops and the garden were reduced to chaos. There was no nurse, so Jean Vanier had to learn how to give injections. One man was a diabetic who needed an injection every morning so the new director found himself practising on an orange.

The need soon attracted help. Volunteers appeared from the village and elsewhere to assist with the book-keeping, the gardening and the cooking. It was a time when the social services were trying to organise themselves a little better and they sent a representative to help straighten out the finance and administration. At a congress in Paris for professionals working with the mentally handicapped Jean Vanier stood up and spoke about community life with mentally handicapped people in a way which he now recognises must have seemed very naive to people with infinitely more experience than he. Nevertheless, a lady psychiatrist present, a Dr Richet who at the time was a psychiatrist at Clermont psychiatric hospital forty kilometres from Trosly, approached him afterwards and they became friends. She would help Jean Vanier and other assistants to a deeper understanding of the suffering and the psychological needs of the men in the Val Fleuri and to increased knowledge of how to help them. Furthermore, despite the protestations of ineptitude and the lack of knowledge of anything but navy gunnery and Aristotle, there can be little doubt that the navy had taught someone gifted with a natural authority something about management and about discipline. It had given a boy who in his sister's recollection was something of a dare-devil non-conformist, constantly up to mischief and disinclined to toe the family line if he could avoid it, a certain respect for discipline. It had developed the capacity to cast aside important issues and go for even more important ones, combined with extreme discipline in areas which he recognised as crucial, such as prayer and work. His disciplined attention to both of these stood him in good stead in the chaos of the early days in the Val Fleuri. Not at any stage did he feel the challenge was not for him.

> There were obviously times when it was hard, when I was angry, but I just kept going because I wanted to keep going. I suppose there is also an element of – I was going to say proving oneself, but that's not entirely true. There's a sort of tenacity. Grace is there but there is also a human element. I had to go through many breakages afterwards, but the Val Fleuri was an interesting time.

The taking over of the Val Fleuri had not only moved

Jean Vanier and l'Arche into the world of regulations and administration. It had also opened up the dimension of the workshops. Work had to be found of a kind which would allow mentally handicapped people to develop their particular gifts and give them access to the dignity of a salary, no matter how small. There was an unmistakable happiness that sprang from a handicapped person's discovery that he or she could make something beautiful or useful. Opportunities to nurture that happiness had to be created. Gradually it would be recognised that on the road to greater autonomy a person might need to feel that he had two places of operation – the home and the workplace – and that there was something to be said for these two places and the relationships that went with them being to a large extent separate. In that way if things were going badly in one, it need not necessarily affect the other. This would prove a strong case for those capable of doing so going out to workplaces outside the community. At the same time, close co-operation between home and workshop could provide a more unified and effective approach to a handicapped person's overall growth and development. Now, in the workshops in Trosly-Breuil, the assistants are quite distinct from those who live in the houses, although the two groups liaise regularly. In the work places the ratio of assistants to people with handicaps is one to three. In the right conditions handicapped people there, and in l'Arche communities elsewhere, have shown themselves to be very gifted in the making of mosaics and pottery, woodwork, weaving, gardening and a wealth of other creative skills. Then, however, such avenues were still being explored and there were possibly one or two assistants for thirty-two people. 'Of course I just opened up the gates. I wasn't going to have thirty-two people controlled by two.'

At midday Jean Vanier would eat his meals at the Val Fleuri in a single vast dining-room which has since been divided into three still sizeable rooms. In the evenings he would return to the Foyer de l'Arche to relax over dinner. His office and his bedroom were at the Val Fleuri. He slept poorly during those initial years, for there were invariably disturbances in the night. Nevertheless, in the tumultuous atmosphere of the Val Fleuri, where there was much shouting and where at times men would go into uncontrollable fits and have to be restrained by force, Jean Vanier was still able to perceive the mysterious presence of God. In all the suffering and the madness there was yet something profoundly of God.

Père Thomas recalls emphasising that it was the religious element which alone could unify the increasingly diverse aspects of home life (be it in the Foyer de l'Arche or the Val Fleuri), of work in the workshops and of external involvement in the form of the growing number of people who came to help. In the village of Trosly-Breuil Père Thomas made himself available in his room behind the chapel in the Place des Fêtes, where the blessed sacrament was reserved, to those who sought his council or simply his presence. Sometimes he would celebrate Mass in the nearby church at Pierrefonds. Often he visited the sick and the elderly. The figure in the white habit pedalling his bicycle or kneeling in silent prayer in the little chapel soon became widely known and accepted by the local people as 'le Père blanc'. He had long felt a calling to be specially present to the dying. Early in his priesthood he had discovered how important it was for the dying to have a priest at their side, and Dr Thompson, who had influenced him so markedly, had maintained – as Freud also had done – that what troubled people most was the fear of death. When he arrived in Trosly-Breuil ninety-year-old Madame Bertrand, one of the village ladies who used to take soup to the Foyer de l'Arche every Friday, confided in Père Thomas that she had been praying to God that there would be a priest with her at her death. She welcomed him precisely as one who would accompany her in her last hours and, as it transpired, she did in fact die with Père Thomas saying the rosary beside her. Thus, very quickly, Père Thomas found an eschatological role.

Within the first year of l'Arche a young person with a handicap died in circumstances that were humanly speaking tragic. One Sunday night he suffocated during a fit. His parents could have taken him quietly away to be buried without much being said about the incident. For Père Thomas, however, it was a very significant event which raised very early on in the history of l'Arche the question of how death was going to be approached. Dr Thompson had maintained that the fear of death, while it remained half conscious and unexplained, acted like an abcess beneath the surface of human consciousness. 'We felt it was a unique opportunity to let the handicapped people face death. Most of them had never seen a dead person before. They all came and prayed around the body.' Père Thomas remembers it as an extraordinary day in his apostolic life, extraordinary for the understanding and maturity their response displayed. 'They came to talk to me about what death was and what happened afterwards.'

In October 1988 I would stay for a week in 'La Petite Source', one of the newer houses in Trosly-Breuil. The youngest and most recent member of the household that made me so extraordinarily welcome for that week was Pascal, whose ability to speak was limited but whose capacity to communicate by means of grunts and smiles and touch was more than eloquent. Each time we met he would press his hands together with a look of entreaty and the word 'Papa' which I came to understand was a request that I should pray for his father. Pascal's mother was already dead; his father to whom the boy was particularly close was now gravely ill in hospital. At lunch one day Pascal gave us all to understand via Joseph, one of the assistants, that he had something to say to us after the meal. Over coffee in the living room Joseph announced on Pascal's behalf that his father had 'gone to be with Jesus'. Little was said in response. There were hugs for Pascal and tears and prayers that were touching in their lack of inhibition. There was no denying Pascal his grief. He would disappear to his room at intervals and I would hear him sobbing in the night; but there was also no mistaking the way in which during the days that followed he was tacitly carried in his suffering by the other members of the *foyer*. Small acts of special consideration, a touch, a look, expressed far better than any words the fact that those about him knew his anguish better than most others, and that he was not alone.

Père Thomas speaks very readily of how among handicapped people he discovered a language of the heart 'which is not written but which passes from person to person'. 'For the Holy Spirit to operate through a sermon', he would say as we sat side by side on his worn settee, 'there needs to be a personal contact.' He recalls asking himself, in the early days of l'Arche, whether he should not teach the handicapped people the rudiments of reasoned theology relating to the God who had created them; but in the years leading up to 1968 he would be struck very powerfully by the fact that it was often the assisted who helped the assistants going through difficult times with regard to religious belief and the sacraments, to discover or rediscover religious faith. There was of course a great diversity amongst people with a mental handicap: not all of them had a highly developed spiritual sensitivity. Nor did all of them live an intimate communion with God. Each one had his own particular struggles and temptations. But, in all his years of pastoral care of people with handicaps, Père Thomas claims never to have come across a mentally handicapped person who was an atheist.

> They were all believers. I won't say practising, but they were believers and they were best helped by introducing them to the Gospels and the sacraments as Jesus presented them – Jesus who is paradoxically head of the Church by virtue of his heart, not because he was capable of giving talks that could unify Aristotelianism and Platonism, not because his teachings were more beautiful than that of the Old Testament prophets. Jesus surpassed the prophets in his littleness.

Père Thomas was to find that handicapped people, who he realised related much more readily to persons than to structures or abstractions, quickly discovered the name of Jesus very powerfully. It was also his experience that they discovered Jesus much more readily through the cross than through the manger:

> The first name which handicapped people respond to is not Christ or Lord, not the social functions of Jesus, but Jesus the person, through the heart of Jesus. I discovered that rather than teaching them about the creator God, through Jesus it was possible to help them discover the Father, the Holy Spirit, Mary. It was very simple to prepare them even for first communion through the cross of Jesus.

If handicapped people were touched in a special way by the cross of Jesus, the recognition would become ever clearer that they also had a way of pointing others into the inner meaning of the crucifixion and the actuality of death leading to life. Years later Bishop Stephen Verney, one of three bishops appointed to 'accompany' l'Arche in the United Kingdom, would recall an incident that occurred one evening at a gathering of handicapped people and assistants in Lambeth.

In the course of that evening a handicapped woman of about forty-five had given voice to that 'primal cry' that the world had abandoned her.

She had been rejected by her family and this was the deep, deep trauma inside her which nothing could ever cure. I tried to comfort her by assuring her that she had a new family in l'Arche, but she made it quite clear that that was nonsense really. She had been rejected. Next morning one of the assistants said to me, 'That woman's cry last night pierced into my heart, broke through my defences and showed me the deep cry within myself which I had never realised was there. I knew last night that cry within myself and this morning for the first time I know that I can be loved.' What went on there is such a mystery, but it seems to me that the handicapped woman's cry somehow unlocked the door in the assistant to her own inner need and longing and at that point she could meet God and discover she was loved. So one begins to see how Jesus actually saves us on the cross. One sees that because he cries out, 'My God, my God why hast thou forsaken me,' which is exactly the same cry as that woman's, he can actually touch the inner cry in my heart, your heart, every-body's heart. If we can stop pretending and all stand there together in compassion, which means after all 'suffering together', then we begin to know that we can be loved. I see the mystery of the death of Christ happening in l'Arche.

The germ of that vision – which saw in the weak, the broken and the rejected, the Jesus who was also rejected by his own, tortured and condemned to death, and which per-ceived also the saving power of those suffering people – was already present in the early days of l'Arche. Père Thomas had seen the gift of the handicapped and allowed himself to be touched and shaped by them. He had discovered too, that handicapped people were particularly sensible to the presence of Jesus in the sacraments and the Eucharist and that, because their primary interest was in the heart, they were less deceived by the exterior beauty of the ceremony and more discerning of the attitude of the celebrant.

I remember once a very lovely midnight mass. One of the assistants serving had made it a most beautiful ceremony and I recall being a little caught up in the beauty of the occasion myself. Afterwards in the sacristy, I commented on how lovely the service had been to one of our handicapped men and he told me that he hadn't been able to receive the sacrament. He had sensed that there was too much concern for the ceremony.

From the very earliest days of l'Arche Père Thomas had understood that when handicapped people serving at Mass placed their sometimes clumsy and often grubby fingers on carefully laundered napkins, he could not be excessively concerned with the outer trappings of the ceremony. He had also understood that something in their approach enabled them to discover the eucharistic presence in a special way. 'With their hearts they went directly to the presence of Jesus, and they needed a priest who was not so much a showman as a man who celebrated the Eucharist with faith and love.'

Père Thomas was not specially present in the *foyer* at the beginning of l'Arche. He had undoubtedly felt the need once more to witness something being born, for he was someone who had always needed to confront his spiritual life with something concrete. To be a Dominican or to be a teacher had never in itself been enough. That was why Eau Vive had been born very spontaneously, as if out of a seed that had somehow been sown in advance. L'Arche was to grow in much the same way. This time, however, Père Thomas was to take upon himself a less obviously central role. He did not involve himself in the daily tasks of the little household. Perhaps once a week he would eat with them and sometimes the small family there would take him food, but he wanted to retain a certain freedom in order to live his priesthood fully, to pray for l'Arche and also for the people in the village and surrounding area. There remains the impression that his unassuming prayerful presence was something absolutely essential to the evolution of l'Arche. In fact, as Xavier Lepichon – an eminent oceanographer and member of the College de France, who has made his home close to l'Arche and is attached to the Val Fleuri – would point out, one of the extraordinary aspects of l'Arche derives from the fact that it is founded not on one but on two complementary but different vocations. Its history has been very largely determined by the tension between the two. The ageing priest made it very clear

from the beginning that the priest in l'Arche could not be a
leader or director. That was to be Jean Vanier's role. In
l'Arche the priest was not to be a Father as in the Foyers de
Charité but something closer to a brother. He was to be the
shepherd and servant of the poor and their advocate in time
of need. His role on the community council, for example, was
to defend the interests of the poor person when personal
problems arose. As a servant of the poor, he was also himself
among the humblest, entrusted by God with the service of
the sacraments which was so vital to the life of the heart
especially in the very poor. Père Thomas was always convinced that it was not for him to lead or to make decisions
but rather to ask the questions, 'Where are we going? What
are our primary values?' In this way he might be considered
to provide a kind of yardstick of the values of the heart against
which the movement and direction of the community could
be measured.

It is not difficult to see that such questions might arouse
tension between the questioner and the one who had actually
to take charge, a man who was by nature inclined 'to go
ahead because I just feel it's right' and who had been trained
to be 'efficient'. There were differences of emphasis. Both men
had been drawn to the poor, both shared the recognition that
the poor were teachers of the heart, that they themselves
could learn from the poor rather than the reverse and that
the poor needed relationships of love and freedom in order to
shine. Both had recognised from the beginning of l'Arche a
fact which constitutes a significant difference between it and
many other places that take in people who are suffering, that
'If you go with the poor it's for life', that if you entered into
a deep relationship with someone you could not simply end
it after a few months or years. For Père Thomas, however,
the emphasis was upon being with the poor person to the end
of his life in order to accompany him to his entry into heaven,
to assist him towards the final step of passing to the Father.
For him the whole community was growing towards what
was really an ascension. Whereas for Jean Vanier, the prag-
matist with an Aristotelian approach to happiness, it was
important to accompany the poor man to the end of his life
but also to spend that life with him and see that he was
happy. The two dimensions – the pull towards heaven and
the simultaneous recognition that life in this world must be

lived with happiness, arguably part of the tension experienced in the Church as a whole – were to be very much present in the history of l'Arche, straining one against the other. Père Thomas would also maintain that a welcome should be extended to any poor person. The door should be open wide especially to marginal people; Jean Vanier on the other hand, on the basis of his experience of having to make choices in relation to Dany, Gabriel and others, would identify the need to be selective; if l'Arche wanted to help handicapped people it could not for their sake have marginal people and drug addicts also.

These tensions would in time be experienced in the different l'Arche communities throughout the world. Indeed, it would seem to be part of the l'Arche vocation to live such tensions – which are the tensions of our modern world – in a very difficult way. They would bring suffering to the communities as they undoubtedly brought pain to the two men whose relationship reflected them. When Jean Vanier referred to Père Thomas as a rock, he qualified his comment with the words, 'and sometimes a wounded rock'. As to his own role: 'I think there had to be a number of knocks on the head. Now I have a much greater consciousness of the "our" and a much greater consciousness that it is God's project. But it wasn't always like that.'

Père Thomas was someone who had given Jean Vanier everything that he most valued. In many ways he had been born from the elderly priest, but there came a time when he felt he must evolve from the child to the maturity of someone who could make judgements for himself. That did not mean that the link between them was broken. If anything it was much deeper. And the tension between them was good. 'Père Thomas has this incredible wholeness and holiness,' Jean Vanier would comment. 'He has the eschatological dimension, the vision, and I am just walking with it.' Their complementary differences would be a great safeguard for both, guarantee the humility and the poverty of both and make possible extraordinary growth.

5

Sharing the Word

'If at Eau Vive we had sought in some way to unify the world through an intellectual elite,' Père Thomas would reflect, 'here we were to realise more fully that there was an elite of the heart which was of even greater relevance to the world.'

In the early years of l'Arche the world began to come to Trosly-Breuil in a very significant way. It came in the form of the growing number of handicapped people needing places, and in the form of young assistants who arrived from as far afield as Canada and the United States. They arrived and offered their services in exchange for their room and board and a small stipend, for it was felt in l'Arche that assistants were coming there with an ideal of community life, and the absence of a regular salary would help them to deepen and clarify their motivation. They usually arrived in just sufficient numbers to keep pace with the community's expansion. By the autumn of 1966, Jean Vanier was writing in his regular circular letter, which the increasing number of people showing an interest in l'Arche and its activities had made necessary, of how he received requests several times a week for places that he could not provide. He was still returning to Canada at intervals to lecture. His courses on artistic inspiration, on friendship and affectivity, and on the cry of the poor attracted large audiences. From Toronto he wrote of how at a talk given to 1,800 students he had felt the current of generosity among them. 'We must create situations in which these young people can dedicate themselves and serve,' he wrote. 'L'Arche must seek to fulfil this function also and so become a sign of hope for many others throughout the world.' Now he disclaims having had any definite ideas about the formation or growth of the community. He knew only that he must go ahead: 'There's something naturally speaking, or supernaturally perhaps, that means I am able to form community, so it just happened.'

The combination of the needs and the increasingly recognised gifts of people with handicaps and the untapped and unfocused energies of the generous-spirited young people he was encountering came about with an extraordinary dynamism. The early letters reflect breathtaking activity: the production of 10,000 paper bags a week in the workshops, the organisation of leisure activities that included a more creative element than watching television – photographic clubs, country dancing, cycling, fishing, stamp collecting, painting, singing – celebrations, excursions that included a flight for the men with handicaps in Canadian Air Force Dakotas from Montmedy, renovations such as the installation of central heating in properties already owned, and in particular the acquisition of new ones. Fortunately, the growing number of requests coming from parents, the social services and psychiatric institutions, especially the nearby Clermont psychiatric hospital, coincided with considerable financial encouragement on the part of the mental health authorities. It became possible to meet arising needs in a way which might not otherwise have been feasible. Some of the men at the Val Fleuri very obviously needed to leave the noise of so large a building for a smaller and more intimate environment. In 1966 Steve and Ann Newroth, who would subsequently found the Daybreak community near Toronto, welcomed three men from the Val Fleuri to another house in the village which became known as 'Les Rameaux'.

L'Arche began to buy up as many available houses as possible in Trosly-Breuil and its environs and to give them the names by which the community would know them. By November 1965 they had acquired the use of 'Les Hirondelles'. In 1968 they opened 'l'Ermitage', and in 1969 'Valhinos' which had once been the old presbytery in the adjacent village of Cuise-la-Motte. The 'little valley', as the name means in Portuguese, provided a home for ten handicapped women. Women had been part of the community at l'Arche from the earliest days. They had numbered quite spontaneously among the assistants who arrived often for a week and found themselves staying for very much longer. The possibility of welcoming handicapped women, however, had occasioned a certain amount of fear in the community about mixing the sexes. Nevertheless, in the conviction that their arrival was something that was meant to be, Jean Vanier did what he calls 'his naval officer stuff': 'I just knew that it had to come and that if I listened to the community here it wouldn't come, so I bought a house. And as I was president of the Board of Directors I just created a new community there.' Afterwards, he acknowledges, he had to pick up the pieces, but by then the important step had been taken. Between 1970 and 1977 l'Arche opened a further twelve houses in Trosly, its neighbouring villages of Breuil and Pierre- fonds and the nearby town of Compiègne. These included 'La Grande Source' which had previously been Trosly- Breuil's café-hotel. Hitherto guests had had to be given accommodation in the various *foyers* but, when the visitors themselves were people in need, such an arrangement had proved to be unsatisfactory. 'La Grande Source' became first a *foyer* and then a place where visitors could stay. So the remarkable growth went on: in 1968 l'Arche had welcomed 73 handicapped people; by 1970, 112; by 1972, 126. Today in the Trosly-Breuil region alone there are more than twenty l'Arche houses.

On 5th March 1967 Jean Vanier's father died quietly and at peace in Ottawa. The day after the General's death, his son was going through his papers and found a number of brief notes which were very simple but clear intimations of a special intimacy with Jesus. It seemed right that the many who had loved General Vanier should be given some insight into the source which had helped him to be what he was. Jean Van- ier's first book, an insight into the spiritual pilgrimage which had been so essential a part of General Vanier's life as a lawyer, soldier, diplomat, ambassador and, for seven years, Canada's Governor-General, was written with no pretensions to biography or completeness. It was the kind of book, the intimation was, that Jean Vanier himself might find accept- able under similar circumstances: written in order only that those who knew and loved him might be allowed to know just a little more of the light and loves that had guided such a man. There was, Jean Vanier would be quick to point out, very little in the book apart from quotations from letters General Vanier had written to some Carmelite Sisters and his notes. His family had no wish to betray the discretion the General himself had exercised.

General Vanier had helped l'Arche financially in its earliest days but he had never visited Trosly-Breuil. Jean Vanier remains uncertain whether or not his father had understood, what people in l'Arche were endeavouring to live. He knew only that his father had loved Père Thomas, sensing that there was a mystery of pain in the priest who meant so much to his son, and that he had trusted them. That trust would enable Jean to look back and say that he and his father had been very close.

After her husband's death Madame Vanier, who had visited the Foyer de l'Arche while her husband was still Governor-General and found her son living 'in a terrible state', paid another visit to the community in Trosly-Breuil. Her mother had also recently died and she had inherited a house in the village in which her mother had intended to live. In her nineties, Madame Vanier would recall with amusement the circumstances under which that house, 'les Marroniers', was acquired and under which she herself had come to live in it:

> Grandma simply told Jean that she wanted to come and live near him and Père Thomas. Oh my – she was eighty-eight and her mind was failing. They had a terrible time finding this house, and when they did it was in a dreadful condition. They started restoring it, and in the meantime grandma was living in a hotel in Paris. The bathroom there was pink and black, so the bathroom here had to be pink and black. Knowing she wouldn't be used to the kind of furniture people had here, particularly in 1968, they acquired two velvet-covered chairs for her, but she died without ever seeing the house.

On her mother's death, Madame Vanier informed her son, in the course of her visit to Trosly-Breuil, that he was to have the house for l'Arche. During that same visit, however, an assistant suggested to her, with what at the time she considered extreme impertinence, that she should come and live in it. The suggestion infuriated her, but the seed was sown. In October 1971, uncertain what she should do with what remained of her life, she would spend a week's retreat in a Carmelite convent in Montreal where she had special permission to enter the enclosure: 'On the very last day it was the Gospel of the rich young man. I came out in floods of tears. I didn't want to come here. I was afraid.'

Nevertheless she left her splendid house in Montreal in the charge of one man-servant and gave herself a six-month trial period in the house set in a garden studded with chestnut trees at Trosly-Breuil. At the end of those six months she sold everything and moved permanently into 'Les Marronners' complete with its black and pink bathroom and its two velvet chairs. Despite her protestations that she was just a 'fat bourgeois amongst the poor', she would find a much valued role as grandmother adviser to the young assistants. 'The gift of youth to community is the gift of wonderment,' Jean Vanier would write in *Community and Growth*, 'that of the elderly the peaceful wisdom of age . . . Grandmothers sense certain things. And there are things which can be confided only to them. They are important to a community.'

The community expanded in a fashion which Jean Vanier would now consider wildly haphazard. At the time he simply acted as the need and the opportunity arose. A house would fall vacant and he would buy it and fill it, without really ascertaining in advance whether it would suit the particular needs of the people who were to live in it. There were times when the arrival of assistants did not keep pace with the number of people with a handicap, and there were days when one single assistant had charge of twenty handicapped men in the workshops. Nevertheless, as early as 1965 Jean Vanier wrote: 'The first months of l'Arche have been lived in poverty and simplicity. Now that the first foundations have been laid, we must give it structure, organise, grow. We must make a solid work that will last.' He also wrote of how he realised that while l'Arche had been profoundly inspired by the Gospels, and while it was to be a community lived in the spirit of the Beatitudes, there was also a need to make full use of medical and psychiatric techniques in close co-operation with the relevant health authorities. He was not one to fail to recognise the importance of professional skills and competence and to encourage them within the community; in any case, government financing involved certain conditions with regard to structure and care, to boards of directors and living conditions.

The story is told of how one government inspector had satisfactorily completed his tour of inspection of the very primitive 'Foyer de l'Arche', much to the relief of Jean Vanier and his fellow residents who had been specifically briefed not to draw attention to the outside lavatory which it was felt left a little to be desired. The inspector was about to leave when Jean-Pierre, with characteristically amiable helpfulness intervened, 'You're welcome to see our toilet.' Another story tells of how a representative from the Department of Health was invited to lunch at a time when l'Arche was seeking the Department's financial support. After the meal this very important person found himself enlisted to help with the washing up. Washing up in l'Arche is still a time of particular fellowship, of relaxed and simple conversation and jostling horseplay in which everybody is invited to take part. In those days the tea-towels were not always very clean or dry. People used to like the hot soapy water and race to do the washing and it was not unheard of for Jean Vanier, then as now, to leap over a table to get to the washing-up bowl first. The official from the Department of Health would afterwards admit to being deeply touched at being asked to help with this simple domestic task. He had felt welcomed as a man and not merely in his official capacity, and it was over the kitchen sink that his enduring friendship for Jean Vanier and l'Arche was born.

Some of the early assistants at Trosly-Breuil who have remained in l'Arche look back with a certain nostalgia to the days when numbers were relatively small, when contact with Jean Vanier was much closer and when, although the need for greater order was recognised, their lack of competence in many fields allowed the poor to reveal themselves in a special way. From the very first Jean Vanier had seen the importance of journeys and celebrations in lives that might otherwise be monotonous and devoid of hope, to keep up spirits and to open hearts and minds to other realities. For centuries Jews, Muslims, Hindus and Christians alike had valued a sense of pilgrimage. The experience of journeying together to a holy place, to a place of prayer was, it was felt, important for everyone but possibly even more so for the poor person and for the person with a handicap. The community would set off on pilgrimage often in processions of private cars to Rome or Lourdes or Fatima or some other distant destination. Often the cars would break down *en route*. There would be other minor setbacks, but ones which were often turned upside down and made mysteriously acceptable and even happy by people like Dédé who would look at a shattered windscreen and see not the brokenness, the inconvenience and the work involved in its replacement but only the beauty, the way it shone like crystal in the sunlight. There would be moments of relaxation, joy, renewed hope, and for some the beginnings of a new and more peaceful life, a life more open to the world, society and other people.

Michel took part in one of these early pilgrimages to Rome as part of a short stay to see whether he would remain in l'Arche. At the hospital where he had been living he had been told simply that he was to stay for a trial period and had not expected anything very different from his hospital life. Suddenly he found himself in a car in St Peter's Square and chattered with great excitement and fluency about his wishes, his fears and his feelings in general. The l'Arche assistants had no official file for him and so it was only later that they discovered that Michel had not uttered a word in hospital for many years. Their lack of knowledge had made it possible for Michel to react to them quite differently from the way he had responded to professionals. One of the early assistants would look back:

> There was a lot of madness. We were incompetent in many ways. We were young and we threw ourselves into this new idea of 'living together' without any regard for how late we went to bed, conserving our energies or having a private life of any kind, but in a way that madness, that incompetence was justified by the fact that we were possibly the first to say to handicapped people, 'You are loved just as you are.'

Though not given an unqualified welcome by all members of the community and not always up to the professional standards of others, greater competence would come. Dr Leone Richet was the first to help the community grasp the particular therapy of l'Arche. For several years she would come for a few hours a week. When she left the area she found another psychiatrist, Dr Erol Franko, who would help and support the community and also play a vital role in Jean Vanier's own intellectual development and the evolution of the therapeutic aspect of l'Arche. None of the psychiatrists and psychologists at Trosly-Breuil, and few working with communities elsewhere, have been people who would call themselves Christian. Asked what it was that had attracted them to l'Arche in the first place, they would cite very practical reasons such as considerations of salary or convenience of location. All, however, have been men and women with a profound respect for people. L'Arche had come into being at a time when professionals in the field of mental handicap had on the whole received a scientific education based on the philosophical ideas of the last century; the ideas of evolution, natural selection, relativism, positivism and Marxist or Freudian interpretations of idealism which have now broadly worked themselves into popular thinking. From such a vantage point it could be considered logical to view a handicapped person as an unfortunate happening, a disastrous mistake of nature. Fortunately, it would seem that the hearts of most people had not fully accepted the message that their heads had been fostering. L'Arche would be greatly encouraged to meet many clear-minded professionals who regarded their clients as people like themselves, who were generous and compassionate and who worked with uncompromising integrity for a more human situation for handicapped people. Some professionals, for their part, would come to see in l'Arche a new vision of how their professional skills could be exercised. One Honduran psychologist had been working for some time on the idea of bringing a group of her colleagues to experience for themselves the life that people with handicaps were leading in the community. At the same time, professional carers presented l'Arche with a challenge to be more competent and confronted it with insights drawn from a different perspective and different reference points.

With the help of Dr Franko who 'worked magic' at a time when the men in the Val Fleuri really needed a magician, Jean Vanier would begin to integrate both professional and spiritual insights into life in l'Arche. He would come to see unusual or abnormal behaviour – such as violence, delirium or the refusal to eat or speak – not as primarily a symptom of mental illness to be categorised and medically cured, but as a language to which people should be listening. Such behaviour showed that the person concerned was living in a world other than the 'normative'. People who were well integrated into society, who lived according to established norms were often afraid of those who acted strangely, were upset by them and neither could nor wanted to listen to them. In their fear they tried by every possible means, even by violence, to change 'abnormal' people, to 'normalise' them, to make them act in an acceptable way. At the same time those who felt excluded and labelled 'mentally ill' tended to build their own isolated world. Their behaviour became more and more odd, and people about them became more and more frightened. It was a vicious circle which often ended in a complete break and hospitalisation. Yet strange behaviour was first and foremost a way of saying: 'I'm suffering, come and help me. I feel alone and unable to find my way in the chaos.' Sadly the response was frequently a fearful and defensive rejection, and the person whose cry for help was the loudest was often the one most categorically rejected. The person who most needed to be understood and supported was often the one who found him or herself most misunderstood and alone.

L'Arche was learning to listen, to listen to the wisdom that could be gleaned from outside the community even when the demands made exposed its own mediocrity, to listen also to what people with handicaps were saying and so discover there a value and a light. On a more recent pilgrimage to Assisi and Rome a group of l'Arche people had an audience with Pope John Paul II. As Père Thomas has often pointed out, for handicapped people who do not relate well to structures but rather to persons, the Roman Catholic Church has the advantage of having at its head an actual father, one person whom they can love, the Pope. On this occasion the Pope went along a line, greeting people who were waiting to meet him. Men bowed their heads, women curtseyed in respectful silence until eventually he came within sight of Alice, one of the handicapped women, who called out as soon as she saw him, 'John Paul, John Paul, we love you.' He sought her out and took her in his arms. 'She had said', reflected one of the assistants, 'what everybody wanted to say but did not feel they had the right to say.'

Whenever there are handicapped people present anything can happen quite spontaneously: a server at Mass will pour the water for the celebrant, then wander off and water a flower, a handicapped person arriving at Tel Aviv airport at a time of great tension can walk up to an armed guard, remove the man's gun from his grasp and hold out his hand to be shaken. 'The basic gift of a handicapped person is that of having kept the heart of a child,' Jean and Anne-Marie de la Selle, two of the first assistants to get married in l'Arche, would point out. 'Much of a handicapped person's personality is still that of the child we can no longer be. Even at the age of forty or fifty a handicapped person can be quite without restraint, can react as a child would and so cast a different perspective on theology, philosophy and our world.'

The de la Selles remember one High Mass in particular at the conclusion of a pilgrimage at which a cardinal sat high up on a throne looking down on the congregation, surrounded by an entourage of bishops. During the communion the cardinal rose from his throne to administer the sacraments and as he did so one of the handicapped men went up into the chancel, sat himself in the cardinal's seat and gazed about him: 'You could see that he really wanted to know what sitting on this throne did to you.' There was much agitation amongst the bishops. Some evidently thought they should do something; others apparently felt they should ignore the figure on the throne completely. In the end nobody did anything. When the cardinal had finished administering the sacrament he took a stool, placed it next to the throne, sat down on it and chatted to the handicapped person.

It was quite a sight: the cardinal sitting on the stool and the handicapped person looking down at him from the throne. The cardinal's humility was very beautiful, and the handicapped person had given him the opportunity to show that for all his importance, he too still had the heart of a child.

Visitors who came to Trosly-Breuil did not fail to be marked, as Jean Vanier and Père Thomas had been, by people who were so poor and so rejected yet were the carriers of so much life and love. Their thirst for friendship and communion, devoid as it was of the masks to which people of power and intellect are given, invariably provoked a strong reaction. There were those who hardened themselves and rejected; more often people opened themselves to a very simple relationship built upon trust and upon those small acts of kindness which precluded the need for too many words. It was true that there were difficult moments in the life of various houses, moments of crisis and violence, but for the most part people were happy together. L'Arche was experiencing the paradox that the people whom the world considered useless and only fit to be put away in institutions – those who were regarded as a heavy burden and a financial problem – were actually sources of light and life. It was also recognising, in that paradox, the paradox of the Beatitudes, of Jesus, of the message of Good News that gave cause for celebration. There was a good deal of laughter in the community over simple things. Mealtimes had become times of relaxation and celebration; people's birthdays were celebrated; their arrivals and their presence were celebrated. There was growing appreciation of celebration as something different from a party at which friends met and drank and laughed, but where often the laughter was hollow and the drinks were necessary to warm hearts and spirits.

'To celebrate', Jean Vanier would write some years later in *A Hope That We Can Grow*,

is to give thanks for the gift God has given us in having brought us together from a place of loneliness into a sense of belonging. I know that you have accepted me and I you. I know your gifts, and I also know your darkness. Yet I accept you as you are, not expecting more and not weeping because you are not exactly what I wanted you to be. So to celebrate is to give thanks for all you are and all we are together.

On this divided earth there was never perfect celebration. A note of suffering was always present: perhaps some members of the community were not there, some were blocked off or in pain, some may have broken away. Whilst celebrating the unity that had been given it was still important, insisted Jean Vanier, to be open to the suffering of our world. Indeed, celebration did not happen if the weak and the frail, if the children or the old were not present. In the same way that the quality of the prayer after the meal in the evening was remarkable precisely because of the special potency of hearts turned in extreme simplicity and sincerity towards God, so at

the heart of every celebration were the eyes and the laughter of
those who were most fragile and most vulnerable.

This witness of handicapped people in daily life was one
which readily engaged the interest and the commitment of
young people in the late 1960s. In the Church it was a time
shortly after the Second Vatican Council. In the world at
large a climate of economic prosperity and security prevailed
and Third World countries were gaining their independence.
There was a great thirst for liberation which gave rise to
problems with authority, in the Church and institutions in
general, but also to the desire to create and to commit oneself
to something purer and new. There was a feeling that most
religious orders had lost sight of the original intuition of their
founders. There was also a desire to get away from the need
to compromise with society, wealth and power. Young people
coming to l'Arche were highly educated and formed in their
ideals and their attitudes and needed in some way to emerge
from that to find their own space and creativity. The idea of
living with the handicapped person as one of the poor offered
a new form of living, a new and purer rule for a harmonious
life together. Assistants of that generation speak readily of the
poignant difference between the community life in l'Arche
and the life they experienced in the 'outside world'. They
committed themselves in a way which produced great dynamism but which was not devoid of problems. It was to cause
difficulties in the tension which would always exist to a greater
or lesser extent in l'Arche between the need for professionalism and the desire to be ever open to divine providence
and the Holy Spirit, between what some would consider a
necessary detachment and a commitment to the point sometimes of self-destruction. It was also to aggravate the problems
which, in the late 1960s, were beginning to arise with the
local people of Trosly-Breuil.

At the very beginning the villagers, though possibly taken
aback by the mentally handicapped people who suddenly
appeared in their streets, accepted their presence with good
grace. The arrival of assistants from all over the world, however, many of whom were not very well dressed and who
behaved in a way which seemed strange to many elderly
residents of the neighbourhood, inevitably gave rise to apprehension. The local people saw Canadians and English people
sitting on the pavement chatting, with their bikes lying on

the ground beside them and they wondered how Monsieur Vanier could possibly have assistants like that to look after mentally handicapped people. Monsieur Vanier, for his part, acknowledges now with regret that in his keenness to help people with handicaps he was undiplomatic and insensitive to the village people. The tension mounted as he bought up more and more houses, a tension which was aggravated by the fact that he was a foreigner. Most of the people in the neighbourhood had lived there for several generations. Their land and their houses represented their history and their cultural patrimony; now these seemed under threat from someone who appeared to have unlimited financial resources, who though he spoke French did not speak their language, and who did not go about things in their way. When Jean Vanier wished to act he did so through the *Préfet*.* He was not aware that in a French village there was a mayor and councillors and that the councillors were there in the very next street. Neither he nor Jacqueline d'Halluin nor Père Thomas had really lived village life before. They noticed a little too late that they had failed to communicate what they were trying to live to the people on their doorstep. Finally, in 1972, l'Arche would recognise the need to stop and to reassure. The community undertook to set a limit to the number of handicapped people it would bring into the village; there would be no more than sixty-six handicapped people living in Trosly-Breuil. The figure was agreed with the mayor of the village and has since been respected. It was also agreed that no more houses would be bought there without the consent of the council.

As it transpired, the arrangement would prove to be in the interests of l'Arche also, for although the growth in Trosly-Breuil had produced a 'motherhouse' equipped to welcome and introduce à large number of assistants to life in l'Arche, who would in their turn go out to found or become part of communities elsewhere in France or the world, it had also meant the very real, if not immediately recognised, danger of creating merely another kind of institution or ghetto in which people with a handicap were set apart and ostracised. The smallness and the attitude of the village had obliged l'Arche to discover that one of their aims was 'insertion'. If one of

* Préfet: local administrator for the region.

the prime objectives was to help the handicapped person to lead as full a life as possible, it was important that his life was integrated with that of his neighbours and the village. L'Arche, however, had failed to make the villagers understand this, and it would take a while for the wound to heal.

This would not be the only incidence of opposition from neighbours experienced by l'Arche. There would be others, perhaps the most significant of which occurred in 1984 when plans were being made for a new community in Kansas, U.S.A. A neighbourhood was chosen and the project explained to many local people, but when it was formally presented to the municipal council it was rejected. Neighbours protested that they did not want to live next door to people with a mental handicap. Three times the founding director went through the same experience, and only in 1988 was the opposition surmounted.

Meanwhile, in 1968, Jean Vanier had been invited by a group of Catholic priests in Toronto to lead a retreat for the Toronto diocese in Marylake. As a layman he was somewhat taken aback by the invitation, and his first reaction was to decline. After an interval of prayer and reflection, however, it seemed very clear that if he was to take the retreat it should not be just for priests but rather for all the people of God. He suggested that the participants should be made up of one-third priests, one-third religious and one-third lay people. The retreat would last eight days and a considerable part would be conducted in silence. Jean Vanier had never given a retreat before, so it was with a feeling of confusion that he entered the room marked 'Retreat Master'. Nevertheless, 'incredible grace was given, something so strong'. With hindsight he would attribute his ability to give things very simply in a way that touched people to the fact that he had never really been in the world of church conflict. At the time, he made a discovery related to his experience as a teacher of 'something inside myself which flowed out with conviction and force and obviously touched people'. Aware of the mystery of the word which can penetrate people's hearts rather than their heads and change them, he would comment,

It's funny how often I find people say, 'You never say anything that I don't know.' It's as if the word penetrates right into the very depths and puts a word on what people already know, gives the revelation. You don't actually teach anybody anything. All you do is give them the consciousness that they know it.

Looking back on that retreat and on the many that would follow, he would value them as experiences of vital importance, both for l'Arche and for him, in that they enabled him to discover the power of the Word of God, the Word which is 'the good news announced to the poor and the promise of the presence, the forgiveness and the sustenance of Jesus, which awakens in us new energies of love, which purifies and liberates, which reveals to each his true identity as a child loved by the Father'. Announcing this Word, he often felt as if he was the first to hear it. He was, he claimed, a long way from living it. Yet it did him good. As far as others were concerned, Jean Vanier was endorsing the gospel message relating to the poor, the sick and the handicapped, those with whom Jesus had so specifically identified himself, with his actual experience of life with disadvantaged people. To them the word born of silence and of personal experience seemed to have a special force. Some were particularly touched by what he had to say about the poor, some by the vision he offered of community, but somewhere beyond it all was a glimpse of the lived actuality of the Word become flesh.

As a layman conducting a retreat for some sixty people of whom approximately a third were priests, Jean Vanier felt the need for the presence of a priest and a friend. He therefore invited Fr O'Conner, a priest whom he had known at Eau Vive and who still comes regularly to l'Arche Trosly-Breuil to join him. Fr O'Conner was very involved in the charismatic movement that had begun in the United States in the early sixties. At the retreat he spoke a number of times about charismatic renewal in the States and every night he had a prayer meeting. Jean Vanier would recall him saying at the end of the gathering that he did not understand why, when at his other prayer meetings gifts had been given, they had apparently not been granted there. Had the gifts of tongues and prophecy to which the priest was referring taken over, which Jean Vanier acknowledges they could have done because he was 'open to anything' at the time, many things would have been different in l'Arche. As it was, what seemed at the time to be most healing for people was the adoration of the blessed sacrament. Jean Vanier felt himself close to the charismatic movement in the Roman Catholic Church, both in the United States and in France. There was 'something incredibly beautiful about it', but somehow he was always more drawn to the more silent worship of Charles de Foucauld and of the Little Sisters of Jesus from whom, in Montreal, he had learned the importance of periods of quiet adoration.

Gifts were given at that retreat in Marylake, though possibly not in the form that some had anticipated. The people who experienced those eight days together were profoundly touched by the talks, by the periods spent in silent adoration, by the Eucharist, and by their times together in groups of eight sharing, as distinct from discussing, their faith. They were left with the impression that the Holy Spirit had been present amongst them and the desire to continue what had begun there. It was decided to arrange two other retreats for the following year: one which Jean Vanier would again give in Marylake and another for those people who had already taken part in the first retreat, organised by one of those participants. So it was that the 'Faith and Sharing' movement was born to organise retreats based on the model of that first one. To whatever place he was invited, after one retreat Jean Vanier would go for the next. A group would be appointed to organise the retreat for the following year. Having given a retreat in Ottawa in French, he was afterwards asked to give one in French in Montreal. If there were people from Quebec at the Ottawa retreat, he decided, he would give a retreat a few months later in Quebec, and so it went on. In this way small groups of people who wished to meet together and pray and share emerged quite spontaneously, as did priests and religious and lay people who were willing to give retreats. The aspect of sharing was an essential one. The initial insight of conducting a retreat for all the people of God was to be remarkably endorsed. Lay people, clergy and religious, married and single people, young and old, all came. From the first also there was an attempt to bring together different social groups, particularly people who were in some way disadvantaged, be it through material poverty, disablement of mind or body or through some other condition which placed them on the margins of society. People were invited from old people's homes together with the mentally and physically handicapped and people who were living alone. In the groups which would eventually meet all over Canada, the United States and Britain there would be one or two active organisers, but often they were predominantly 'little people'. As in the parable of the wedding feast, Jean Vanier would point out, there were many in our world who had no time to come to such gatherings, but there was also a whole class of people – the elderly, the handicapped, the lonely who had too much time and who were glad to come. Their presence would prove invaluable.

Often new l'Arche communities would spring up in the wake of one of these retreats. The communities in Edmonton, Calgary, Mobile, Cleveland, Victoria, Winnipeg, St Malachie and Erie all had their roots in the retreat movement. Among the many who were deeply and lastingly touched by Jean Vanier's talks was a Canadian religious studying at the University of Toronto. Sue Mosteller had first heard him speak at the university and had been greatly moved by what he had said about the circle of poverty:

> I remember him saying that the person who is poor or suffering does not take care of himself, looks as if he is suffering and is therefore not attractive. Consequently we are not attracted to him and he feels rejected. He is stuck in this circle that ostracises him, while we who are stronger, who have education, friends and wealth and who can get out of our own pain are in another circle with people who like us. We stay in that circle and don't step out, so we don't have any ugliness. If we don't like people we walk away and so we keep our circle going while the circle of the poor spirals down.

On the strength of this insight and of Jean Vanier's emphasis on the message of Corinthians that the poor would bring the message to the wise and the prudent, Sue Mosteller went to the retreat in 1968.

> I was at a point in my religious life where I was searching because I wasn't finding. Jean called us to prayer. He called us to silence, and it was the first time in the whole of my religious life that I felt that the silence was not empty, that it was full of the presence of God, that God was acting in my emptiness. There was a need in me, and that word

came and filled the vacuum for me. I wanted to be more faithful, more radical.

Three years later she would find herself at Daybreak, the first of the l'Arche communities to open in Canada.

Also at the Marylake retreat in 1968 was a Superior General of Our Lady's Missionaries, Sister Rosemarie Donovan. At the end of the eight-day gathering she felt moved to offer l'Arche a house and some seven acres of land in Richmond Hill, once the site of the order's novitiate on the outskirts of Toronto. The offer coincided in an extraordinary way with the return of Steve and Ann Newroth to Canada. The Newroths were Anglicans; Steve had in fact completed studies for the Anglican ministry. Since opening the 'Rameaux' in Trosly-Breuil, they had spent a year at the Ecumenical Institute of Bossey near Geneva. The couple's creativity combined with Jean Vanier's Toronto retreat and the offer of the property suggested that the 'Daybreak' community in Richmond Hill was given in a very particular sense. A board of directors was formed and 'Daybreak' opened its doors in October 1969. In addition to the seven acres which had been given by the Our Lady's Missionaries the new l'Arche was able to take up an option the Sisters had held on another 13 acres owned by the Basilian Fathers. They also leased a further 150 acres directly from the Basilian Fathers for the princely sum of one dollar a year. Against the background of a move in North America towards the introduction of group homes instead of large institutions for the mentally handicapped, Steve and Ann Newroth brought with them to Canada their experience of Trosly-Breuil and the vision of working towards the building of ten homes which would be not exactly a village but in some ways self-contained, like the community at Trosly – the limitations of that self-containment had not yet been identified. Also integral to their initial vision was a farm. Steve Newroth was the son of a farmer and he was attracted to farmwork as good, physical, meaningful work which could be therapeutic.

To the 'Big House', originally the home of the Our Lady's Missionaries, the 'New House' was swiftly added in 1969. From there most of the 'folks', as the handicapped people became known in l'Arche in North America, went out to a local sheltered workshop, but some remained to look after the cattle, sheep, horses and, at one stage, a milking cow. In the early days it was also very much the pattern that all the male assistants went out to work on the farm while the women assistants remained in the house to do the cooking. It was inevitable that that initial vision would be subject to change. As it transpired, the 'Green House', built in 1974, would be the last constructed on the original land to provide living accommodation for the people with handicaps. The philosophical trend in North America towards 'normalisation' would highlight the value of living, not on a farm which in those days was somewhat isolated from the city centre, but in an 'ordinary' street from which people could walk to the local store or doctor or bakery.

Steve Newroth, and through him Jean Vanier, had come to know Wolf Wolfensberger, one of the exponents of 'normalisation' in the United States, who was fighting most effectively for the rights of people with handicaps and denouncing the structures that oppressed them. There was a beauty and a truth in this theory which did not fail to appeal to l'Arche. People with handicaps, it maintained, had the same rights as any one else, and should be welcomed into society on an equal footing. They should be able to go to the municipal swimming baths, to the cinema or to church like any one else. They should even be able to go to school like other children. The worst thing for a handicapped person was exclusion which brought about a wounded self-image and ultimately feelings of guilt. Everything should be done to help people with handicaps to have confidence in themselves, to rediscover their human dignity and develop their intellectual and manual capacity. The dynamic in North America in this direction raised a number of salutary questions in l'Arche. Were the communities sometimes over protective? Did they show enough belief in the ability of the people they welcomed to grow towards greater independence and the rediscovery of their dignity? Was there not perhaps a danger inherent in the Gospel vision of the prophetic poor of being too quick to spiritualise the handicapped person's need to grow, of being too ready to see his poverty as something 'divine' and therefore of not helping him sufficiently towards greater liberty in human terms? Love should never inhibit the competence necessary to help someone to develop to his full potential.

In 1974 Daybreak opened its first house off the main prop-

erty, in downtown Toronto, and the experience would show
that many of the 'folks' could learn to take the subway and
the buses and benefit from access to more vocational opportunities. One house for more independent people in the city
had been part of the original vision, but by 1989 there would
be more people living off the original property than on it.
The boom in building development around the city of Toronto
would fill the community's once rural setting with an ever
increasing number of newly built houses in such a way that
it would no longer be 'normal' to maintain a farm there,
and in any case the community would recognise that many
assistants and handicapped people, coming as they did from
a restless, hectic consumer society, were not naturally drawn
to farming. The farm would eventually be gradually phased
out in what was a relatively late departure from the founding
vision.

Much earlier in its history the community would have to
acknowledge that l'Arche in North America would not be
able to draw on quite the same spiritual resources as l'Arche
in Trosly-Breuil. In France, as Henri Nouwen would later
point out, there were at least pockets of spiritual intensity,
which were not so readily found in North America. Daybreak
had no Père Thomas, and in any case Richmond Hill was not
Trosly. 'This is the Americas and we are in a very hedonistic
country. There is an American religious life that is very
young, a reality of religious pragmatism and good works,
but where do you go when you really want to be nourished
spiritually, when you want to be surrounded by the mystical
knowledge of God?'

Here as elsewhere in Canada and the United States – where
in the delicate and constantly shifting balance in l'Arche
between the two complementary elements of professionalism
and spirituality people would perhaps more readily align
themselves with the former – the challenge would be to find
a life that was North American but deeply spiritual. In this
challenge, retreats would once again have a crucial role to
play as a call to prayer and as a reminder not only to the
communities in North America but to l'Arche as a whole
that it was founded first upon the Gospels before being a
professionally run home for people with a handicap. They
were a reminder also that whilst l'Arche set out to encourage
maximum autonomy and normalisation for those capable of

it, the ultimate aim for people with handicaps – as for all human beings – was growth in love, in the welcoming of others and in service and holiness. At the same time, this growth did not in any way preclude the communities from seeking every possible means of helping handicapped people to achieve as much independence, knowledge and ability as they could or to be better integrated into society and the Church.

For Steve and Ann Newroth, the founding directors of Daybreak, there was an additional challenge which Trosly-Breuil, for all its universality of heart, had not as yet had to confront in quite the same way. Given the recognised need for a spiritual life, what form should that life take when' they themselves were Anglicans, an increasing number of assistants were Roman Catholics and the handicapped people came from a culture which included Anglicans, Catholics and members of the United Church? Theirs was the first experience of trying to express the vision of Trosly-Breuil in terms of a different culture. They had brought their own modifications to it, and the culture and the community rooted in it would bring others. By 1970 a newly formed community in Bangalore, India was facing similar questions, questions which in time would be confronted by communities all over the world – namely, what were the elements of life in l'Arche on which it was inappropriate to compromise and in what ways was it right that the original intuition should remain open and receptive to creative change?

6

Between Two Worlds

'It is such a great grace to be here,' Jean Vanier would write from India in November 1970, 'I sense such a change taking place in me. I would like to become poorer, much less aggressive, more gentle and non-violent ... more welcoming ... pray for me that I may be faithful.'

Extraordinary circumstances had once again contrived to bring a small l'Arche community to birth in the land of Mahatma Gandhi. Among the assistants who had come to l'Arche in Trosly-Breuil as early as May 1965 was an Indian girl, Mira, the Roman Catholic daughter of a Hindu mother and a Muslim father who were still living in Madras. When her father subsequently fell ill she found herself torn between the need to return to her homeland and what she felt was a calling to l'Arche and a life in the spirit of the Beatitudes. To use Jean Vanier's expression, 'This triggered something.'

Could l'Arche begin in India? In Canada Jean Vanier mentioned the idea to Gabrielle Einsle, a German woman then in charge of the 'Carrefour', a centre for foreign students in Montreal. She too felt called in a particular way to the Indian subcontinent. At the same time he found himself in contact with a Major Ramachandra, a follower of Gandhi who wanted to create schools for handicapped people in India. A fortuitous encounter with General Spears, head of the Canadian International Development Agency who was responsible for allocating government funds to voluntary agencies provided the necessary finance. Finding himself with a surfeit of funds at his disposal for that financial year, the General agreed that if Jean Vanier could provide a profile and compile a budget for his proposed project in India as quickly as possible, CIDA would provide a third of it. 'Gabrielle and I started working on a budget, although I had no idea how to go about it. To cut a long story short, we worked out a budget for 100,000 dollars and within a few weeks we had 33,000 dollars in the bank'. The 'folly' of l'Arche in India was no longer a dream but a reality.

On 30th October 1969 Gabrielle and Mira set out on a three-month exploratory journey in India. Shortly afterwards Jean Vanier followed them to a country where he already sensed that the role of l'Arche would be not only to help the handicapped but also to become in some ways like the people of India whom he had no wish to wound by adopting an attitude of superiority. It was his first journey to the East. He was prepared for it in the sense that he had read and digested the spirituality and teachings of Mahatma Gandhi, but that did not diminish the impact on him of the Indian culture, of a people that was profoundly religious and not motivated by the individualistic materialism so often found in Western countries, of the continuing relevance of the teachings of the Mahatma and of the suffering poor. 'I suppose there are two things that left a very, very deep impression,' he would say nearly twenty years later, as he reviewed the experience with a certain critical detachment in constantly modified phrases:

> One is the immense poverty, the poverty of humanity, the littleness of humanity and the relativisation of everything that I had done before that was so small in size compared with what was happening in India. The other is what I call the whole mystery of Mahatma Gandhi – a gift to humanity, a spirituality, a prophetic vision, the vision of the Harijans and the vision of *ahimsa* or non-violence, and in both cases a depth of spirituality and union with God and a sense of prayer, a sense of the continual presence of God in his heart, in his flesh, in his being.

The fact that Gandhi had had a very deep sense of his own littleness and poverty had, Jean Vanier would confide, 'imprinted itself, given new certitudes, enlarged my tent'. Non-violence was 'being prepared to be vulnerable'.

During his first travels in India and on numerous subsequent visits he wrote back to friends, ever more widely distributed throughout the globe, in a way which suggested a new sense of his own poverty. He visited schools for mentally handicapped children, homes for the physically handicapped, psychiatric hospitals and leper asylums. He met Mother

Teresa in the United States when together they received the
Kennedy Foundation Award and she invited him to come to
the city where she had first experienced the call to serve and
live amongst the poorest of the poor as one of them. In
her company he visited the refugee camps shortly after the
Bangladeshi war, went into homes for the dying run by the
Missionaries of Charity, and met the people who lived out
their poverty-stricken lives and died on the filthy pavements
of Calcutta. The encounter with so much suffering seems to
have tempered the energy and dynamism of the beginnings
of l'Arche with a deeper sense of his own limitations but also
more markedly with the desire to be poor and through that
poverty to put his trust in the Holy Spirit.

As he moved increasingly between the material affluence
of Europe and North America and the poverty of 'Third
World' countries, between the people of power and influence
and the little people, he was touched by a more acute awareness of the gulf between the two and by a feeling of his own
hypocrisy when he found himself introduced as someone who
had 'dedicated himself to the mentally deficient' or dined with
the Governor of Bengal while others starved in the streets. Yet
there was justification for his apparently dual role: 'Everything I say,' he wrote in 1972, 'I can say because I want to
work in silent and hidden identification with the little people,
but at the same time I know that I must try and work within
society, speak, spur others to act, manipulate money, act
externally, use contacts, chair administrative councils, meet
governors, etc.' His notes written during a visit to India that
year refer to:

> The two worlds which exist outside and within me . . . the
> need to be really transformed by the grace of Jesus . . . by
> the Holy Spirit . . . to become poor not externally, but poor
> internally because I am possessed by the Spirit, transfor-
> med by it . . . to discover the security of God's love . . . if
> not, these divisions between rich and poor will continue to
> bursting point, to the point of hatred and destruction. Unity
> must come between those who are entrenched in the world
> of wealth and human security and those who are in the
> world of poverty, but it can only come when the rich start
> to abandon their security to live the security of God and
> thus really draw near to the poor and the little ones.

Yet in all the suffering Jean Vanier encountered, in fact precisely in those situations where human solutions no longer
seemed possible, he discerned the works of the Holy Spirit
wrought little by little in the hearts of men – 'a very slow
process for God works in such poverty, so slowly, like the
flower that grows a little at a time'. Nevertheless the signs of
God's presence were strong and real. Within a week of Jean
Vanier's first arrival in Bangalore l'Arche had acquired a
property with two hectares of land and two wells, thanks to
Major Ramchandra and his associates who were committed
to furthering education in the slums. A board of directors,
made up of people who supported the spirit of l'Arche but
who were also competent in human affairs, was equally swiftly
established to serve as a recognised association and lasting
and legal guarantee of the community and its leader. By the
end of 1970 the first 'Asha Niketan', 'a Home of Hope' was
opened to be a place of hope for those who, with wounded
minds and psyches, waited in the psychiatric hospitals of
India. There were men and women in those 'hospitals' who
were confined naked in 'lion-cages' built more than a hundred
years previously, with no toilet and no bed, only the bare
floor and bars. There were others kept in enclosed wards
who almost never went out except to receive electric-shock
treatment.

It was, Jean Vanier would quickly acknowledge, pure madness to start a house for mentally handicapped people in
India, knowing virtually nothing of the language, the traditions and the culture. It was a question, however, of being
poor enough and trusting enough to allow a new kind of
community to develop, a community for which there was no
prototype other than the idea of living with handicapped
people, be they Muslim, Hindu or Christian, praying with
them, eating with them and generally walking with them on
the journey that was life. Gandhi had recognised the need to
follow his path with God as his only guide. He had also
admitted that, in the face of all the deception and the suffering
he encountered, he would have gone mad were it not for his
sense of the presence of God in him.

A guiding hand appeared to be at work in the tiny foundation in Bangalore. In no time at all Gabrielle had arranged
for electricity and sanitation to be installed. The gardens
flourished. A nearby factory provided very basic work of the

kind three of the handicapped people could undertake for
1,000 rupees a month. Other 'Asha Niketan's would follow.
In 1972 a couple from the United States founded a community
in Kotagiri, 2,000 metres up in the mountains, although this
would in fact prove to be one of the very few l'Arche communities that would founder. It had happened too quickly,
without sufficient preparation with the national board of
directors. Within nine months of its inception it was compelled to close and the handicapped people it had welcomed
went to join the community in Bangalore. In Calcutta, in
1973, Archbishop Picachy would offer l'Arche the use of an
almost empty two-storey parish house located between all the
noise and bustle of Sealdah station, where some half a million
people arrived and departed daily, and St John's Church
with its adjoining cemetery. The substantial basement to the
church was provided as a workshop and in time a contract
with Philips India Ltd would make it possible to provide
the men at Asha Niketan, Calcutta, with work adapted to
individual capacities. In their basement workshop they cut,
twisted, stripped, soldered and counted radio wires. Their
earnings would enable the community to pay for daily food.

Communities in Madras would follow in 1975, and in Calicut in Kerala in 1978. Nearly all of them came into being in
a way which suggested that they were in some mysterious
sense meant to be, but pehaps none had more extraordinary
beginnings than the foundation near Calicut, the city of coco-
nut palms beside the Arabian Sea. Mr Pramanand, an Indian
travelling on a train one day from Calicut to Bangalore, read
an article in a newspaper about the l'Arche foundations in
India. His response was to arrive at Asha Niketan in Bangalore with a story of how his father had owned a soap factory
in the south of India until the military authorities had closed
it down. Mr Premanand's father had been a devout and
prayerful Hindu who, having relinquished his ownership of
the factory, had chanced upon a beautiful property by the
sea in Calicut which he knew immediately he must buy. The
price was 500 rupees but he had no money. On the very day,
however, on which he was due to pay for the property, the
sum of 525 rupees, the cost of the property plus his travelling
expenses, arrived by post accompanied by a letter from a
man in Mysore who had had a dream telling him that he
must send the money. On the newly purchased site Mr Pre-

manand's father had once more started up a factory, this
time to produce furniture wax, but when the Communist
government came to power in Kerala, despite Mr Preman-
and's father's warnings that this was a property given to him
by God and that if the government took it over the venture
would fold within three weeks, it did so. Sure enough, within
three weeks the factory folded. 'It's a very strange thing,'
Jean Vanier would recall,

> Mr Premanand's father had written a document which has
> since been lost and which I've never been able to refind.
> In it he wrote of how he saw on one side of this property
> a place that would welcome people with leprosy and people
> with handicaps. There would be no drinking of tea or
> coffee. Nor is there now in Asha Niketan in Kerala. He
> had had this Gandhian vision of welcoming the poor, and
> in recognition of this Mr Premanand offered us forty or
> fifty acres of this huge and beautiful property that his father
> had regarded as belonging to God.

The full estate was far too large for l'Arche, but the community accepted with gratitude five or six acres. This land
was unused for a while because of the lack of a director, until
Chris Sadler, an English woman who had been living and
working with the *harijans* in South India, felt called to start a
community there. In time Asha Niketan at Nandi Bazaar
became an 'incredibly beautiful' community – beautiful in
the gift of its people, of Mitran who called others to look
afresh at the frog which he called a chicken, the lizard he
named a mongoose or the banana he insisted was laughing;
beautiful in its physical setting of golden beaches and natural
silence, which Jean Vanier did not fail to appreciate; beautiful
too in its fragility.

In India centuries of the absence of any separation between
life and religion meant that there was no lack of spiritual
wealth to be tapped. Everything was a religious act, and
prayer came very naturally in a land which, despite the gradual influence of Western materialism, was still steeped in a
sense of the sacred. There was something in the culture and
the climate, especially in rural settings where life was lived
in close contact with nature and its daily and seasonal
rhythms, that was conducive to the recognition of the deeper
meanings of life. The very simplicity of existence – the depen-

dence on earth and sky, sun and rain, to meet the fundamental necessities of eating and drinking, bathing and washing – called upon people to relate more fully to the reality of matter, to each other and to the source of life itself. The Indian assistants did not rebel, as assistants might in the West, when invited to pray twice a day. Yet only a tiny minority among both the assistants and the handicapped people were Christians. The majority were Hindus but there were also Muslims amongst them, and the Christians themselves included not only Catholics but Protestants and Syrian Orthodox. Finding a prayer life which was acceptable to all would not be devoid of problems. In Bangalore the community quite spontaneously elected to have a prayer room in which Gabrielle Einsle put a picture of Mary. A Christian assistant subsequently added a cross he had made. Then a Hindu member of the community added a picture of Ganesh, the elephant god. Some of the men went home to their families for the weekend and returned with pictures of other Hindu deities. Quite spontaneously the room came to contain a number of pictures of various gods. It had seemed right that if people wanted to hang pictures of their gods they should do so, that their way of worshipping should be respected, but there were Christians who visited the community and were shocked to find a room where the image of Jesus was just one among several.

The diversity of religious faith was inseparable from the diversity and complexity of culture. Furthermore, in India it would be a question of expressing the vision of l'Arche, not so much in terms of the national culture (in itself a difficult task for community leaders who were initially all European) as of the Indian cultures which varied not only between different states but also between castes. In Bangalore many of the mentally handicapped people who came to the community were Brahmins, possibly owing to widespread intermarriage, possibly because their families were more educated and therefore the most likely to hear of the existence of Asha Niketan. The Brahmin caste was a culture in itself, one accustomed to subservience from others and not one well suited to showing ways of tending the country's poor to Europeans who were ignorant even of the complexities of Indian eating habits or of cultural beliefs – such as that it was a mortal sin to step over another's body, even over his legs. What was acceptable in Bangalore, which had been subject to strong Western influence, might not be acceptable elsewhere in India. This was apparent at the most fundamental level: in Bangalore, partly no doubt because of climatic conditions, people wore heavy shoes everywhere. Elsewhere, in Madras for example, it was unacceptable to enter even a rich man's house without removing one's shoes.

It would become swiftly apparent also that in a country where material poverty was so extreme it would be a particular challenge not to appear rich in relation to the majority of people and very rich in the eyes of the poor. 'Calcutta is not India. India is the villages. India is united families. India is the faces of the poor whose smiles radiate peace,' wrote Jean Vanier, but he was not one to disregard the fact that Calcutta existed, Bombay existed and so too did the lepers, the street dwellers and the inhabitants of the asylums in numbers too vast to contemplate. It would be difficult to retain a sense of the meaning of l'Arche's existence here and easy to despair at the smallness of the four tiny communities, each made up of no more than a dozen people, in relation to the magnitude of India's need. In the context of that need it was indeed folly to choose to live with and to love a few individuals deeply, but perhaps it was that each Asha Niketan was meant to be but a small sign of what the world could be if only each person sought to live as a child of God open to the Spirit.

India was only the first of many countries in which l'Arche would have to face a particular challenge in relation to the poverty and simplicity of its life, together with other problems which the attempt to lead a life integrated with local people and their culture would inevitably present. Very soon there would be a community on the Ivory Coast where, as in most 'Third World' countries, there would be no government funding and l'Arche would be entirely dependent on money raised locally through the board of directors and through their own labour, and on gifts from abroad.

'In Africa,' Claire de Miribel, now international co-ordinator but earlier one of the first l'Arche directors on the Ivory Coast, would recall, 'there was no problem about being a Christian community. I think Africans can only come to our communities if they are Christian. Otherwise all their traditional beliefs in relation to handicapped people would make it impossible.' On the Ivory Coast some handicapped children

Jean Vanier in naval uniform

Père Thomas Philippe

Jean and members of his family

Jean with Raphael, one of the first members of the Trosly community *(Photo: G Dysart, MSC, Journey Communications)*

Père Thomas gives the Host to a member of the community in Trosly

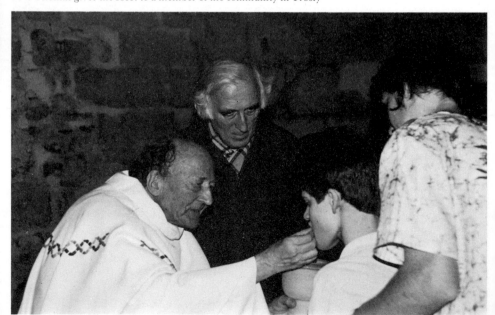

The founder members of the Daybreak community in Canada

Sharing a meal in the Erie community, USA

Robert Larouche (top) and Nadine Tokar with the community in Tegucigalpa, Honduras

Praying together in Ouagadougou, Burkina Faso

Bill and Jan from the community in Kent, England

Faith and Light: the pilgrimage to Rome, 1975

Robert Runcie, Archbishop of Canterbury, during an ecumenical retreat in 1983

Thierry and Paul at the Lambeth workshop in South London

Kashi from Asha Niketan, Calcutta

Michelle from the Lambeth community

Jean, Père Thomas and Pope John Paul II

Celebrating at 'La Forestière', Trosly

could not be kept in the family because they were believed to bring bad luck and the interests of the group, rather than those of the individual, were regarded as paramount. Some parents would take their child to a witchdoctor who would then abandon it in the bush and tell people that it had turned back into a snake. A pregnant woman could not eat at the same table as a handicapped person for fear that her unborn child would be contaminated. In general there were strong fears about taking meals in the company of handicapped people, especially those suffering from epilepsy. How could one impress upon the people of the Ivory Coast the mysterious value of their wounded and rejected children?

How do you articulate l'Arche in a culture like that? Even the whole way of running a meeting, of working through a conflict is different. There are all those rules of African tradition and when you don't know them, even if you speak the same language, the words don't necessarily mean the same thing. In France a thing is black *or* white. In Africa it can be both.

There was much that Africa had to teach l'Arche. The quality of the welcome it afforded its foreign guests was one illustration among many of the hospitality and warmth of the materially poor. In time the small family in Bouaké and another in Ouagadougou would flourish as witnesses, in a world of so much material poverty, to the value of the person with a mental handicap. But the young assistants who came from Europe would at times be confronted with the accusation that they had large eyes but saw nothing.

Communities would swiftly follow in Haiti, in Honduras and a rapidly increasing number of other countries where material poverty was an all too evident source of suffering yet, remarkably, not of bitterness or resentment. Often these communities were born as a result of invitations to Jean Vanier to talk or take retreats. He would arrive and grasp the essentials of the political, cultural and religious climate with extraordinary speed and energy. A need, an opportunity, a call would be perceived by him or by others and – through meetings with ministers of health, psychiatrists, religious and a multitude of others with or without influence – the means would be discovered to meet it in some small and frequently precarious way. Often too, the call to l'Arche would find its

incarnation in a particular handicapped person whose cry for
love and relationship was articulated in his very flesh.

L'Arche in Haiti began when Robert Larouche, at one time
a philosophy teacher in Quebec, accompanied Jean Vanier
on a trip to Haiti and Brazil and felt called to remain in
Haiti. They had gone to Port-au-Prince without really knowing whether l'Arche had a place in Haiti, realising only that
the model of community which had been established in
Europe and North America could not necessarily be repro-
duced there. For three months Robert stayed in a Haitian
community in a poor neighbourhood on the outskirts of Port-
au-Prince, discovering the place of the handicapped person
in Haitian society. The perception of the person with the
handicap as a heavy burden, a perception which frequently
led to his exclusion and placement in a special institution was
not so very different in Haiti from that of people in North
America or Europe, only less camouflaged. It was more
openly expressed in jeering and mockery on the part of neighbours. Handicapped people often learned how to become not
only the buffoons and the clowns of the neighbourhood but
also the beggars. In this way they could contribute to the
financial upkeep of their family, but they lost all sense of
personal dignity in the process. Institutions, usually adminis-
tered by the government, were reserved for those whose needs
were extreme or who had been abandoned altogether.

It was in a psychiatric centre that Robert Larouche met
Yveline. She was an emotionally disturbed ten-year-old who
used to run up to passers-by in the city streets, singing at the
top of her voice, until eventually she had been picked up and
placed in the institution. When Robert met her she had been
there for a year, the only child in the ward. No one had
succeeded in tracing her family. The director asked whether
she might not have a future in l'Arche. Until that time l'Arche
had accepted no children, but the encounter with Yveline had
made it clear to Robert that a l'Arche house should be opened
in Haiti. The child psychiatrists in another hospital offered
their collaboration and, together with several others, were
able to help form a board of directors to support the new
community. In time there would be three different homes, a
small school for the children of the community and of the
neighbourhood and a workshop producing, among other
things, exceptionally good peanut butter.

In the courtyard of Casa Nazaret, the blue-and-green-painted wooden building in Tegucigalpa which had once been a tiny seminary and subsequently a school, Nadine Tokar, founder of the first community in Honduras, would speak of her own call to a country where the poor were 'hungry for the good news'. Against the chatter of parrots in the trees and the din of a fair erected in the square nearby to celebrate the festival of Our Lady of Suyapa, she spoke of how she had first come there to prepare for Jean Vanier to give a retreat in the capital. Touched by the country and eager to know more of it, she had climbed aboard a bus and found herself in the poverty-stricken suburb of Suyapa on a hillside overlooking the city where an incongruously imposing basilica erected to the glory of the patron saint of Honduras is the focal point for pilgrimages. Suyapa, where now the community occupies the wooden structure that, for all its extreme simplicity, Nadine Tokar initially declined as being too large in relation to the neighbouring houses, is more like a village than part of a modern metropolis. Often the small, one or two-room houses are not only homes for sizeable families but also improvised food shops. In the market in the central square next to the church, women sell bread, fruit, holy pictures and *tacos* which they cook on little stoves set up on the pavement. An inordinately large number of *estancos* (shops) selling the national liquor provide the men with a much travelled route to oblivion. Further up the mountain on the other side of the river is Nueva Suyapa, even poorer than Suyapa itself. Born in the wake of hurricane 'Fifi', the district grew up when large numbers of poor people who had seen their homes swept away by one of the greatest natural disasters to have struck Honduras, made their way to the capital in search of work and housing. On the mountainside behind Suyapa they were reduced to making their own shelters out of cardboard, wood and whatever else they could find. By the time Nadine arrived there, there was still no water or electricity supply and no tarred roads.

The extreme poverty of the people, their simplicity and their struggle for life called to her, as did the spirit and devotion of the truly poor. Entering the local church, a much more modest building than the basilica of Our Lady of Suyapa, on that first chance arrival in the square, she was moved by the old women she discovered reciting the rosary there. When Jean Vanier came to give his retreat they returned together one Saturday night to a Celebration of the Word. The experience of hearing those local women, virtually illiterate though they were, struggling to read the word of God, was one which would remain with her for years to come.

In Honduras, as in Haiti, a particular need had been identified amongst the young people, who in their poverty dreamed only of going to the material affluence of North America in pursuit of a better life. Nadine returned to Honduras to organise another retreat with these young people specifically in mind. 'There was so much poverty, so many lost young people and so many handicapped children.' She visited psychiatric hospitals and asylums. One asylum in particular she recalls as another of those places of horror: 'It was a terrible, dirty place where there was nothing but all kinds of people who were just waiting for death: mentally sick people, old people, anyone who was abandoned or rejected.' It was there that she met Marcia who had been abandoned at the age of three and who spent twenty years of her life within its walls before coming to live in the l'Arche house in Suyapa.

At a children's hospital Nadine asked a social worker if she could see any abandoned handicapped children. She was directed to a room set apart from the main wards with the warning that its occupant was dangerous:

> In an empty room was a cage and Raphael was in there. He was completely naked with nothing in his cage but a fragment of food. He was severely handicapped and epileptic and had been abandoned as a baby. He had been born in the hospital, left there and grown up there. He had never had a relationship of any kind and he was quite violent, incapable of touching or being touched, but with the face of an angel. I spent half an hour trying to play with him and touch him and during that half hour I felt deeply that he needed a home and that he was calling l'Arche, and it became clear that that call was my call.

Nadine was French. She was happy in Trosly-Breuil but at that moment, without giving such factors undue consideration, she found herself saying 'yes' to Raphael and to Honduras.

It was equally clear to her that it was not just a question of transporting a French community to Honduras. Before

doing anything else she must live there for a while and begin
to understand the language and the reality that the poor of
Honduras were living. For a year she lived in Nueva Suyapa
with Dona Maria, a local woman and her family in a small
room with two beds, a fire and a table. It was not easy at
first. When she entered the house the men and any visitors
would go out. The colonisation of Honduras had meant that
any foreigner was perceived to be educated and clever, a
person of power, money and influence. The men of Honduras
were suffering from a general sense of inferiority and a lack
of their own national identity and dignity, and this found its
compensation in *machismo*, the resort to excessive alcohol and
violence. In the congested houses of Suyapa, however, the
people soon realised that this particular *gringita* (young foreign
girl) had nothing to give them in the way that they had
expected and everything to receive and to learn:

> I was like a little child. They taught me how to speak.
> Each night we would all sit on the two beds while Dona
> Maria cooked corn to make tortillas which she sold next
> morning to make a little money, and they would point to
> my nose or my mouth and I would repeat the words after
> them. They taught me how to wash my body, how to go
> to the bathroom when there wasn't one, how to wash my
> clothes in the river or buy food in the market.

For that year Nadine learnt how to live as a poor person in
Honduras. She came to know many of the local families and
visited the handicapped people of which, owing to malnu-
trition and poor medical facilities, there were many. It was
hard to be amongst strangers and have an image of power
and wealth thrust upon her when that was not what she
wanted to live, hard too to feel the eyes upon her as she
walked alone in the dusty streets, but it enabled her to touch
upon the feelings of the poor: 'the mixed-up feelings of rejection and curiosity, something very strange'.

If l'Arche had entered into a broader and a deeper understanding of the needs and the nature of the poor and the
handicapped of this world, so too had Jean Vanier. He had
been journeying: journeying to give talks and retreats,
journeying to help found and nurture the small communities

that were springing to life across the continents. As the communities grew in number, he too was growing. 'To grow', he would write some years later in *Community and Growth*, 'is to emerge gradually from a land where our vision is limited, where we are seeking and governed by egotistical pleasure, by our sympathies and antipathies, to a land of unlimited horizons and universal love, where we will love all men and desire their happiness.' He was manifestly emerging from some of his own 'antipathies'. He had been an outspoken critic of the 'normal' who failed to treat the handicapped as people, one who was not afraid to stand up and state in the baldest terms that, 'normal people, not the handicapped, are the strange people. It is they who are the ones with the problems.' By his own admission, there had been a time when, in his compassion for handicapped people, he had been ready to point an accusing finger at the parents and families who had, albeit sometimes unconsciously, added to their wounds. Had some of them not rejected their children? Was it not because of their cultural values and lack of competence that their son or daughter felt unloved, unworthy and useless? Yet, in the same way as he would come to recognise that he had been insufficiently aware of the needs of the villagers of Trosly-Breuil and the importance of co-operation between l'Arche and the village people based on mutual respect for each other's gifts, so he would come to a greater understanding of the suffering and the needs of parents of people with a handicap and to the realisation of the importance of working in co-operation with families.

It was during a pilgrimage to Lourdes in 1971 that Faith and Light, an international Christian association for the mentally handicapped, their families and friends, came into being. The seed of the idea had originally been sown at a meeting with Marie-Hélène Mathieu, General Secretary of the Christian office for people with a mental handicap in Paris. She had been deeply touched by a meeting with the parents of two severely mentally handicapped sons who wanted to organise a pilgrimage to Lourdes in which their boys could participate. In those days parents with handicapped children in Lourdes – as in hotels, beaches and holiday resorts elsewhere – could find themselves hurt and isolated. Yet l'Arche's experience of previous pilgrimages to Lourdes, La Salette, Fatima and Banneux had shown how handicapped people were transformed by these journeys, how unity was cemented en route by their sensitivity to water, light, processions and all the other signs that spoke to their hearts. With Marie-Hélène Mathieu l'Arche decided to organise an international pilgrimage for people who had a mental handicap, their parents and friends, especially young people.

At Easter 1971, 12,000 pilgrims from fourteen countries gathered on the esplanade at Lourdes. A third of those present were people with mental handicaps. It was an important occasion for celebration and joy, a time of discovery for many parents that they were not alone, that their child was not a source of shame and that they could celebrate together. For many of the young people there it was an occasion for real commitment to people with a mental handicap, and for many of those with a mental handicap it was a moment of great joy and a meeting with God.

Five days together in Lourdes brought so much hope that when the time came to leave it did not seem possible that the experience should end there. 'Do whatever the Holy Spirit inspires you to do to build up a world of love around the handicapped person,' was Jean Vanier's directive. The Faith and Light movement, which he would describe as 'a kind of first cousin to l'Arche' was born. It too would spread throughout the world. By 1989 there would be more than 750 communities in over fifty countries.

These 'communities' each made up of thirty or so people – children, teenagers or adults who were mentally handicapped together with their parents and friends, particularly the young – would meet regularly for sharing, prayer and celebration. They were centred on the discovery of the mystery hidden in the handicapped person, who was so often very close to the Beatitudes, to gentleness and humility, and whose frailty, it was recognised, broke down the barriers in people's hearts. They were also centred on the awareness of the deep suffering that the birth of a handicapped child could bring. In France thirty years ago many people hid their handicapped child in the bedroom. In some countries this is still the case. Parents too were wounded and, in their pain, tended to isolate themselves. More and more, therefore, the Faith and Light communities would gear themselves to mutual help and the dis-

pelling of loneliness between meetings, to looking after a child
for an afternoon, inviting disheartened parents for a meal,
organising a holiday camp or simply keeping in touch by
telephone. Through Faith and Light a number of people
would discover their vocation to live with handicapped people
and joined an existing l'Arche community or founded another
– in Rome, Sao Paolo, Switzerland and elsewhere. Through
Faith and Light, Jean Vanier would be able to state years
later, thousands of mothers and fathers were 'beginning to
dance and laugh with their children'. He would recall a
mother in Yugoslavia who had four children, three of whom
were mentally handicapped. 'My three handicapped children
are so beautiful,' she had told him, 'The one who's normal
has a lot of problems.' In a multitude of other instances a
total inner transformation had been brought about.

Meanwhile the growth towards a 'more realistic and a truer
love' was to take Jean Vanier into the enclosed and pain-
ridden world of prisons. He found himself invited to talk even
in maximum security prisons and, as he spoke of the pain
and the brokenness of the mentally handicapped people with
whom he lived, he found that he was speaking too of the pain
of the prisoners he was addressing.

> One of the most moving moments for me was when I was
> talking about our people and their pain and depression and
> rejection and a man got up and screamed, 'You know
> nothing about our pain. You've had it easy.' He explained
> about his life, about how he had seen his mother raped
> when he was four, how he had been sold into homosexuality
> so that his father could drink. Then, when he was just
> thirteen, the men in blue had come. Finally he really
> screamed at me, 'If one more person comes into this prison
> and talks about love, I'll kick his bloody head in.' You can
> imagine the sort of silence that followed. I knew that for
> me this was a make-or-break situation.

Jean Vanier sought to remain peaceful in the face of this
explosion and was able to acknowledge that he had indeed
had it easy. He asked whether he could repeat what the
prisoner had said to others who did not know what he was
living. 'He said I could and I said, "If people outside need
to listen to you, then it might be important to listen to what
those outside have to say to you."' When the talk was over

he went and shook the distraught man by the hand and asked him where he came from and whether he was married.

I asked about his wife, and his eyes filled with tears. I still remember him saying that his wife was in a wheelchair. At that moment I saw his immense wound, his cry for love. Here was a guy coming to talk about just what he needed, and this immense explosion had been because I had touched his wound.

Entering the prison world was for Jean Vanier an 'incredible revelation which taught me more about people'. It dispelled some of the naivety of which he knew he was capable. 'Instinctively when you're in a prison the guards are the baddies, but reality isn't quite like that.' He remembers, not without laughter, the prisoner who had acted as his secretary during a retreat at Calgary prison. They had talked a good deal together, and as the man had nearly completed his sentence he asked the retreat leader for some addresses to contact on his release. Jean Vanier obligingly gave him some. A few months later he received a succession of letters from people across Canada informing him that a friend of his had been and stolen their stereo, television and a whole series of other items.

More significantly, contact with people who occupied a world of cells and locks and metal doors would reveal to him that the most fundamental characteristic of a human being was a heart crying out for love. It was a characteristic common not only to the mentally handicapped or the imprisoned but to all mankind. What was more, so much depended upon the response that cry received.

If that heart is listened and responded to then people don't create barriers but if the heart and the cry for communion is wounded at a very early age the barriers are stronger, so strong that it can cause psychosis in people. If the heart receives love it flowers, but if it is hurt it becomes angry and seeks revenge. It resorts to anti-social behaviour.

'The world in l'Arche, the Third World, the prison world – they all seemed so close together.' Like the barriers between the mentally handicapped and the 'normal', or between the 'First' and the 'Third' World, in Jean Vanier's understanding the barriers between the wounded inside and outside prison

walls were dissolving. At times that dissolution was mani-
fested in a very concrete way. In Ottawa he took part in a
weekend gathering in a disused prison in which prisoners, ex-
prisoners, police, prison guards and directors, psychologists
and government officials came together for two nights and
two days without anyone knowing who the others were or
what their usual role was. They slept together in dormitories,
not knowing whether the man in the next bunk was the
director of a prison or one of its inmates. Sadly the idea did
not, as Jean Vanier had hoped, lead to other similar gatherings, but it was nonetheless a much valued experience.
Another Canadian prison had linked its prisoners with
severely handicapped people. Once a week they would go out
together for a picnic. The 'beauty of those men from the
prison, their kindness towards those very handicapped people,
the bringing together of the marginal of society for a picnic
on the beach' would not be forgotten.

   At the very beginning of l'Arche, the community at Trosly-
Breuil had itself welcomed two men who had been condemned
to death but were subsequently reprieved. As a way of rehabil-
itating them into society, the arrangement had worked quite
well; after ten years they left to work elsewhere. From the
point of view of community life, however, it was less satisfac-
tory. They were, Jean Vanier would acknowledge, a bit too
wounded. Now he is somewhat reluctant to take people direct
from prison, feeling that they should spend a period in the
outside world doing what they want, rather than opting for
community life whilst still in a position of weakness and
vulnerability. 'The demands and exigencies of community are
too similar to those of prison.' He himself admits that it has
never been easy for him to go into prisons, that the experience
– though life-giving – evoked in him fear and revulsion. He
has difficulty in going into hospitals where there may be
twenty or thirty handicapped people smelling of urine, or
picking up a child and then having to put it down: "When
you touch a child who has never been touched except for
functional things, when you hold him close to your body and
play with him, the child immediately starts to open and
blossom out, and then you put him down . . . ' Similarly he
has difficulty going into prisons, meeting men with whom he
gets on well, and then leaving them to the clang of metal
doors.

'What people do to people in prison and what people do to people with handicaps', Jean Vanier would comment, 'is a measure of what society is, of how hard and broken it is,' a measure in fact of how deeply society too is wounded. To him there is a strange similarity between two men, one of whom was told by his mother when he was eight years old that, if only the contraceptives had worked, he would not be here now and who subsequently took part in the kidnapping of a child, and the other who, though less wounded, is yet sufficiently hurt for the growth of his heart to be stunted and who throws himself into activity seeking admiration because he cannot believe in communion. The prisoner's wounded heart has turned him towards anti-social behaviour; in the factory director, who is bent on competitive work at all costs, who is unjust to his workers in the pursuit of his own project, the wounded heart has driven him to behaviour that is apparently social but in reality also anti-social. 'The two poles seem to be the same, just as the prodigal son and the elder son are the same reality. In a way it's easier for the prodigal son because the truth about him becomes more visible, whereas the elder son doesn't know the truth about himself.' We are, Jean Vanier asserts, all Pharisees, thinking we are good, thinking we have knowledge, thinking we have power and should dictate to others what they should do. In reality we are crushing the little people with our imposing ways. 'That is the mystery of the two poles of humanity: at the heart of each is the wound.'

7

Towards Communion

'One of the things I discover more and more is that it takes months and years to build community,' Jean Vanier would claim long after the surging energy of 'take off'. The creation of new communities had continued, each one slightly different in roots, orientation and character. In North America a considerable number had been born out of the Faith and Sharing retreats or through filiation with Daybreak. In general the seventeen communities founded there between 1972 and 1977 subscribed to two models. There were those modelled on Trosly-Breuil and Daybreak, which wanted to be Christian communities centred on the poor. These were financed, supported and controlled by the State and wanted to take full advantage of any professional resources available; they also had solid and reliable boards of directors. There were other communities, however, which wanted to draw closer to the poor by sharing their insecurity and declining state control and assistance. They set themselves up in poor areas of large towns or in the country, close to the land, and often they took in other marginalised people as well as those with mental handicaps. Despite being slightly different in their orientation, nearly all the communities took in people from large institutions, many of whom had suffered from long years of separation from their families. There were consequently times when the burden on fragile communities was almost too great.

In France, most of the communities were modelled on Trosly-Breuil and received a grant from the State, although two later communities would choose not to be state subsidised but to live instead off the proceeds of their own agricultural labour and the pensions and salaries of the handicapped people and assistants who took on work outside the community. Other communities were born out of Faith and Light pilgrimages: two in Scandinavia, which had some difficulty in rooting themselves in the social and church fabric of the country. Another, in Belgium, had already been established as a place where men and women suffering from cerebral palsy could live but, having taken part in the Faith and Light Pilgrimage to Lourdes in 1971, its founder had asked that it be recognised as a l'Arche community. His request was accepted, and in time another two Belgian l'Arche communities would be established. L'Arche in Africa began in Bouaké, on the Ivory Coast, largely because the prior of a Benedictine monastery very much wanted l'Arche to start a community there and offered his help and support. L'Arche in Africa, as in Haiti, Honduras and other Third World countries, was characterised by the clear option to live in the poorest neighbourhoods and to welcome people who had been completely abandoned. Also, because there were fewer regulations in these countries, it was easier to welcome adults and children with handicaps together, a fact which gave these foundations a very particular character.

Looking back on the 'sixties and 'seventies Jean Vanier would identify three different models for community life in society and the Church. There was the religious life, exemplified by Mother Teresa's Missionary Brothers and Sisters of Charity, the Taizé Brothers and others. There were the residential homes for people with handicaps which had begun in the United States, Canada, the United Kingdom and Scandinavia with a professional vision of 'reinsertion' into society. There were also all the new-style communities that sprang up, particularly in North America, as a reaction against the consumer society, large impersonal institutions and a certain legal rigidity. 'Friendship House' and 'Benedict Labre House' were among these. So too were all the communities that wanted to live close to nature and the 'communes' which often had very high human and spiritual ideals reflecting a desire to live very simply, without the constraints of society, and sometimes in greater proximity to the poor. The various l'Arche communities which began during that same period reflected these elements to different degrees: some inclined more to the professional model, others to that of the religious life, and yet others to that of the new communities close to the land and the poor. Their different characteristics brought to the broad banner of l'Arche all the richness of diversity. They also meant that communities sometimes suffered from a lack of clarity when it came to the question of their identity. Only with the passage of the years would l'Arche acquire a clearer and deeper sense of its identity and with this a better understanding of its role in relation to professionals, to boards of directors and to the Church. With that understanding l'Arche would find the confidence to announce what it was living. In the meantime the journey was very much one of sometimes painful discovery.

There were, Jean Vanier discovered, always plenty of courageous people who were ready to be heroes, to sleep on the ground, to work long hours and live in dilapidated houses. The problems arose when it came to living with brothers and sisters who had not been chosen but given, and to maintaining fidelity in the simple things that made up the daily round. After the beginnings that were so evidently given, some communities would come very close to closure. In most there would be times of tension and trial, related not only to the problem of integrating l'Arche into different countries and cultures – to such very practical questions as whether meals should be taken at table or on the floor, to the establishing of appropriate wages for assistants in Third World countries, and to the preservation of an appropriate simplicity of life in relation to the poverty of those amongst whom they lived – but also to the very spirit of communion which must be nurtured and sustained if communities made up of people from a wide diversity of backgrounds were to live and grow and belong together. Most of the early foundations had come about by virtue of personal contact between their individual founders and Jean Vanier. They did not necessarily know each other. In the early years there was no support or decision-making structure. Nor was there any means to ensure a common vision. In 1972, in an attempt to establish and maintain greater unity between the individual communities, all the founders met together in Ambleteuse for what was to be the first meeting of the Federation of l'Arche Communities. Those present began to put the vision of l'Arche into writing. This draft would in time be reworked and amended to become the International Charter of l'Arche. In time also a small International Council, of which Jean Vanier himself was the co-ordinator, would be formed to watch over and guide new foundations.

Internationally, nationally and at the level of individual

communities – of those little groupings of people who had left a wide variety of backgrounds to live with others under the same roof and work from a new vision of human beings and their relationships with each other and with God – it was apparent that what was being sought after was something more profound, more subtle and more lasting than mere collaboration. Today Jean Vanier speaks often of 'communion':

> Generally speaking communion is a sense of unity deeper than working together. It is more on the level of being, and somewhere it breaks down the barriers of loneliness and gives people a sense of freedom. It has a very deep respect of difference. It is very close to the things of God. It is frequently deepened in silence and is linked much more to the body.

Jean Vanier had begun l'Arche in the desire to live the Gospel and to follow Jesus Christ more closely. He was himself a man of prayer who appears in some sense to have been grounded in the mysticism of Père Thomas and in oneness with him. He was also a man for whom relationship with handicapped people, with the poor with whom the Christ of St Matthew's Gospel had so specifically identified himself, was a religious experience profoundly linked to his understanding of communion. Often he refers to gentle moments lived with the profoundly handicapped, to bathtime with Eric for example, who was almost completely blind and deaf:

> It was an occasion when a deep communion could be established; when we would touch his body with gentleness, respect and love. In hot water Eric relaxes; he likes it. Water refreshes and cleanses. He has a feeling of being enveloped in a gentle warmth. Through water and the touch of the body there was a deep communion that was created between Eric and myself. It was good to be together. And because Eric was relaxed, it made me feel more relaxed. He has complete trust in the person who gives him a bath. He is completely abandoned. He no longer defends himself. He feels secure because he senses he is respected and loved. The way he welcomed me, the way he trusted me, called forth trust in me. Yes, Eric called me forth to greater gentleness and respect for his body and his being. He called forth in me all that is best. His weakness, his

littleness, his yearning to be loved touched my heart and awakened in me unsuspected forces of love and tenderness. I gave him life; he also gave me life . . . These moments of communion are the revelation that God has created deep bonds between us. (From *Our Inner Journey*)

Asked once in what way the handicapped were religious, Jean Vanier referred to such a moment of peace and contentment at bathtime and added, 'How do you hold those moments?' Somewhere, this touches upon the way in which all who live in l'Arche, regardless of their professed creed or world-view, are religious. Those who stay in l'Arche are responding to the cry of the handicapped person for communion which, whether perceived as such or not, is 'very close to the things of God'. 'L'Arche', Père Thomas has said, 'brings together all people of good will, whatever their country, their age, their race or their culture. Without knowing his name, they sincerely and loyally seek the Saviour.' Most people in the communities, be they atheist or agnostic, Hindu or Christian, can sooner or later identify with those quiet moments in which deep bonds are created. The desire, even the need, to hold and nourish those moments very often leads naturally to prayer.

The early recognition of the right to 'choose in freedom', brought about by Philippe's timely questioning as to why he had to go to Mass every day, would mean that there was no obligation to hold any religious belief or to participate in the daily prayer or worship of the various communities. In the beginning Jean Vanier had had to recognise that whilst he wanted to create a Christian community, this was not Raphael and Philippe's primary concern. They needed, above all, friendship and security. The religious foundation of a community was not automatically present. Many communities did not have a spiritual guide, priest or minister, but in the experience of most, relationship with handicapped people had a way of opening individuals to the spirit of prayer which many would see as essential if that 'deep sense of unity' was to be nurtured and sustained. Chris Sadler would refer to one of the Muslim assistants who, when he came to Asha Niketan, felt that prayer was rather meaningless.

He came freely to the house prayer because he could see that it was of value for others, so it was very interesting watching him over the years. I feel he really prays and it's through his relationship with one of the handicapped men who does not speak that something has opened up in him. There is a real transforming effect. Even his presence is quite different.

Even, perhaps particularly, where the pull towards meeting the requirements of the State and away from the spiritual dimension is especially strong, where the pressures of an achievement-orientated society and the demands of an exceptionally rapid pace of life overtaxes energies and allows little time for those gentler moments, the need for prayer is increasingly felt. In what Father George Strohmeyer would describe as the 'beautiful blend in l'Arche between the French vision and the North American sense of how to go about things', the strength of the Erie community would reveal itself to be competence as opposed to Trosly's gift for being a community of love, creating links and caring for people: 'We're always very good at competence, at looking for people's growth needs because we're never free not to. But if we needed anything, it was always more to create the community dimension of caring, spending time, appreciating the mystery of the person.' Increasingly the need has been felt for a spiritual centre to the community's life. 'For years we have been able to meet the demands of the State and still keep reaching for community, because when we're exhausted from trying to carry both we come to the spiritual centre to be nourished.' Recently the Erie community has set aside a building called the 'Waterspring', along similar if smaller lines to Daybreak's 'Dayspring', a place of prayer and quietness and worship to which people may come for spiritual nourishment. They have also welcomed a young man who feels his particular vocation as a lay person is to be a man of prayer at the heart of the community.

In Choluteca, the second tiny Honduran foundation on a dusty barrio not far from the Nicaraguan border, the first instinct of its Mexican founder, Pilar Hernandez was to set aside a tiny corner for prayer in which the sacrament could be reserved. She was a young woman about to live alone amongst the handicapped men she was to welcome, but if the sacrament was there in the middle of the community she felt sure the people of the neighbourhood would understand. They

did, as did intuitively the people with handicaps who came
to live with her. Not wishing to impose her own desire to pray
upon her companions, she would rise early and go quietly to
the chapel until one day Santos enquired why she did not
invite them. At a little meeting it was decided that each
morning they would all go together to the chapel to offer the
day to Jesus and to take part in a liturgy at which they could
receive communion. 'Felipe did not know Jesus at all before
he came to live here, but little by little he understood that in
the small tabernacle was someone who loved him.' With his
wasted legs he could only pull himself along the rough ground
by his arms and in his frustration he was often angry. 'He
would go to the chapel when he was very angry and tell Jesus
he was angry with me or with whatever other cause.' In the
evening when the community gathered once again for prayer
Felipe would murmur over and over again, 'Padre in cielo,
Padre in cielo, Padre in cielo' – Our Father who art in heaven.
Sometimes at night he would cry out his suffering with Jesus.
Sulema used to bang her head so much that she would cause
an open wound, but she too seemed to sense some relief
simply in being in the chapel. When she was very angry
she would go there to shout, and afterwards would emerge
strangely at peace. 'I sense', Pilar would say, 'that Jesus
really is amongst us.' Her experience was, she felt, a lived
endorsement of the words of St Paul: 'God hath chosen the
foolish things of the world to confound the wise; and God
hath chosen the weak things of the world to confound the
things that are mighty' (1 Corinthians 1:27).

The actual experience of communion with handicapped
people was a point of profound unity. There was too, in
communities founded upon the spirit of the Beatitudes, a
unity to be sensed in the idea that, as Père Thomas would
point out, 'all those who truly believe in the Spirit are
attracted to the Sermon on the Mount.' Handicapped people
themselves have a way of cutting across the barriers potentially created by the diversity of religious faith and denomi-
nation. Asked by a visitor to the community which God
he worshipped, Viswanathan at Nandi Bazaar near Calicut
responded unhesitatingly, 'I don't know which God I
worship. Can that be known? There is a little light and in
that we pray, that's all.' Most handicapped people taken to
any church would respond not according to whether it was

in the Roman Catholic, Anglican or United Church tradition but, as Père Thomas had early realised, according to the faith and the love which went into it. They listened to Père Thomas's homilies, and it was not the Thomist theology to which they related but the tone of his voice. Indeed, they would relate to any voice that had that quality regardless of what language it spoke. For others, for whom tradition and ritual were an indispensable part of their faith however, the issue was less straightforward. At the point of the profoundly religious act of l'Arche, the act of meeting handicapped people person to person, there was profound union of all diversity, but at the point where that experience was given articulation, for those who needed that articulation, tensions arose.

L'Arche had begun in France, founded by members of the Roman Catholic Church. At Trosly-Breuil the language, the vocabulary and the values were, despite the insistence on respect for other religions and other Christian denominations, very French and very Catholic. Despite the growing appreciation of the value of married members of the community in terms of what they could contribute in helping the community to become part of the wider local community and of what might be called the 'naturalness' of their children in relationships with people who were handicapped, there were some married people at Trosly-Breuil who sensed that they did not quite fit into a scheme of things in which celibacy appeared a higher form of life. There were also those who felt that, even in the absence of any tangible imposition of the Catholic faith, not to be Roman Catholic at Trosly was a serious limitation. 'There are two forms of ecumenism in the Catholic Church that are in continual tension,' Jean Vanier would comment years later, 'One is an openness to help people become Catholics. The other is an openness to help people become themselves.' In the early days of l'Arche there were some who felt that l'Arche, particularly in Catholic countries but elsewhere also, was unduly inclined to the former. Jean Vanier himself would acknowledge that there had been a time when he had regarded Protestants as people to be converted rather than sisters and brothers with whom he was called to live and grow in Christ.

In India, despite the endeavour to find a form of worship of songs, prayers and readings that was universal – in the sense that it would speak to Hindus, Muslims and Christians alike and at the same time give space to the celebration of each one's personal faith – the assistants who came from abroad did, albeit innocently and blindly, tend to dominate the life of the community with their Christian faith. The celebration of Christmas, for example, far outweighed the celebration of any of the Hindu festivals. Yet for a while this domination passed unnoticed, precisely because Hindus were so open and so disinclined to be upset by it. A similar unconscious domination, some non-Catholics would say, existed in communities that were predominantly Catholic, and even where the communities were made up of a number of different Christian denominations the tensions were far from negligible.

Steve and Ann Newroth, the founders of Daybreak, were Anglican and married. Many of the first handicapped people who came to Daybreak were also Anglican. Links were accordingly established with the local Anglican churches. A very high proportion of the assistants who came were Roman Catholic. They, in their turn, forged links with the local Catholic church. There followed, in the words of one of the early members to join the community, 'the tremendous pain of living so intensely together and then on Sundays going up the driveway in two different directions.' It was a pain which was all the more acute for the fact that everything about l'Arche tended to be articulated in terms of relationship, of family and of love, in a way which made the revelation on the seventh day that these qualities no longer prevailed shocking. Furthermore, the pain was even more intense if it was not quite mutual. 'It's quite different to be in pain as a minority out of step with the majority, if you're not quite as good, not quite as religious.' Even in the United States the majority of people in l'Arche were Catholic; Erie today has no Protestant assistants. Not surprisingly, sensitivity to other religious traditions was at times slower in its actual practice than some might have wished – to a degree where one community director at a retreat in Winnipeg was reduced to exclaiming with considerable emotion, 'I feel like I'm a member of a Roman Catholic club.'

Just as the history of each l'Arche community was different, so each community where such issues arose would have its own story to tell in relation to the ecumenical journey. It should also be said that l'Arche had not set out to be ecumenical in the sense of consciously bringing together people of different Christian denominations or different religions, any more than its founders had envisaged communities outside France. Nevertheless, in a number of different contexts the l'Arche journey would, because of the needs of its people in different countries, become an ecumenical one and perhaps nowhere was the call to become ecumenical more clear than in the communities which began in the United Kingdom where the majority of the handicapped people belonged, at least nominally, to the Anglican Church.

In 1971 Dr Thérèse Vanier, who was by that time a clinical haematologist on the staff of St Thomas' Hospital in London, took part in the Faith and Light pilgrimage to Lourdes. Having spent the very first Christmas at Trosly with her brother, she had been involved with l'Arche since its beginnings, if somewhat discreetly in the background. As someone of great compassion and understanding but equally considerable competence as a doctor, she had found herself intrigued by it but at the same time distanced from it by her professional training and by certain reservations about much of the incompetence of l'Arche. When she first visited Trosly-Breuil she had been both attracted and repelled by l'Arche:

> The attractive thing was and still is the very simple attitude of just bringing people together who are very different and saying, 'This is actually possible.' What to me has always been the repelling side is to assume that you can go on doing this without more space for everybody, and I would include the handicapped people. People need space and silence and other aspects to their lives apart from a constant movement from work to meals to celebrations.

Her pilgrimage to Lourdes was undertaken as a doctor in a group of people for whom she was medically responsible. In the course of it she found herself very much occupied with a fifty-year-old Welshman called Billy and his mother who was in her eighties:

> Between them they must have weighed about thirty stone. Billy had the most appalling asthma and his mother had chronic heart disease so both of them were in wheel chairs. I saw quite a lot of them and not just medically. It didn't

take me long to discover that Billy's one prayer was not to have to go back to hospital and that his mother's one prayer was that Billy would die before she did, because if she didn't outlive him nobody would ever visit him.

At the end of the pilgrimage Thérèse Vanier saw them both off on a train to Wales and for a time, in the process of getting back to ordinary life at St Thomas', she almost forgot about them. A couple of weeks later she was informed that Billy was dead. He had arrived back in Wales too late to go back to the hospital until the following day and during the night had suffered a fatal attack of asthma. After the initial shock, his mother had realised that both their prayers had been answered. The meeting with mother and son had touched Thérèse in a somewhat indefinable way:

I decided I would get more involved. As with so many of these things it wasn't for any particularly rational or intellectual reason. But in fact that story rather fitted in with the work I would go on to do with the hospice and the people with a mental handicap.

Thérèse Vanier started working together with Ann and Geoffrey Morgan, a couple who had previously been at Daybreak, towards the opening of a community in England. At the same time she took up part-time work for two days a week at St Christopher's Hospice. The two roles would prove to be complementary:

It wasn't just remembering Billy and his story. It was the whole question of being with powerless people, people whose defences have gone or are going, who are confronted with reality and who confront you with reality. Just as the handicapped person is stripped of many sophistications and concealments and adornments, the same is true of someone who is seriously ill and indeed of their family. Also in terms of the meaning of these people in present-day society or in the Church today, there are many common factors. Our experience in l'Arche and the hospice experience is that just as very needy people, very powerless people, can be a tremendous source of disruption with pain around them, so they can also be an incredible focus of unity when you begin to really care for their needs and when you begin to see the value that is there. The caring for their needs and the appreciation of their value really go together, because it's making a big demand to see the value of something that is alien, like death or like someone who is mentally handicapped, until you actually enable people to meet it. We all need to be able to give if we're going to receive.

To Thérèse Vanier, with all her professionalism and expertise, the greatest gift of the dying or the handicapped person was the way in which he or she could teach her her own incapacity.

At the same time, her work as a highly capable doctor in the hospice was a relief and a support to her in relation to her life in l'Arche in which she professes to have had no idea what she was doing. Thérèse herself was a Roman Catholic, as was Geoffrey Morgan. His wife, however, was Anglican, and in an extraordinary way the first l'Arche community in England began at the very centre of Anglicanism. Jean Vanier had been contacted by a French woman living in Paris who owned a house in Canterbury which she wished to sell specifically for the use of handicapped people. His sister went to view it and considered it unsuitable, sited as it was between a busy road on one side and a housing development on the other. Nevertheless, struck by the strangeness of the unexpected contact with the unknown house owner and uncertain of her own judgement, she asked Jean Vanier to come to England and help in the decision. Meanwhile this same woman had been in touch once again, with the unexpected suggestion that if l'Arche was going to establish anything in Canterbury, they should first of all go and see the Archbishop of Canterbury. On a cold and snowy New Year's Day in 1972 Thérèse and Jean Vanier visited Archbishop Michael Ramsey at his home in the cathedral close and told him what they were trying to do. The Archbishop, eager to help, put them in touch with the Anglican authorities who would give them first refusal on any church property that came up for sale. Eventually they bought what had been the rectory at Barfrestone, a small village with an old Norman church ten miles from Canterbury, where 'Little Ewell' has been ever since. 'We had been led to make contact with the centre of Anglicanism; we found opening up before us a whole series of friendships with members of the Anglican communion and the hierarchy of that Church', Thérèse Vanier would recall.

'Curiously, it did not spell out to us at the time that of course our people would be members of that Church; we discovered that as they came to live with us. It is the only house in the U.K. l'Arche communities in which we built a chapel.'

A greater awareness of the ecumenical dimension of the new foundation, and the questions it would have to face, arose in connection with an offer on the part of a Roman Catholic priest who wished to spend part of his sabbatical year at Little Ewell to celebrate Mass for the community. There were other l'Arche communities made up of people of different faiths where the issue of division at the Eucharist did not arise. In India where the majority of community members were not necessarily Christians the difficulties of finding a form of worship in which all could share would with time and patience and forgiveness resolve itself around the need to simplify what faith was really all about and link it to daily life. Prayer centred around times of trial, when for example the community was without water, and times of rejoicing: the appearance of the first cashew nuts or the first mangoes. When water was first drawn from a new well, that water was drunk as part of the worship. People brought to the prayer the fruits of nature and the fruits of their labours – the harvest of yams or a bunch of bananas, giving thanks to the One who had given the life-bearing seed, which they had planted and tended, to the One who had prospered the work of their hands as he prospered the work of their hearts. Without seeking a superficial syncretic oneness it became possible to speak of a profound unity which grew through the meeting of their hearts in the little moments of the day, through the shared experience of the love, the forgiveness and the mercy of God, by which they were forgiven and learnt to forgive and respect each other. In communities where times of prayer did not include everyone and where leisure activities were much needed opportunities for individual privacy, celebration was often discovered as a source of unity – the celebration of local fiestas, of the gift of members of the community on the anniversary of their arrival, of birthdays – occasions which lifted people out of their daily routine, their fatigue, their tension and their worries.

In communities, however, where people belonged to different denominations of the Christian Church each of which would normally look to the Eucharist as a focus of shared thanksgiving, forgiveness, repentance and reconciliation, and where the similarities in eucharistic celebration became increasingly apparent, it was perhaps inevitable that the issue of the Eucharist should feature prominently in their concerns. The initial vision had been of 'a Christian community'. At a time when the question of the sharing of the Eucharist was first becoming a prominent one for l'Arche in England, Thérèse Vanier recalls reading in a declaration of Vatican II: 'No Christian community, however, can be built up unless it has its basis and centre in the celebration of the Most Holy Eucharist. Here, therefore, all education in the spirit of the community must originate.'*

Jean Vanier's own more recent words would reflect a not dissimilar train of thought although, significantly, related to that particular religious experience that is at the very heart of l'Arche: 'It is very clear to me that the Eucharist is at the very heart of every community that is body-centred, and maybe every community should be body-centred.' He was speaking of another of those 'gentle moments':

About two and a half years ago we welcomed a guy who was very disturbed. He couldn't stay still. We were using a lot of words with him, but then we discovered that he had athlete's foot and the doctor told us to wash his feet three times a day. There was a transformation. His language became more coherent when we were washing his feet. There is something about the touch of the body, holding the body, respecting the body. That is the initial communication. We forget that, and yet that is at the heart of everything. Somewhere that brings us very close to the whole relationship between the Word and the Eucharist. Then, as you touch the eucharistic body you touch the division of the churches, the pain, but then maybe you're touching the whole mystery of the broken body of Jesus.

At Little Ewell in England, with the gradual arrival of handicapped people who were all Anglicans and the simultaneous appearance of a Roman Catholic priest prepared to celebrate Mass, the question arose as to the position regarding Anglicans receiving communion. In the French communities,

* 'Decree on the Ministry and Life of Priests', in *Documents of Vatican II* (Geoffrey Chapman 1966).

with the permission of the bishop and local priest, Anglicans and Christians of other denominations could receive communion if there was no church of their own communion accessible to them. At Daybreak in Canada, in the climate of experimentation that had followed the Second Vatican Council, all kinds of solutions had been tried including that of a Catholic priest and an Anglican priest concelebrating the Eucharist. Ann Morgan had had no difficulty in receiving communion there regularly. There were, however, those at Daybreak who found it hard to let go of the old order and join in the spirit of experimentation. There was also a reluctance in l'Arche in general to pursue a path within the community which did not match what was happening outside and so create in a sense their own church. It was clear in Jean Vanier's vision that l'Arche was not to become another church in itself. When, therefore, it became apparent that in England, as a country which was not predominantly Roman Catholic, permission from the Roman Catholic Church for Anglicans to receive the sacraments at a Roman Catholic Mass would not be readily forthcoming, it was decided, although not without difficulty, anger and sadness, that the idea of no inter-communion should be accepted. There were other factors involved in the decision to conform to the rules of the Roman Catholic Church. Within the community there were potent arguments relating to the attitude and understanding of the handicapped people themselves: handicapped people could not understand the differences and difficulties, the rules and regulations. Left to themselves they would disregard them. Why impose incomprehensible rules? Why not follow their simplicity and directness? They were leading the assistants in their own need for unity. Why not follow them? Offset against these was the fact that the path along which handicapped people were happy to lead was sometimes determined by factors as random as which assistant they liked accompanying them. Mgr Richard Stewart, the priest who advised on ecumenical affairs in the Roman Catholic diocese of Southwark, raised a number of pertinent questions:

If your Anglican people who are handicapped have permission to receive communion at a Roman Catholic Mass, they may well wish to do so but what will their families think? Will they feel this is a Roman Catholic take-over?

Should not your handicapped people, if they wish to attend the Eucharist, have a choice as to whether they attend that of the Anglican Church if that is their Church.

In the experience of l'Arche, handicapped people needed to *belong*. Might not belonging include for many of them a sense of belonging to their own Church, the Church of their family?

The importance of building relationships between handicapped people and their families, who had sometimes long been estranged, was recognised. Such links could be a source of healing for families who had often undergone years of suffering and guilt because they had not had the resources to care for the person with the handicap at home and had 'abandoned' them to a hospital or institution. It also sometimes happened that the person with a mental handicap became a source of reconciliation in drawing different family members together. A similar idea of the place of the poor, of handicapped people, in creating unity between the churches was germinating. In 1971 the World Council of Churches had published a Study Encounter entitled 'The Unity of the Church and the Handicapped in Society'. It was felt by people in l'Arche that if handicapped people had indeed a role to play in church unity, it was not for others to take steps on their behalf, but rather to look to their needs within their own Church and then help them to be the leaven in that Church. It became increasingly clear in l'Arche in general that ecumenism was not just a melting pot, and that it was important to help each person to be rooted in his or her own tradition. As to the families of the handicapped people, for some it was important that their son or daughter belonged to the Church of their origins, because it was confirmation of their value to that Church. For others, their own break with the Church related directly or indirectly to what they had experienced as the rejection by the Church of their child. A path to healing this rift might be opening.

In Little Ewell it was agreed that Anglicans and Roman Catholics would go to their different parish churches on Sundays and that once a week there would be both an Anglican Eucharist and a Roman Catholic Eucharist in the community chapel. All would be invited to attend both if they wished but there would not be intercommunion. Other communities would follow in the United Kingdom with other questions and other solutions. In 1973 l'Arche was offered a house in Inverness, Scotland. The decision to open a community some 800 miles away from the first l'Arche community in the United Kingdom might again have been considered foolhardy; it presented a challenge far beyond the problems of distance. The challenge was accepted by an American Roman Catholic working in l'Arche, Trosly-Breuil, who found herself in a city where her people would belong to the Church of Scotland, a reformed church stemming from Calvinist roots. Expressed in the simplest terms, the ecumenical arguments could rest there upon the question of whether or not to pray around a lighted candle, let alone upon much more delicate matters concerning the Eucharist.

Very soon after coming to England, the l'Arche community had recognised that it would not be appropriate simply to translate into English the prayer of l'Arche in the form in which it had very early been said by people gathered around the table in the first small house in Trosly-Breuil. In its original form it was a prayer largely addressed to the Virgin Mary. In England it was rewritten in such a way that it was addressed to God, the Father, through Jesus, but it accorded a small place to Mary. In Presbyterian Scotland even that small place was conceded to the Holy Spirit:

Father, through Jesus our Lord and our Brother,
    we ask you to bless us.
Grant that l'Arche be a true home,
    where the poor in spirit may find life,
    where those who suffer may find hope.
Keep in your loving care all those who come.

Spirit of God give us greatness of heart,
    that we may welcome all those you send.
Make us compassionate, that we may heal and bring
    peace.
Help us to see, to serve and to love.

O Lord, through the hands of your little ones bless us,
    through the eyes of those who are rejected, smile on
    us.
O Lord, grant freedom, fellowship and unity to all your
    people; and welcome everyone into your kingdom.

Liverpool in 1976, London in 1977 and Bognor Regis in

1978 would all see the opening of other l'Arche communities. Their respective ecumenical journeys would vary. In London, before the community opened, the decision was made that there would be no community eucharists. People would simply go to their own parish churches. Although this decision would change with the years, at the time no one had the courage to impose or have imposed on them the pain of division at the Eucharist.

Amongst all the suffering and the inevitable negative reactions that arose at times in connection with decisions taken along the way, there was much that was positive that would enable l'Arche (U.K.) to see its beginnings near Canterbury as an important sign. There was a constructive aspect to the need to find means of expressing community unity throughout the Christian year other than through the Eucharist. The value of celebration and of pilgrimages as a means of expressing and living the spiritual values they shared was increasingly recognised. The creation and use of symbolism would become a tool to express deep truths.

In the struggle to express Christian unity without individuals divorcing themselves from their own churches, many l'Arche communities discovered the importance as a healing gesture of a blessing during the Eucharist for those not actually receiving communion. That this healing could be extended beyond l'Arche communities would be brought home to them in 1985 during a retreat given by Jean Vanier in the crypt of Canterbury Cathedral. During the Anglican and Roman Catholic Eucharists people came up for a blessing. Thérèse Vanier would subsequently write* of this occasion:

> I remember how touched the Bishop of Dover was by the fact that not only Roman Catholic lay people but priests were coming up for the blessing. I remember also a mysterious little intervention by Robert from Liverpool l'Arche. Robert is Anglican and knows and values this because he goes regularly to his own local church. He is also used to mixed gatherings when he may ask for a blessing at one Eucharist and communicate at another. On this occasion, at the Anglican Eucharist which was presided over by

* In *An Ecumenical Journey – L'Arche in the U.K.* (a l'Arche Publication, December 1989).

the Archbishop of Canterbury, Robert presented himself apparently uncertain as to whether he was asking to receive communion or a blessing. The Archbishop waited and had just decided that Robert was asking for a blessing when Robert suddenly put out his hands. He received the host, looked at it lengthily and broke it in two, handing one half back to the Archbishop and eating the other half himself. He then came back to sit in a totally different part of the crypt. I know this because he came to sit near me, where there was a vacant place at the end of the row on the central aisle. At the end of the liturgy, the Archbishop, visibly moved, came down the aisle near Robert.

After the Eucharist Robert was taken to meet the Archbishop who was also on the lookout for him. Holding out a small quivering hand Robert introduced himself: 'I'm Robert, Robert from Liverpool.' The Archbishop bent his 6ft 4ins down to Robert's 4ft 6ins and said: 'Oh really, I'm Robert too and I'm also from Liverpool. Today we are brothers.' The incident had come at a moment of great healing and pain together. As Thérèse Vanier would later reflect:

> Few if any of us are likely to extend a hand to an Archbishop who is visibly moved, whether in compassion, solidarity or friendship. Maybe we need to ask ourselves why . . . but for Robert from Liverpool, who had broken the host and given half back to the Archbishop, it was no problem. For the Archbishop I suspect this was a gift.

Some time later Bishop Stephen Verney would acknowledge that the fact that the l'Arche communities in the United Kingdom could not receive the Eucharist together had led him to 'some exciting insights' on how otherwise their people could be a eucharistic community:

> What Jesus said is, 'Do this in remembrance of me. Did he mean just do the Eucharist in remembrance of me? He did not die upon the cross in order that there should be hundreds of thousands of Eucharists performed all over the world. He died on the cross in order that the truth of the Eucharist might be set free in the world. What he did in the Eucharist was actually take the bread, or as the Greek word says 'received' it, gave thanks for it, held it up to

God to be blessed, then broke it and gave it. I wonder whether when he said, 'Do this in remembrance of me,' he didn't mean us to do as he did, in the sense that we should take, or receive from him our whole selves, offer them to God in thanksgiving so that God may transform us, then break us and give us. To be a eucharistic community would then be to be people, not hiding behind the Eucharist, but saying, 'We're actually challenged to do these four things'.

St John in his account of the Last Supper did not mention the Eucharist but rather the washing of the disciples' feet, as if to imply that this was the actual truth of what Jesus was doing. So perhaps the washing of the feet, or some other simple human action through which 'we take, give thanks, break and give,' could actually represent the inner truth of the Eucharist. While people in l'Arche obeyed the Church in the realm of ecclesiastical ritual, nothing prevented them from offering these ordinary actions to God to become extraordinary.

Jean Vanier and l'Arche, Bishop Verney would acknowledge, had turned his understanding 'upside down and inside out'. He recalls once being asked to take a retreat for handicapped people and wondering beforehand how on earth that would be possible. Afterwards he found himself wondering how on earth he would be able to give retreats in future without handicapped people.

For months beforehand we tried to think of themes that would be intelligible to people with handicaps and to do that I had to get closer and closer to the heart of the truth. During the retreat they mimed some of the Gospel stories, and their mimes brought a freshness and an actuality to the humanity of Jesus. Then, after the Eucharist we danced. Seeing all those handicapped people dancing and us dancing one realised somehow what heaven should be, that we should all be set free to dance together. Whether we were handicapped or not, clumsy or graceful, somehow didn't matter.

Slowly the importance for the churches of having handicapped people in their midst would become apparent. Canterbury Cathedral, the l'Arche people were told, would never be quite the same after a pilgrimage came over from l'Arche communities in Canada and the U.S.A. in 1974 and joined the huge Easter congregation at the sung Eucharist. It was one of their contributions to a more recent general shift of attitude to handicapped people in the Church of England, as in other Churches. Such contributions did not, however, need to be on the Canterbury pilgrimage scale. Paul, in the London community, would be largely responsible for the introduction of the 'sign of peace' in the local Anglican parish church, because he consistently disregarded the provisional decision not to adopt it. In a multitude of ways the weak and the broken were potentially a reminder – to churches inclined at times to lose sight of the gospel of the weak – that the poor could be a focus and a source of unity and love.

A story relating to Doris who is hemiplegic reminded Thérèse Vanier of an essential aspect of ecumenism:

> Doris is a strong-minded woman in her fifties who has survived nearly half a century of hospital life and remained resilient and full of life, but angry too. She did not always know where to fix her anger and we were not always sensitive to her fears and wounds. She did not like people to hold her paralysed hand. One night at prayers we joined hands to say the Our Father and a new assistant tried to take Doris' paralysed hand. She had not been warned – that was our fault – she was too insistent. Doris got angry and stamped out shouting, 'I don't like the way you Catholics pray.' The focus was wrong. The anger was right. So much hurt within and between the churches as between people, has more to do with insensitivity than doctrine.

The need for sensitivity of this kind was one which would impress itself with varying degrees of immediacy and intensity upon l'Arche communities throughout the world. In Erie Father George Strohmeyer would acknowledge that it was only as the greater l'Arche discovered its ecumenical life that the Erie community would begin to pay attention at home to the fact that whilst the majority of assistants were Roman Catholic some of the handicapped people were Protestants. The Waterspring in Erie has both an oratory in which the blessed sacrament is reserved and a larger chapel in which the daily liturgy is held. That larger chapel is adorned only with a plain cross on the wall and an icon. On the table which serves as an altar the Word is enthroned. 'Symbolic small beginnings for us, but we have to be constantly vigilant because we don't have any Protestant assistants and it's really hard for Catholics to think ecumenically for others.'

During a recent week of prayer for Christian unity, daily prayer services at Erie found their expression in terms, not only of different Christian traditions, but also of Hindu, Islamic, Buddhist and Jewish, in 'a real attempt for us to find our deepest communion'. 'Roman Catholic with growing ecumenical mission and vision' is the description to which the Erie community would most comfortably lay claim, but that description would not fit every l'Arche by any means. Jean Vanier himself would refer in time to 'non-homogeneous communities', for any attempt at definition even of l'Arche in London would need to accommodate the presence of people who were not necessarily Christian.

By 1985 a Dutch Buddhist in the Lambeth community would experience no difficulty in living Buddhist teachings in the day-to-day life of l'Arche: 'The teachings of Jesus and those of Buddha are very close together, so in that way I can feel that I can live a very harmonious life.' For her there had been a period of difficulty related to her own need to learn to find personal space and discover what time she could actually take out of community life for her own faith and in what ways it was appropriate for her to respect the Christian life of the community. She had left for a while, but after a period of working in institutions and hospitals in Holland without the support of a community with a spiritual life, she would come to the conclusion that l'Arche was one of the few places where she could really live what she believed. It felt very right for her to take part in the evening prayers in the house and often she would join in with her own form of Buddhist prayer to the beat of a drum. Her Buddhist faith was treated in a very respectful way by the community as a whole, and the handicapped people in particular were very supportive: 'Most people in Western society ask what is Buddhism, why do you beat the drum and why do people shave their heads? – and before they have the answers to those questions they can't really support it, let alone join. But people who need no worldly explanations are very supportive.'

There were and are those who would see the danger of the

'melting pot' as ever present, but l'Arche in general would embark upon an evolution which retained a sense of what the churches were doing. The churches were on the move too, but in a way l'Arche's position would always be unique. As one Canadian would put it: 'What the theology of ecumenism says is wonderful, but in some ways we're not at a theological place. We're at an experiential place.' L'Arche was trying to live that deep unity that is communion on a day-to-day basis. They would be helped along the way by 'their people' – by Sulema in Honduras for example, who, by repeatedly placing one person's hand in that of the next and insisting that they greet each other, makes lack of communication or forgiveness almost impossible.

At the same time they would not be allowed the relief of avoiding confronting the questions, the escape into collaboration. There would always be those who tugged at their hand and their heartstrings when it came to the time to walk in a different direction. Yet talking to long-term members of various l'Arche communities I would encounter again and again a sense of privilege on their part at their close proximity to the poor whom they recognised as a path to unity, and if there was suffering in the search for communion in diversity, then suffering and the wound and its mysterious power for effecting communion was at the source of life in l'Arche. For those who wished to see it, the mysterious relationship between the broken bread and body upon the altar and the broken bodies of the poor and the suffering was ever present, and if for some there was pain in the division of the mystical body of Christ that is the Church, and pain in their own broken hearts, then that in itself was surely a form of communion. 'Slowly I discovered', Chris Sadler would claim of her life in Nandi Bazaar, 'how deeply I carry in my own yearning for God, the yearning of each one here, and as we become more one body, I sense a little bit of the great groaning of the universe.'

The extent to which l'Arche was being called to live in communion with the wider community and the world would become apparent in all kinds of ways. For Pilar and the community in Choluteca there was something missing if the discovery of the spiritual treasure of the poor was not shared with their neighbours: 'We have been given a treasure and our neighbours are thirsting for that treasure, even if sometimes they don't know it. For me the gift of l'Arche is to discover the gifts of our people and to help our neighbours discover that gift.' From her first arrival in the barrio the poor people in the parish made it clear that if l'Arche was coming to Choluteca they wished to involve themselves in it. At the foot of the altar in the church, where only once a month a priest would come to say Mass, they placed a small basket with a piece of paper on it marked, 'For l'Arche'. 'People here have hardly anything, but what they had they wanted to share.' With the pile of tiny coins they gave during the first months Casa San José bought Felipe a pair of shoes, and the people of the barrio were proud of their achievement. 'I sense,' Pilar would explain as she sipped water from a shell, 'that we mustn't change our style of life, because if we do we shall no longer belong to them any more.' We were enjoying the hospitality of neighbours who gave so generously of the little that they had, as we swung in the hammocks that formed their only furnishings. Like most others in the tiny houses of the barrio, they had viewed the community's comings and goings initially with a certain guardedness, but they had watched and eventually visited and gradually come to see in the life of the l'Arche house something to which their family could aspire.

It was important that in Casa San José the community made their own tortillas and cooked them over a wood stove rather than buying them ready made, because that was how others on the barrio had to live. It was important that despite the heat they did not have a fridge, because that gave a privileged neighbour, who did have one, the opportunity to offer them the use of his. It was important that, although perhaps now with the help of the board of directors they could buy a little car, they did not do so, because when Santos, Sulema, Vilma or Felipe travelled on the local bus to the nearby town they met and talked to other people who could in their turn see that the life of the people with handicaps at Casa San José was not out of reach of their own handicapped children. As it was, in a society of broken families where men often had several common-law wives and children that were all too frequently handicapped, the neighbours watched the little community living amongst them and saw in some way a tiny model of what family life and the place of the handicapped person could be.

In the small courtyard of Casa Nazaret in Tegucigalpa, amongst a number of frail and often underwatered fruit trees, grows an avocado pear tree. In the early days of the house Nadine had been joined by Régine, another French assistant from Trosly-Breuil who had also felt a special call to Honduras, but they had had to wait what seemed to them an interminable time before they could obtain the legal recognition from the government which was necessary before they could take in children. While they waited, one night the neighbour's wooden house caught fire and with it much of Casa Nazaret. It was, Nadine was able to perceive, providential that the children had not been in the house at the time – the board of directors had been right to insist that they waited – and she planted the stone of an avocado pear in the arid ground as a symbol of new life. Not long afterwards, with the necessary repairs carried out and with government endorsement, the house welcomed the children Régine and Nadine had been visiting regularly in hospital. The small community had started with a fervent desire to be part of the life of the local people, but the presence of Raphael who had spent all his life in a hospital cage, and of Claudia who was blind and autistic and who screamed day and night for a year, absorbed so much time and attention that the community became a little more enclosed. After a while it was realised that something was disappearing from their special relationships with the neighbouring people. Then Raphael, for whom the community had been founded and for whom it had had to wait so long, became more seriously ill. The tiny community had to live through his gradual deterioration and eventual death, but his funeral was an occasion of extraordinary communion between the community and its neighbours who carried it in a time of trial, and between the rich and the poor who so rarely otherwise met in any real sense in the tragically divided capital of Honduras. Raphael's death, and that of Suyapa a short while later in another house built a little higher up the hill overlooking the city, brought communion with the community in the wider sense of the word. The avocado pear tree grew and flourished. No one who visited the two houses in Nueva Suyapa with their tiny school and busy workshop could doubt that whilst l'Arche was being brought in a very concrete way to recognise that there was a universality in the call to drink from the cup of suffering, here as elsewhere, it was equally tangibly being shown the mystery of death and resurrection.

8

Servants of Communion

Jean Vanier had a gift for drawing out the abilities and the sense of responsibility in others, and for giving them the confidence to follow the call of God into places where they would otherwise fear to tread. His understanding of authority was based upon the role of Jesus as a good shepherd as described in the tenth chapter of St John's Gospel. 'The qualities Jesus gives to this good shepherd are truly those that every shepherd of a community needs. Shepherds lead the flock and give direction. They must also "know each one by name".' In the biblical vision the *name* signified the person's gift and call or mission. Shepherds must therefore have a personal relationship with each one. They must know an individual's particular gifts in order to help them grow, know their wounds in order to give strength, comfort and compassion, especially in times of pain. Shepherds must be bonded to people with bonds of love and be ready to give their lives for them, sacrificing their own personal interests.

From the early days of l'Arche its founder had endeavoured to give others a role in the direction of the community. Early on at Trosly-Breuil he had formed a community council of six people to share his responsibilities and to nominate heads of houses and workshops. He had also set up a board of directors which years later he would acknowledge he had regarded at first as a necessary evil but which in time he had come to value and to honour:

At first I just wanted to get on with it, and there were these guys asking awkward questions. Gradually I saw that I needed them for finance, for contacts with governments and so on, that I couldn't do it alone. Then I saw that as a community we needed them, that they could bring wisdom to the community and another understanding to the way we were dealing with situations. They were not just useful when it came to financial matters but also, in many instances, really knew what community was about.

The establishing of a good board of directors would become recognised as an essential part of the formation of any l'Arche community, not simply as a body legally responsible for property, finance and other such issues but also as people who, if they exercised their authority with a real understanding of the vocation of l'Arche, could help the community to work through crises, to define and set up structures and enable it to be clear about its established goals. As an external authority with an 'outsider's eye' they also, it would be increasingly recognised, had a role in relation to leaders of communities. They were there to confirm, give support and encourage leaders. They were also there to supervise and challenge them when necessary.

One of the distinctive characteristics of l'Arche is what Jean Vanier refers to as the 'triple-authority'. He believes firmly in the delicate balance between the authority of the priest or minister, that of the doctor/psychiatrist and that of the community leader or director, all of whom have areas of responsibility in relation to the community and to the individuals in it and none of whom have exclusive control. This safeguarding balance built itself quite spontaneously into the fabric of the community at Trosly-Breuil. The role of the priest was based very largely upon Père Thomas's understanding of his place, not as a director and decision maker in the community but as a defender of the interests of the poor. In a sense there was a parallel to be drawn between his role and that of the psychiatrist/doctor, for he too was there to defend people's well-being. Together they were responsible for the physical, psychic and spiritual health of individuals and this would oblige them at times to adopt a position that was somewhat counter to the movement of the community as a whole, a movement which did not always allow an individual what was in his best personal interests. At the same time, a further tension was inherent in their own particular roles, for whilst they must protect the interests of individuals they were also the community priest and the community psychiatrist/doctor. The health of the individual was also to a large extent dependent on the well-being of the community.

There were at times uneasy complexities associated with each one of these roles. Although in a way a priest who was answerable to his bishop had slightly greater independence than the psychiatrist who was paid by the director, time would show that not all priests would tread the path adopted by Père Thomas quite so willingly. Whilst, with the passage of the years, in many parishes and dioceses the presence of handicapped people would come to be valued as a gift and the influx of energetic young people welcomed, priests and pastors would not always be as supportive as their local l'Arche communities might wish. Part of the difficulty would arise because l'Arche communities did not fit into preordained categories. If the community was not Roman Catholic, then what was it and under whose jurisdiction did it fall? To the problems of specific religious identity was added the fundamental challenge of the person with the handicap with whom most people outside the community might well feel initially ill at ease. There were priests who were very shy of people with handicaps and who could not open their hearts to them. Then, for the secular Roman Catholic priest the whole concept of a community, particularly one in which men and women lived together under the same roof, could represent an uncomfortable challenge to his personal experience. Many priests and bishops of various denominations who grew close to l'Arche would claim that they found in it something which not only challenged but actually affirmed their priesthood. The ecumenical dimension, the simplicity, the way in which communities touched the heart, the relationships involved, the manner in which handicapped people saw beyond the cassock and remembered them as individuals, the fact that people were hungry to be affirmed in the Gospel, to be told that they were leading a Christian life – all these factors could give meaning to the lives of priests. They could also be very demanding. Furthermore, to respond to l'Arche's desire to share the sacraments and the Word might be something radical. It was also something very small, based simply on relationships with little people. The unpretentious role of the priest or pastor as servant of the poor was one to which some would subscribe more readily than others.

Yet from the very beginning of l'Arche the desire to be a Christian community had been there. Jean Vanier had begun with an approach to a secular authority and the formation of an association, but almost immediately, in 1965, he had gone to the then Bishop of Beauvais to speak about l'Arche and express his desire to be in communion with him. He had subsequently been greatly touched and encouraged by the bishop's friendship, encouragement and ultimate retirement to a small house in Trosly. Thereafter he made similar approaches to the local bishop each time a new foundation was in the process of being formed. Invariably the response was one of interest and support. Some communities were actually founded by priests, but although little by little l'Arche would discover another more active example than the hidden, contemplative, mystical model set by Père Thomas, it always encouraged priest-founders gradually to leave the role of community leader and to assume a more priestly role in the community: the role of a man of prayer, the sacraments and the Eucharist, of spiritual guide. 'I believe', Jean Vanier would elaborate, 'that to live in l'Arche we have to espouse the gospel values. That means a *metanoia*, a conversion at such a depth that it isn't just a question of a knowledge of Christ but rather of espousing the vision of Christ. This is so contrary to anything of this world that we need the Holy Spirit. The role of the priest as a man of God, who is close to each person and who brings the sacrament, is to be a constant reminder of the spiritual dimension to our lives. And where there is a priest who really understands the gift of the poor as people who receive with the greatest simplicity the message of Christ, he has a very specific role.'

In 1978 two former assistants would be ordained in Compiègne to be priests for l'Arche but also to have a ministry in the diocese. Both would experience some difficulty in finding an appropriate role within their respective l'Arche communities. Other bishops in Belgium and France would thereafter accompany other young people in their preparation for the priesthood in and for l'Arche. These ordinations were taken as a welcome confirmation of the Church's acceptance of l'Arche. The role of the priest in l'Arche, however, would be for some years a role continuously subjected to evaluation and a process of discovery. In time a distinction would come to be drawn between priests 'of' l'Arche and priests 'for' l'Arche. Priests of l'Arche were those whose main ministry was in a l'Arche community. Priests for l'Arche were those who exercised a ministry in l'Arche in a limited way for a limited time. Priests of l'Arche were called to help other priests in the region find an appropriate place within the communities. They also frequently took part in events, meetings and retreats organised by l'Arche. Some priests in l'Arche were also members of their community council and participated in the working out of the priorities and fundamental orientations of the community. In general, however, they were called to a rather hidden role at the service of the spiritual growth of individual members and of the community as a whole. It could be difficult for priests to be accountable to the community for what they did and to be evaluated by it and called to growth and progress. Their area of responsibility and authority was not clearly defined, and tensions would sometimes arise in the various communities between the priest and the director, the parameters of whose authority were also somewhat complex.

Because of the double identity of l'Arche, both as a community 'espoused to the gospel values' and as an establishment responsible to public and government authorities for the welfare of the handicapped people committed to their care, the role of director was at very least a dual one. The very term 'director' was one which derived from the necessity to denote a function which would have recognisable standing in the eyes of both public authorities from which l'Arche received financial support and relatives who entrusted their people to the communities. At the same time this 'director' must also serve as shepherd and servant of the community. It was not always easy to find the balance between directing and ensuring a certain level of efficiency on the one hand and, on the other, the more pastoral role of listening, being attentive to those who suffered most and were not perhaps happily settled in their place, and watching over the spirit of the community. There were times when it was almost impossible to unify the two aspects. Alain Saint-Macary, the present director at Trosly-Breuil, would describe how sometimes in correspondence he signed himself 'director', while at others, such as when writing to the bishop, 'community leader' would seem more appropriate.

In essence the three roles of priest, psychiatrist/doctor and director were complementary, overlapping and subject to tensions both between one another and within themselves, in a way which safeguarded against over emphasis of any one aspect of life in l'Arche, against abuse of authority and against authority becoming too onerous, especially as communities grew in size. Joe Egan, the outgoing director of Daybreak, would speak of how at times he had been greatly relieved to be able to refer particular problems to the community psychiatrist or a priest. The more critical view would be that the result is an authority which is only weakly grounded. Ultimately its effectiveness depended on trust, a respect for the other person's ministry and on good personal interaction and relationships. It depended on each person exercising authority recognising that authority in the light of the role of the Good Shepherd.

Now, Jean Vanier is greatly attracted to the title which Brother Roger of Taizé has elected as most suitable for the leader of the Taizé community: a 'servant of communion'. Although, earlier in the history of l'Arche Jean Vanier would probably not have articulated his understanding in quite that way, somewhere at each level of authority and responsibility was the idea of authority exercised as a servant of God's plan of communion. In *Community and Growth* (1989 edn) he would write:

> Yes, the leader's role is to facilitate communion; a community is fundamentally more a place of communion than a place of collaboration. If the leader or prior is a servant of communion, then he or she must be a person of communion, seeking communion with the Father and communion with people. Then the leader will create space for communion in the community. We must remember that all of us, and not only the leader, are called to be servants of communion.

Within this framework there is and was, even in the 'sixties and 'seventies when Jean Vanier was often absent from Trosly-Breuil for six months of the year or more, still scope for his charisma and personal authority to carry considerable weight. Despite his early formation of the community council, the structures at Trosly had remained fairly vertical and hierarchical and people still referred directly to him and found their support and authority in him. It was Jean Vanier who drew up the agendas and ran nearly all the meetings. Consequently, when he was away the community had to await his return to settle most of its problems. Finally, in 1974, in recognition that the director could not, while he was so active in other parts of the world, also direct the community at Trosly-Breuil entirely on his own, a special meeting of the council was called. On its agenda was a study of the deficiencies of structures which did not provide for more collective decision-making. (There had been occasions while Jean Vanier was in residence when long queues formed outside his room late into the night, to such an extent that he had taken to sleeping in a cubby-hole in his office.) Alain Saint-Macary recalls the meeting being approached with a certain nervousness. After all, it was to touch upon the role of the community's charismatic and much loved founder, and if sometimes people in l'Arche suffered from too much dependency, they were aware that they also found security in him. As if to confirm the need for less dependence and greater provision for the future, however, shortly before the meeting the news was announced that Père Thomas had come close to a life-threatening cerebral haemorrhage.

For twenty-four hours the elderly priest lived the present moment, but could not remember what had happened on the previous day and had no grasp of the future. He had asked Jacqueline d'Halluin to go to Paris to get him a ticket for Lourdes but, when she telephoned to tell him that there were no tickets available for the day he had wanted, he had no recollection of his own request. So normal was his behaviour at the time that the friends with whom he had just eaten a meal noticed nothing wrong. Nevertheless Jacqueline d'Halluin alerted a doctor. Père Thomas was treated immediately and the clot on his brain was dispelled. The incident was sufficiently serious, however, to bring home to the community in a painfully vivid way the fact that their founders would not be with them for ever. The need for a deputy director to share in the director's responsibilities was confirmed.

A new constitution was set up in January 1975. This stipulated that the council would consist of fifteen members instead of six. All of these would now be elected by the core of permanent assistants, whereas previously the appointment of half the council had fallen to Jean Vanier as community leader. In time this constitution too would be subject to change. In 1976, for example, a new stage was reached with the decentralisation of the houses into geographical areas. The main principles introduced in January 1975 would, however, hold good, the general movement being away from a constitution which was essentially vertical to one which was horizontal, in the sense that at each level of community decisions would be taken collectively from within the group concerned.

A similar process would be undergone on the international level. The second meeting of the International Federation in October 1973 brought together thirty-five representatives from a dozen communities. During that meeting the existence of two charters was confirmed: the specifically Christian Charter born out of the first Federation meeting and the Indian Charter which provided for inter-religious communities. It had been decided not to try to agree on one Charter, which would remain vague at the Christian level in order to be acceptable to everyone. It was also decided to create a structure which would sustain the links between the increasing number of communities. A small council was formed around Jean Vanier, the 'international co-ordinator'. In reality, however, this council was never able to meet; the unity of the Federation was still maintained almost exclusively through Jean Vanier's regular visits to America, Europe and India and his personal links with individual communities.

At the third meeting of the Federation, at Shadow Lake in Canada in 1975, there were almost one hundred delegates representing some thirty existing communities, including the new foundations in Haiti and Africa. At this meeting Jean Vanier announced his decision to step down as international co-ordinator. Work began on an international constitution creating eight regions in the Federation, each one with a regional co-ordinator elected for a three-year term. These eight regional co-ordinators, along with the international co-ordinator, a vice-co-ordinator, and Jean Vanier as founder, formed the international council of the Federation which was to meet once or twice a year. Again, this constitution would be subject to evolution and change. Essentially, however, l'Arche was feeling its way towards structures which would allow for the decisions, vision, mutual aid and support to be dependent not on one person but on the group. The Federation meeting held in Rome in May 1987, which brought together 350 people from 82 communities and which was highlighted by a visit from Mother Teresa and a meeting with Pope John Paul II, would adopt a new constitution which divided the regions into three zones. Two years later the number of zones would be increased in order to bring better, closer support to the regions and through them to individual communities.

Inevitably, the process was initially slow. For the person who first had to assume the role of international co-ordinator in place of Jean Vanier the step was far from easy. Sue Mosteller found herself suddenly not only director of Daybreak but called at an international level to step into Jean Vanier's shoes. She had agreed to assume the former role temporarily while Steve and Ann Newroth took a sabbatical year and found, when at the end of that year they decided not to return to l'Arche, that it was assumed she would continue. Her nomination to a second role, on the international level, filled her with a sense of inadequacy:

> After a spell of feeling I hadn't really had any choice, I was happy being a director. I'm good at being a community leader. I can call and listen to people although I was poor administratively, hopeless at financial and administrative things, so there were people who had to help me. I grew and the community grew. But being called to the international role was horrible for me. I hadn't travelled very much. I'd been a nun in a convent. I hadn't read widely. I didn't know anything about other cultures. I was afraid of aeroplanes.

For the first couple of years Jean Vanier continued to steer the international co-ordination, if now from behind the scenes. 'But', Sue Mosteller would recall, 'he was always pushing me into the centre. I couldn't speak French and I'd have to go and give talks in France. I would be so scared I was weeping. Jean told me the first thing we had to do was get the international constitution written, so we worked on it together. He would suggest where I should go and visit, and I just went.'

Jean Vanier had a strong and exceptionally attractive personality and an understanding of what community is all about. He was caught up in a vision to the extent that there were those who felt that if they trod too closely upon it he simply did not hear them. But hand in hand with that went the gift for catching others up in the same vision and a capacity really to listen to other people that was rooted in his early discovery of the gifts of the weak. He had developed the ability to be extremely patient. Some might say that he was too patient at times with the wrong people, but his patience was based upon a ready acceptance of the way an individual was at a given time and on an awareness of the fruits of waiting. Experience had shown him how people and situations could change. He had in fact outstanding ability at every level. To those around him he seemed invariably to know how to go about things and, if he did not, he knew how to find the person who did.

If the survival of the transition from a charismatic founder is one of the classic difficulties in the history of a community, Jean Vanier had hardly failed to recognise it. Perhaps his decision to take a step backwards and let others assume authority touched in some way upon the point in the life of Jesus at which he told his disciples that it was expedient for him to leave, because only then would the Comforter come to them (John 16:7). Certainly the withdrawal had to be made as the leader felt called by God to make it.

By 1976 Jean Vanier was still director of the community in Trosly-Breuil. At a gathering of the more permanent assistants that year, however, Odile Ceyrac found herself nominated deputy director to assist him in the overall leadership of the community. She had been in l'Arche since 1969, had been previously put in charge of the Val Fleuri and had managed, whilst an assistant at Trosly, to undertake more formal studies outside the community in the psychology and education of handicapped people. All the same, she considered herself hardly competent to become responsible for a community which was by that time made up of more than a hundred people. On the very day that she was appointed deputy director, Jean Vanier left once more for India. On his return, she collected him from the airport still looking to him to make decisions and give advice, but Jean Vanier, who sleeps very easily when he is tired, fell asleep in the car. In fact he was ill. During the two months of hospitalisation and a further two months of convalescence that followed, the community predictably went through a period of unrest. Hitherto, even in his absences Jean Vanier had been very present. Whatever his official title, he had still been very much the person on whom everybody relied. His illness, following the period of Père Thomas's ill health, was very much an endorsement of the already recognised need in Trosly-Breuil to find a way of going forward and of taking decisions as a community, if necessary without him.

Internationally also, his illness might be said to have achieved what his more deliberate attempts to prepare for that ultimately inevitable transition could not. Thérèse Vanier recalls one important consequence of it as a new assumption of responsibility on the part of the Federation. It was significant that despite Jean Vanier's absence the meeting due to take place in Africa was not cancelled. It was he who had initiated l'Arche in Africa; the remainder of the Federation representatives knew little about what was happening there. Nevertheless the international meeting was held in Africa, and it was probably crucial for future development that it passed off successfully without him. Sue Mosteller remembers a point in the year 1977 when she realised that she did not have to be Jean Vanier, that her own calling was to be different and that she could be accepted in her own right. In a multitude of other ways people were forced to get to work and assume responsibility regardless of how timid and apprehensive they were, and they did so in a way which could only inspire confidence for the future.

It was a mark of Jean Vanier's vision that, in the interests of the future of the community, he recognised the necessity to leave even his role as director at Trosly-Breuil. Following his illness he returned briefly to the directorship of the community of Trosly-Breuil, but in 1980 stepped down as director and asked Odile Ceyrac, who took over the position, if he could take a sabbatical year during which he would have no major responsibilities in the community. He did not again return to the role of director. 'Many things have happened,' he would reflect years later, 'I've lost many things in the community. I have no specific place in the community. The same is true on the international plane and on most other decisional planes in l'Arche. But I can see the rightness of it, and at the same time God is giving me other things to do, moving me in other directions – which gives me a lot of light.'

There are those who would debate whether even now Jean Vanier has really 'let go' emotionally. His influence remains unquestionably strong. Although in the United Kingdom, for example, he tends to be known as Thérèse Vanier's brother, and although the dependence on him may be hidden, it is nonetheless real. Be it in Canada, the United States, Honduras or France, l'Arche has its own vocabulary which is all the more distinctive because it can sound slightly strange in English. Undoubtedly it reflects a community experience and undoubtedly language, as Jean Vanier is quick to point out, is an evolving entity, but the vocabulary of l'Arche is very much the vocabulary of Jean Vanier: of 'journeys', 'passages', 'breakages', 'accompaniment', 'formation' and 'celebration'. Travelling to the various communities, just as I would meet again in a multitude of subtle ways the hidden presence of Père Thomas, so I would rediscover Jean Vanier's words, his thinking, his mannerisms and even his distinctive laugh. And if there were those whom I met who had light this was still, it was suggested to me, very largely reflected light.

The transition to the new structures at Trosly-Breuil was not easily made by all. Père Thomas was a Dominican who thought most readily in terms of religious orders. In his old age he could not make the change to the community's new way of living without some difficulty. He had always occupied a position on the council, but the larger numbers represented a greater trial in relation to his deafness. He found meetings in general difficult. There was also a generation gap for him to contend with and, in a community where a growing number of people belonged to different Churches or did not profess any specific belief, the whole question of the attachment of l'Arche to the Church he represented was not entirely clear. His role in relation to the community, though vital, was becoming even more hidden.

In 1971 l'Arche had acquired what had been a farm in the village, and Jacqueline d'Halluin, whose artistic and creative talents had been repeatedly called upon to refurbish and furnish successive houses, had informed Jean Vanier that she was tired. As an artist, she had never felt particularly drawn to community life. The moving from one house to the next and the constant new challenges had given her a degree of personal space that had made life in community more acceptable, but the time had now come, she felt, to create a place of rest for herself and for Père Thomas. In fact, the old buildings surrounding two shingled courtyards would become a complex of accommodation, library, oratory and chapel in which to welcome the many guests coming to Trosly-Breuil. In the atmosphere of peace and spiritual intensity enveloping

these converted stables and outhouses, Père Thomas, who
still has an exceptional memory for individuals and names
and for theology and philosophy, would find himself 'eaten
up' by people and constantly engaged in those 'little conversations' which he recognised without a trace of egoism, 'could
go very far'.

For Jean Vanier himself the departure from the role of
director would bring difficult moments when his susceptibility
and egoism were bruised, but not, he would insist, too much
suffering. Living the example of the shepherd who must be
'ready to sacrifice his own personal interests' and taking every
opportunity to express his confidence in those who were in
new positions of responsibility, he embarked upon a passage
which would bring 'liberation' for his heart and mind.

9

More Earthy and More Heavenly

The plan, according to which everything had happened so swiftly, had also made use of 'the fragility of the person in it'. That was the way God worked, Jean Vanier was able to recognise – 'through what is clean and what is dirty'. As to his own fragility it was, he felt, very complex. He could easily become the naval officer, but behind the capacity of the naval officer was a vulnerability. Power in people invariably hid vulnerability in a way which gave him occasion often to speak with characteristically vivid imagery of 'the wolf at the door of the wound'. There was a wolf in each person which was frequently orientated to efficacy. What in his case, the vulnerability was behind the wolf he was not quite certain. He sensed only that 'in each of us there is an immense anguish, a fragility which can come out in different ways, confronted by relationships that could lead to anguish, confronted by people whose anguish reveals our own anguish, our fear of contradiction. You're never quite sure what is a power that is given you to go forward which shouldn't be contradicted and what is the fragility that would have to be contradicted.' In the journey which he believed each person was undertaking there would inevitably be moments when he or she would go through 'passages' or 'breakages' in the process of bringing together the poor and the rich person inside each one. His illness in the spring of 1976 had been one such moment in his own life. With hindsight he could see that he had been moving at a speed that was much too fast for his body. The frequent air travel, the nights spent at times on airport benches, the contact with suffering in all its multifarious forms which he found himself 'carrying a little in my flesh', the strains of being constantly available to people, of being the bearer of the message of the poor to the sometimes reluctantly receptive rich, of sleeping in different beds in different climates had finally taken their toll. 'I wasn't listening sufficiently to Jesus in my body, and so at one moment my body said, "Stop".'

L'Arche has a way of calling for the body to be given its appropriate recognition: in the understanding of the Church, in the formation of community, in the lives of individuals. It was as if Jean Vanier had in some way to live that recognition in his own flesh. He had contracted amoebic hepatitis together with a secondary infection to which the doctors did not put a name but which was undoubtedly related to exhaustion and the failure to take proper medical precautions in tropical climates. During the two months he spent in the Cochin hospital in Paris he discovered in a more personal way the path of death and resurrection. There he experienced also, and possibly for the first time, what it was to be assisted rather than to be an assistant. He learned new lessons in patience, for the doctors were unable to tell him how long he would be confined to bed, and he very soon realised that it would take time in his weakened condition before he was able to walk let alone fly again. Jean Vanier professes not to have had too much difficulty in accepting illness any more than any other 'breakage' in life. 'That doesn't mean to say there haven't been difficult moments, moments when I've touched anger and so on, but I can't say I'm someone who has suffered a great deal. I've matured I think but I can't say I've had difficulty accepting. I think there is something in me which gives me a possibility of advancing peacefully.' When he looks at others in their suffering he senses his own limits. 'My capacity to bear inner pain or anguish is probably less than many others, so God can't give me too much. Of course he can, but I think we each have our psyche which permits us to go only a certain distance. It has always been very gentle for me.' Confined to his sick bed, Jean Vanier did not lose the ability to exclaim, 'Allelulia', a much used exclamation in l'Arche, at the smallest intimation of good fortune. His capacity to find humour wherever there was the least potential for it did not fail him. The fall of the mercury after it had nearly burst the thermometer was cause for amused satisfaction. So too was the fact that his height had induced the hospital staff to provide him with the bed in which General de Gaulle had slept when he had undergone an operation in the Cochin hospital: 'It's just a simple hospital bed, only

longer than the others. Praise the Lord!' Nevertheless the
message of the experience, namely to rest, was undoubtedly
a sacrifice for him in which the regular presence of Père
Thomas at his bedside was a necessary source of support. It
was the first time in the twelve years since l'Arche had begun
that they had spent so much time together. 'He helps me to
abandon myself, to be more inwardly silent', Jean Vanier
would write at the time. He would also write to the l'Arche
communities asking them to pray that he might remain faithful and able to take advantage of this period of inactivity to
discover a new 'activity', for this, he realised, was perhaps
the time to discover the Jesus who 'dwells in our hearts and
asks only that we remain in his love'. In the sleeplessness of
those hospital nights he had time to think of the men and
women in prison cells, of all those who were alone, and to
recognise how spoilt he was in having so many brothers and
sisters who loved him.

There are so many people who are all alone, hidden in
hospitals, prisons, flats and rooms, so many rejected,
wounded, unloved people. Let us pray together for them,
and give thanks for all the love and peace that Jesus gives
us, which unites us and which we are called to share. And
at the heart of this unity and peace for all the 'Raphaels'
of this world in whom the hidden Jesus is a source of peace
and joy.

Jean Vanier appears to have emerged from the 'breakage'
of his illness in a state of greater equilibrium than had previously been his. Thérèse Vanier is quite certain that the
doctors advising him told him a few home truths which no
one else could have put to him. The experience would prevent
him from pushing himself to quite the same extremes, from
spending nights without sleep and completely disregarding
his own fatigue. It would also point him on the road to a
somewhat more reflective role. It would not, however, prevent
him from continuing to rush round the world.

New Year's Eve of 1976 saw both Jean and Thérèse Vanier
knocking on the door of Stephen Verney's house in Graffham,
Sussex. Books have a way of finding their way into Jean
Vanier's hands at a time when they are likely to strike a
special chord of recognition. On this occasion the book was

Stephen Verney's *Into the New Age.** The title of the book was a translation of the Greek words, *eis ton aiona* which occur like a refrain through St John's Gospel. In recognition that humanity was standing at the edge of a new epoch, Stephen Verney had written of how he believed that the new age could be entered for good rather than for ill through the discovery of interdependence.

> It was a time when we were seeing the dawning of ecology, a time when new scientific insights were emerging. One was beginning to see the universe in terms of energy and matter being two ways of talking about the same thing. We seemed to be moving into a new world on that side; and on the Church side there was a feeling of great hope and renewal. In the Roman Catholic Church there was all the aftermath of the Second Vatican Council. There was the Pentecostal movement and all kinds of renewal in the Anglican Church. I was trying to write a book that would bring together the vision of a renewed earth and a renewed heaven with the idea that we at the heart of it could be very earthy and very heavenly.

In his foreword to the book Canon Verney wrote of how good and evil were interlocked in everybody and everything, and chiefly within ourselves. As people discovered their potential for good, they uncovered at the same time their potential for evil. The way out of this predicament was through the way of death and resurrection. There was, he acknowledged, nothing new about saying this. What was needed in the crisis of this generation was a new courage in choosing it, new depth in feeling it and a new perspective in understanding it.

Deeply moved by the book, Jean Vanier wrote a note to its author that was 'so charming and so gracious' that Canon Verney felt he must somehow 'get to know this man'. They talked late into the night and saw in the New Year of 1977 together. Many things had struck a chord of recognition in Jean Vanier. There was the fact that the book had been born out of the author's personal experience of the death of his wife and was a witness to the life that is born out of death. There was the vision it offered of a new Church. There was also the assertion that at the heart of Christian community

* Stephen Verney, *Into the New Age*, Fontana/Collins, London, 1976.

lay forgiveness and that part of the role of the leader was to assume the anguish and the aggression of those he was leading and to be a leader in forgiveness.

If when faced with aggression or servility, Stephen Verney had written, the leader aspired to enable the group to live the life of the new age, then he must be

> one step ahead of the group in this very process of forgive-ness which is its essence. That is to say, he must become more aware of the good and evil that interlock both in himself and in the group, and he must pass through the experience of death and resurrection by which they may be unlocked and transformed. This he will have to do not once, but continuously. As Jesus puts it, hyperbolically but realistically, he must 'take up his cross daily'.*

The passage had sufficient impact on Jean Vanier for him to quote directly from it in his own book, *Community and Growth*. What moved him above all, however, was the state-ment, 'We are more earthy, and more heavenly, than we have cared to admit.' The sentence touched, it may be inferred, upon all that was at the heart of l'Arche: upon the relationship between the body and the Word; upon the relationship between the poor and the presence of Jesus in them; upon the challenge and the gifts of scientific knowledge and the call to spirituality; upon the interlocking of good and evil in terms of both the community and personal experience. With hind-sight, Jean Vanier would comment, 'I'd read quite a lot of theology, but somehow in that book human experience and the Gospel message were being intertwined in a very beautiful way.' At the time, the relationship between the human experi-ence of l'Arche and the theology and spirituality of the Gos-pels seemed to him to be becoming more defined.

In 1976 a new house, 'La Forestière' was opened at Trosly-Breuil, to welcome ten people with severe handicaps. None of them could talk. Their autonomy in general was limited in the extreme. L'Arche had begun with people who had a certain degree of ability. They had been able to work in the workshops. Some had even left to live independently in their own apartments in Compiègne. However, as group homes and workshops began to develop in France under the influence of

* Stephen Verney, op. cit.

various parents' associations, l'Arche had come to a greater appreciation of the pain and rejection of those who were more severely handicapped, those whose abilities were too limited for them to fit into a workshop programme or to be part of a group home.

The welcoming of the severely handicapped was a project which had long been close to Jean Vanier's heart. Fortunately, as he himself now acknowledges, his original plan to have eight buildings on the edge of Trosly to which l'Arche could welcome eighty people, had been overruled by a group of permanent assistants. It had been replaced with a more modest undertaking to have one house in Trosly and one in Cuise or Pierrefonds which would permit better integration into the existing community. The occupants of the newly built and carefully designed 'La Forestière' brought to l'Arche a fresh recognition of the presence of God in those who could not speak and who could barely move their inert limbs.

It was in 'La Forestière' that Jean Vanier requested permission to spend his sabbatical year. It was there that he lived many of those 'gentle moments' with Eric, with Lucien and with the other men and women who, though severely restricted on the verbal, rational level, and though physically almost totally dependent, still had a capacity for relationship. Though poor in many other ways they were extraordinarily rich in qualities of the heart, yet really to recognise this required in itself a certain openness of heart. In their company Jean Vanier came to appreciate more fully that, in order to perceive all the treasure of Eric's heart, he must himself become poor, move into a slower pace of life, become more attentive and ready to listen, be more centred and contemplative. Eric, whose loneliness was reflected in the tension of his whole body and who relaxed only when he sensed that he was loved, called Jean Vanier to greater love. Eric, who was completely blind and deaf and unable to speak, invited him to interior silence and to receive him in his silence. After dinner, in the evening, the assistants would help the handicapped men and women into their pyjamas. Then they would all meet together in the living room for a time of quiet and sharing. Some of the men and women would sit on the assistants' laps; others on the floor beside them. They would sing, pray or simply be there silently, content to be together. If the rush of activity of the years of the community's rapid growth had left him less time than in the earliest days to pray in the little oratory or chapel, Jean Vanier still had the gift of taking advantage of any given moment to find a contemplative still-ness. One member of the community recalls watching him stretched out by the fire at 'La Forestière' and envying him the capacity to take full advantage of the moment, 'resting in God'. In such moments Jean Vanier loved having Eric on his lap. The handicapped man's slight form became more peace-ful and sometimes a faint smile would pass across his face.

In *Our Inner Journey* Jean Vanier would acknowledge:

Eric revealed to me the mutual openness which is at the heart of l'Arche. He opened his doors, his person to me, to my person, to my touch. I opened my doors, my person, to his presence. He gave himself to me and I gave myself to him in service and a spirit of communion. We trusted one another. His weakness touched me and called forth love. These moments of communion are the revelation that God has created deep bonds between us. For 'to love is to win over, to establish ties'. As the Little Prince says: 'We become responsible for the one we have won over.' It is such a gentle thing to discover this covenant which unites us; to know that we are made for one another in order to communicate life to one another.

Yet there were also darker moments in their relationship. There were times when Eric or the other men and women at 'La Forestière' would yell in their distress or hit themselves or close in upon themselves, refusing all relationship. This refusal could provoke all kinds of reactions. Initially hurt by the rejection, Jean Vanier would refer to the gradual communication of anguish:

I too became anguished. His closing up on himself would make me do the same. His violence and aggression aroused my own. And I was horrified to discover the sources of violence within my own self, to discover that in certain circumstances I myself could do harm to a weaker person. At certain moments, I touched the sources of psychological hatred within me. I could understand how a human being could try to hurt and destroy another. I saw how the weak person can draw out what is beautiful in me but also what is worst.

The men and women of 'La Forestière' were able to call him forth to new life, to tenderness, openness and patience, but they also made him discover the world of blockages, fear, hardness and even violence that was in him: everything that was an obstacle to mutual trust. Their wounds, he found, revealed his own wounds. The experience of his own darkness, the revelation of a part of his being at which he did not like to look, was humiliating. At the same time he recognised how crucial was the way in which people reacted when a relationship was no longer apparently a source of life, when it exposed instead their fears and defence mechanisms. It was vital that they should not flee it but rather undertake to continue in the knowledge that they needed God's help and the help of others. For Jean Vanier it was the recognition that

> I can only continue if I recognise that God has created a covenant between Eric and myself. Because of these bonds we are responsible for each other. And if it is God who has established them, it will be he also who will help us to deepen them. He will give me the grace and the patience to accept my darkness and, even more deeply, he will help me to trust that it can disappear in his time.

The confrontation with his own poverty and wounds was to bring home to him, not for the first time but possibly in a more profound way, the impossibility of feeling superior to the handicapped person. Brought back to the deepest reality and truth of his being, where divisions no longer existed between the 'carer' and the 'cared for', or the 'educator' and the 'educated', he felt he could come to be himself. He did not have to be the 'adult', to strive to be important or powerful:

> I no longer need to pretend to be someone. I can now accept to be the child I am, a child of God. . . . And now that I have become more realistic, and I hope more humble. I can enter into a truer relationship with the handicapped person. I am his brother, a brother responsible for his brother.

Writing of his experiences during that year of living with the most severely handicapped, he would emphasise the importance for any human being of not denying the darkness inside him, and of the forgiveness which he had discovered more than ever before was at the heart of l'Arche. He had also discovered how demanding l'Arche must be in encouraging growth: the growth of others and his own. It was not just a question of living the bonds of affective communion: the community must grow together towards greater autonomy, truer identity and stronger hope. At the beginning of Jean Vanier's time at 'La Forestière', Edith, one of the severely handicapped women, had thrown herself out of her wheel chair. An assistant had insisted that she got back into her chair herself and a minor struggle had ensued. Jean Vanier acknowledges feeling that the assistant had been too severe. Then, however, Edith had begun to make an effort and once she had done so the assistant had helped her. Reflecting upon what had happened Jean Vanier found himself asking: Am I as demanding with myself for my own growth, as I am with people who have severe handicaps? 'I do not want to elaborate too much on this question of pedagogy and growth,' was his conclusion, 'but I am convinced that we have no right to expect so much from others if we are not just as demanding with ourselves. Each one of us has to grow in love and in fidelity.'

The 'passage' that followed the 'breakage' of his illness had brought Jean Vanier to a state of greater well-being, psychologically, spiritually and in every respect, a state which he has not since lost. He had come to recognise a need to be more completely present, not only in body but also in mind and heart, to the people with whom he lived at 'La Forestière' and subsequently at the Val Fleuri. He had also come to a new valuation of the simple, hidden life. The first disciples of Jesus – the twelve apostles who were possessed of a very creative spirituality and travelled from place to place proclaiming the Good News, healing the sick, creating communities of prayer and sharing – were not, it seemed to him then, the models for life in l'Arche. Rather he felt called more and more to live what Jesus, Mary and Joseph had lived, and to deepen his life of simplicity and littleness. Jesus had lived for thirty years in Nazareth before he began to announce the Good News or to perform miracles. Before entering into the struggle, he had lived like the other people around him – a life of work, celebration and prayer in a small town. He had loved the people and suffered with them. He had not exercised any special charism.

There was, Jean Vanier realised, immense value and even
healing in the unspectacular. This was why at times he felt
hurt when members of the Charismatic Renewal Movement
wanted to pray over people with handicaps for healings to
take place in l'Arche. He did not deny the value and importance of charismatic healing but he sensed that the way of
healing in l'Arche was through the daily life together, through
the covenant that existed between the assistants and 'their
people', through a love that accepted all, believed all and
bore with all.

He had lived the confrontation with some of his own
wounds at 'La Forestière'. In that same year he would hear
Fred Blum, a psychotherapist, give talks to a 'renewal' gathering of those assistants who had been in l'Arche for more
than five years, on the subject of the 'wounded healer'. Blum
maintained that only the healer in contact with his own
wounds could be an agent of healing for another person. Only
if he had touched his own vulnerability would he be able to
welcome the vulnerability of another. Jean Vanier's understanding of healing, like that of Blum, would become based
upon a common experience and recognition of a certain value
in vulnerability. There were those who cited the example
of psychotic children who became university teachers and
directors of banks as instances of healing: 'That worries me,'
Jean Vanier would explain,

> because there are plenty of directors of banks who are not
> actually labelled psychotic but who are so caught up in
> their own project that they are unable to be truly open.
> The only healing which seems to me to be true healing is
> the gradual opening up of people to other people in true
> relationship. It's not pedestal healing. It's not integration.
> There are integrated psychotics, people in our society in
> whom the barriers around their vulnerability are so strong
> that they are unable really to listen to other people or be
> peaceful.

A gradual deepening of Jean Vanier's consciousness of the
wound would take place, of his own wound in relation to that
of other people and in relation to the Word made flesh as a
source of life in the broken bodies of humanity. 'Can it be
that as we touch the discarded, entering into communion
with them, we are healed?' he would ask some time later.

Can it be that in the bowels of the earth and in the mud of life we find the Word made flesh? Can it be that in all that is apparently ugly and sinful and painful we find a secret source of communion, a touch of God? Can it be that the Word made flesh is hidden in our broken bodies and flesh? Must we ourselves be broken so that the source of life, the spring of water may flow from our very brokenness?

He had touched his own brokenness and shadows and experienced in a very profound way the truth of the claim that 'we are more earthy and more heavenly than we have cared to admit':

In all this I feel very vulnerable, for on one side I have seen, I have caught a glimpse of the kingdom and the new vision of Jesus. I have even tasted it in my flesh and heart, but yet I am so aware of my own barriers and inner fears and am sometimes paralysed. By what? I do not know. I am frightened maybe by an inner world too broken, too terrible to be brought up into consciousness, where madness and agony and pain are intertwined. But yet I believe too that under all that pain there is a yearning for the kiss of God, a communion where we can drink from each other's chalices, and from the chalice of Jesus delicious wine of the kingdom but also the wine of his blood and pain.

Having come face to face with his own vulnerability, he had in some way drawn nearer to the mystery of the vulnerability of Jesus. It was a vulnerability which moved him deeply:

The whole tension in the life of Jesus is his bigness and his littleness. The words around the Eucharist reveal that he wants to give his body to eat, which is impossible. People say, 'We want a good prophetic leader and here we have someone offering his body to eat,' so they all leave him as of that day. Then there is the incredible revelation that Jesus is a lover and vulnerable . . .

Years ago he had read the Gospel of St John from beginning to end and he had gone on to read St Luke's Gospel in a similar fashion. There was for him a special value in relating experience to the Gospels. At Trosly-Breuil he would lead a weekly sharing on the Gospels. If the Word touched people it was firstly because Jesus was in that process but also because of the relationship of life to the Gospels. Whilst Jean Vanier was frightened of too much symbolic interpretation of the Gospels, he was profoundly struck by the way in which they were 'so incredibly human, so historical, so true'. Behind them was such a philosophy and theology, such a unity. A 'blue print' of reality was not quite the right expression but they fitted so clearly into what people were.

So it was that from the intertwining of human experience and the gospel message he drew his reflections on love, paternity and a multitude of other themes that had a specific bearing on life in l'Arche: on growth, on the yearning for God and the cry of the poor, on the importance of spiritual nourishment, on the welcoming of the vulnerable and of vulnerability, on the sharing of weakness and on celibacy. Contemplating Joseph in his love for Mary, it seemed to him that those who had been called to the celibate life had much to learn about the quality of their love for one another. It was important for handicapped people, many of whom were unable to marry, to live and celebrate with assistants who had accepted this gift of celibacy in order to be able to create a family life with their people. By choosing celibacy these assistants were identifying more fully with the struggles and the suffering of people with handicaps. Through the quality of their love for one another, as exemplified by Mary and Joseph, they were called to strengthen and sustain each other in their choice. Joseph and Mary also had much to teach married couples. They were a model of a privileged and unique relationship which was also very necessary in l'Arche. Couples and families not only helped to integrate communities into the town or neighbourhood, they also brought to l'Arche a witness of stable faithful relationship.

Jean Vanier also saw in Joseph a particular model of paternity, as the father of Jesus not 'according to the flesh' but through his love:

He is more of a father than any father who has adopted a child. He accepted the responsibility of this fatherhood even before Jesus was born, from the day the Angel told him to take Mary into his home and to call the child 'Jesus'. Joseph became responsible for the Word made flesh, Jesus, so that he might grow and accomplish his mission of love.

The paternity of Joseph was of course unique and special, but it could still provide a model for those to whom handicapped people had been entrusted. Many people with handicaps had suffered rejection by their fathers. It was up to the people in l'Arche to call them forth, to be responsible for them, to liberate them through love, and to give them confidence in themselves by having confidence in them. In a way which, it may be suggested, reflected his own relationship with a father who had trusted him at a very early age, Jean Vanier went on to reflect upon paternity:

It is an extraordinary gift. It implies a communication of life, a liberation of what is deepest within another . . . A father (or the father figure) loves the other with a very personal, unique love and desires his growth. There is a relationship of mutual trust between the two. They love each other. The father sustains, encourages, counsels, confirms and when necessary corrects. He knows the personal gift of each child and helps each one to find his/her place in the community and in society. A true father also knows that no one is perfect. He realises that in each one there are wounds, fragility, anger and depression. He is patient. He prepares, sustains and encourages growth. He knows how to forgive and comfort; he also knows how to call forth and challenge.*

The process of dying a little to his own project, of becoming more aware of the way in which good and evil were interlocked in himself as in everything, of touching the darkness within and living the truth of the resurrection – all these experiences would enable him to put the right word on the experiences of others, not only orally but in the form of numerous books and articles. Personal and community realities were given expression in his talks and his writing, invariably in the light of the gospel message, and especially in the light of the words of 1 Corinthians 13:

Though I speak with the tongues of men and of angels, and have not charity, I am become as sounding brass, or a tinkling cymbal. And though I have the gift of prophecy, and understand all mysteries, and all knowledge; and

---

* *Our Inner Journey* (l'Arche publication.)

though I have all faith, so that I could remove mountains, and have not charity, I am nothing.

Jean Vanier had heard the cry for love that flows from the heart of people in need. He had seen that that cry was often mixed with pain and anguish, that the appeal for communion could unleash not only the love in those to whom it was addressed but also their hardness of heart and their fears. He had also recognised that even in communities that strove to develop relationships of communion there was a certain loneliness. In particular people who carried final authority in communities were always in a sense alone. Many people would say that Jean Vanier knew them well; not so many that they really knew him well, and there were times, some suggested, when he did not perhaps share what needed to be shared. Jean Vanier himself was not sure about the truth of such an assertion but in any case perhaps it was part of the necessary reality/mythology of a man in his position.

He had never felt called to marry. Celibacy had been part of his original option for the priesthood which had since been endorsed by the realisation of how important it was for people with handicaps to have about them not only the secure relationships provided by married couples but also models which revealed an alternative to marriage. It was important now to show that celibacy could be not simply a negation but something very positive. In marriage or outside it, men and women were called to love each other in a relationship of affective communion and not just to be collaborators: 'Where there is affective communion, fecundity and life flows from them, but where there is division between men and women, all kinds of breakages follow – there is a breakage with the child.' Men and women were moving into a world of collaboration rather than communion. Jean Vanier was not sure that people were really conscious of the gravity of the problem, but it was one which he sensed very deeply.

His vision of 'family' had grown to embrace communities and people throughout the world, in a way which made even the discomforts of long and frequent travel justifiable because of the people and the warmth that awaited him on his arrival. As to his relationships with his brothers and sister 'in the flesh', Jean Vanier would now describe them as 'close but distant'. As a child he had been very close to Bernard. They

were close in age and had been the two mischievous ones –
but Bernard had embarked upon a different spiritual path.
He was an artist who had lived for many years to the south-
west of Paris. Michel, the youngest, had taken a degree in
the field of education which had always been his great interest
and had taught at university level. Married for the second
time, he was now living in Montreal. His eldest brother,
Benedict who had become a Trappist and whom Madame
Vanier sees as in some way the power-house behind Jean, he
would describe as 'incredibly holy and God-filled but not a
communicator'. For the last seven years Benedict had been
chaplain to the Sisters in a Cistercian convent near Quebec.
With Thérèse he shares the commitment to l'Arche but both
would acknowledge that they are very different in tem-
perament.

'In a community', Jean Vanier would say, 'you have a lot
of deep relationships' and if the loneliness of people with final
authority was their cross, he would also (in *Community and
Growth*, 1989 edition) write of how it was 'the guarantee of
the presence, light and the strength of God. That is why they,
more than anyone else in the community, must have time to
be alone with God. It is in these moments of solitude that
inspiration is born in them and they will sense what direction
to take.'

In the opening chapter of the same book he wrote:

My people are my community, which is both the small
community, those who live together, and the larger community which surrounds it and for which it is there. 'My
people' are those who are written in my flesh as I am in
theirs. Whether we are near each other or far away, my
brothers and sisters remain written within me. I carry
them, and they, me; we know each other again when we
meet. To call them 'my people' doesn't mean that I feel
superior to them, or that I am their shepherd or that I look
after them. It means that they are mine as I am theirs.
There is a solidarity between us. What touches them, touches me. And when I say 'my people', I don't imply that
there are others I reject. My people is my community,
made up of those who know me and carry me. They are a
springboard towards all humanity. I cannot be a universal
brother unless I first love my people.

It had taken time for him to assimilate intellectually what he and the others in l'Arche were really living in terms of the components of community life which had happened naively and spontaneously and only afterwards been discovered to be right or wrong. He claims to have an 'integrating but a slow mind'. In 1976, however, he was asked to give four conferences in Paris for four weeks running on the theme of 'Community'. The large church was packed on every occasion and he began to realise that l'Arche had something to say on the subject. The first draft of his book, *Community and Growth* consisted largely of these talks. It was shown to the publishers Laffont who liked it but suggested that parts of the final chapter were rewritten. Jean Vanier did not get round to doing so for two years, and when he did return to it he found it 'absolute trash', a fact which he would later see as an indication that during the intervening years he had grown to a certain maturity of thought.

In 1978 he travelled to Fatima by bus. During the three-day journey there and the three days back he dictated for eight hours a day little snippets about community to different people who wrote it down in relays. Those dictated thoughts became the basis for the actual book which he would subsequently begin to order into chapters. In 1989 he would work on a revised edition of the book which he was satisfied was much clearer. Reviewing his own progress, things seemed to him to have been revealed very gradually. Over twenty years of living with people with handicaps and their assistants had provided him nonetheless with a deep well from which to draw when others were confronted with similar 'breakages' and 'passages' to his own, and from which to pass on the message that living waters flowed not just from the heavens and the places of light, but also from the broken earth.

Man and Woman He Made Them was written in 1984 because so many questions were being raised both in and outside the community around the subject of sexuality. A well known figure in French literary circles who had a child with Downs syndrome had written a book which criticised Jean Vanier to some extent and stated in particular that his daughter was now happy at last because she had access to contraceptives. Disturbed and unhappy, Jean Vanier went to see him and eventually felt inspired to write a book which explored the relationship between men and women from a Christian and a community standpoint. Tackling the most intimate and searching questions in relation to whether love necessarily implied sexual relationship, how people could live with anguish and loneliness and how they reached emotional maturity, it reflected the way in which men and women who were often unable to develop sexual relationships could demonstrate what true intimacy was, how men and women who could not have children or live outwardly productive lives could show what true fruitfulness was.

Most of his other books, Jean Vanier claims, simply have not been written by him. *Tears of Silence*, for instance, his second book, was the result of a request for him to publish something relating to the lectures he was giving at the end of the 'sixties to groups of students in Toronto. He handed over his notes to a publisher who built up a book from them on which Jean Vanier subsequently did a little work. *The Broken Body* on the other hand was, in Jean Vanier's own words, 'just given'. A call to the reader to draw nearer to those who suffer, to follow Jesus on the path to wholeness and discover peace and joy by first accepting the reality of suffering, he wrote it in about ten days.

Whilst some tasks, such as his current revision of *Community and Growth*, were a matter of blood, sweat and tears, he did, he acknowledged, experience urges to write on particular themes. At the moment he felt very strongly drawn to produce an article or a book on communion and broken communion. It was a subject upon which Père Thomas, and before him Dr Thompson, had been touching for years, but one which now seemed to Jean Vanier to have special need of airing:

> I feel people are talking too much about sexuality and not enough about communion, the fundamental need of the human being, the relationship between communion and the body, and the relationship between collaboration and communion. What broken communion is and the consequences of it. Then, going deeper, to the mystery of the incarnation: that God is three persons in communion and that Jesus came in order to share that communion.

The urge to write was there but, sadly, the time in which to do it was not. Time had on one previous occasion been so short that he had been reduced to correcting proofs over the telephone from France to England. In any case, his books were structured in a somewhat unusual way, a fact which he felt irritated some, for when he wrote, he wrote as if in diminishing circles which spiralled down, trying to pick up threads and delving ever deeper.

10

Part of our Broken World

In writing of the growth and development of l'Arche, I am ever more conscious of the illusive nature of its real substance, of the difficulty of holding on to the actuality of the relationship between the Word and the flesh, between the hidden Jesus and the broken bodies and wounded hearts and minds of the people with handicaps, between the silent presence and the necessary doing. It was a problem to which some of the assistants also would give expression: that of retaining a real sense of the relationship between the poor as prophets for our world, as paths to unity and wholeness, and the small, humdrum and sometimes even distasteful tasks of their days and nights spent with handicapped people. There were inevitably times when one side of the equation would far outweigh the other.

Jean Vanier had from the very beginning stressed the importance of 'living with', of *living* rather even than experiencing, for somehow experiencing implied too much detachment. Living l'Arche was as illusive as the twinkle in Maurice's eyes as he accentuated his disability to win the sympathetic and supportive embrace of well-intentioned ladies. It was as tangible as the bathmat found stuffed each morning down a lavatory. Living l'Arche was the sudden appearance in the night of one of the 'folks' who had completely ignored you all day but who chose just as you were falling asleep to sit companionably if unspeaking on the end of your bed with no evident intention of leaving. Being stared at as you walked with Johnny to share a bottle of Coca Cola bought with his hard-earned money from a Honduran street stall; the envious preoccupation with a visitor's wedding ring; the cooking of meals balanced to suit the medical and dietary requirements of people with handicaps; the careful administration of drugs; hours spent assisting with exercises designed to foster the tiniest step towards autonomy; the laundering of clothes soiled because of limbs and mouths that defied control; deriving pleasure not only from a chocolate but from the shiny coloured paper in which it was wrapped; the endless repetition, at first welcome but gradually more irritating, of 'She's my friend'; seizures, sudden floods of tears and unpredictable rushes of anger or affection . . . all these were part of living l'Arche, as were the broken chairs and glasses, the concrete reflection of less visible damage to rejected hearts and restricted minds.

Those who came to be assistants in l'Arche, be it in Brussels or Brazil, came for an almost infinite variety of reasons. They were drawn to the idea of community, to handicapped people, to Jean Vanier or Père Thomas. They had read Henri Nouwen's, Odile Ceyrac's, Bill Clarke's or Jean Vanier's own books or were in the process of rejecting all reading in the pursuit of 'first-hand experience'. They had drifted there almost by accident, reacting against something that had gone before or searching for something they could not really define or, in countries where jobs were scarce and money short, they identified in it some sort of security. They came with definite ideas of what their life in l'Arche should entail and they came without the slightest notion. They came for a week and remained for life; or they came for life and left after only a month. They stemmed from the country in which the community was founded or they were called there from the other side of the world; in India in time most of the assistants would be Indian – the recognition of the need to find local directors and assistants was increasingly recognised; in London the assistants were English, German, American, Lebanese and a multitude of other nationalities. In India and Africa and countries of extreme poverty there was fever and diarrhoea and physical discomfort with which to contend. Showers could take the form of buckets, meals could be beans three times a day. In other cultures where l'Arche was 'counter-cultural' there were the pressures of disappointed families and lost friends and the isolation born of the failure of others to comprehend.

Among the assistants there were students, religious, linguists, former teachers, psychiatric nurses, bankers, law graduates and people who were potentially capable of achieving the kind of professional status outside l'Arche which the world would much more readily applaud. Some came with the approval and support of their families; some were indulged in what, it was felt, must be a passing whim; some had to face a barrage of criticism or of silent disinterest on the occasions when they returned home. Few found it easy to explain the full significance of what they were living in what was neither a religious order nor an institution for the mentally handicapped that could supply them with a good salary and job security. Often even approbation took the form of praise for a son or daughter who was wonderful because he or she was 'working with the mentally handicapped'. Many would experience the tensions between their life in l'Arche and the world from which they had come in quite a painful way.

When assistants arrived they were thrown in at the deep end, some never having had much if any previous contact with people with a handicap. There was the fear of hurting them, of not being able to understand people whose ability to speak was often very limited, of not being able to cope with their needs once they had been identified, or simply of being rejected. There was the challenge of being suddenly called upon to cater for twelve or possibly even more people when there was little time in which to do the cooking, and starch and a number of other ingredients could not be used because the handicapped people could not eat them. There were the complexities of living in close proximity to people of both sexes, the difficulties of choosing between a life of celibacy and that of marriage and, if an individual felt called to married life, the problem of finding the opportunity to build relationships not necessarily within the community which might lead in that direction. There were particular pressures on women in male-dominated cultures and there were additional pressures on men in societies which measured people in general but particularly men in terms of their achievement, position and earning power. It was easier on the whole for women to find fulfilment in l'Arche than for men, perhaps mainly because compassion was a primarily feminine quality but also because the lack of identity, the 'disappearance' entailed in a life made up of simple daily household chores and joys, in which choosing what coloured socks to wear for the day could represent a major decision, tended to be more difficult for men. In general, there were the difficulties of relating to the other assistants in the house and to the community as a whole.

Now in many communities there is a system of trial periods in which both the new assistant and the community can decide whether they are mutually suited. There is also a system of accompaniment and support in which a more long-term member of the community is assigned to listen to and guide and share experiences with a particular newcomer. In time l'Arche would come to see that not only individual members but also individual communities needed 'accompaniment', someone who in a relationship of trust could listen, pick up the anguish, reassure and probably find meaning in the pain. Eventually it would recognise the need for accompaniment of assistants on three levels: work accompaniment to enable assistants to carry out the daily tasks entrusted to them, community accompaniment to help them to put down roots and advance along the path of love and gift of self within the community, and spiritual accompaniment by a priest or pastor to help them to discover their call from God and to deepen their life of prayer and communion with the Father. There was a time, however, when the need for assistants was so great that people simply asked to come, arrived, were welcomed almost irrespective of their suitability for such a life, and were then left to a large extent to find their own way.

Inevitably assistants were often themselves deeply wounded people, for they came as part of a broken world. Still there was a limit, it had to be recognised, and Jean Vanier had recognised it almost from the very beginning of l'Arche, to the number of people who had difficulty in forming relationships any one community could carry. As one community leader would say in the course of explaining her difficulty in turning away some people who were seeking a welcome as assistants:

If I had to summarise it I would say I am looking for someone who can take responsibility for someone else and for himself. If I can direct people elsewhere all the better, but often there isn't anywhere to which you can refer really needy people. It's hard but there is something about recognising our limitations. We just can't be a boat for everyone.

On average the London community houses were called upon
to welcome two new people every year, two new people who
would affect the way the entire household inter-related. Usually people were taken from the age of eighteen upwards but
there was a certain caution to be exercised in welcoming
individuals over forty: 'Often there is a lot of idealism and
need for change but not actually the flexibility to fit into
households that demand an enormous amount of it.' On the
other hand, an eighteen-year-old would need a fair degree of
maturity. It was true that they brought an injection of life
into a community in which the other assistants might be
predominantly in their thirties. Often they knew they were
only there for a year before going up to university and for
that year they gave totally.

At the same time there were older people with handicaps
who did not necessarily appreciate the presence of unbridled
youthful vigour. Doris who was fifty-four did not particularly
want to live with the pace and enthusiasm of an eighteen-
year-old bounding with energy. Nor was a person not yet in
her twenties necessarily aware of what was appropriate for
Doris. As Katharine Hall would explain in one of the Victorian houses that form part of the London community:

> You notice it in clothing when people go shopping, depend-
> ing of course on how able the handicapped people are to
> choose for themselves. I could probably tell you who has
> been shopping with whom. I remember vividly Doris was
> heavily into pink frills and bows when she was already
> forty-five. I was constantly saying to her, 'You're not a
> little girl any more. You're an adult woman with mature
> relationships. You can't be a little girl, however much you
> might want to be mummy's little girl. Mummy's dead and
> you're an older woman and there are people much younger
> than you coming into the community.' It is Doris' dream
> to be somebody's child again. So when we went to buy
> clothes I bought her serious clothes, but then an eighteen-
> year-old assistant living in the house at the time took her
> shopping and Doris came back with this enormously bright
> yellow and orange flouncy dress.

Irrespective of nationality, background or age, people who
came to l'Arche as assistants would sooner or later be called
upon to confront their own wounds. Most would speak of a

period of euphoria, and possibly naivety, during which the discovery of the gifts of the handicapped people was paramount; many would refer to a period of darkness, breakage and disillusionment with community that followed: 'You have really to be hurt by l'Arche, not just to be fatigued but to hit a wall of something you can't penetrate and then to say, "What does this mean and where am I?"' Often it was only then that the word born of Jean Vanier's own experience would really touch them, that his books about suffering and growth and community gained a deeper relevance. There were those who did not remain to work with that experience, who left still disillusioned. For those who stayed, invariably it was a relationship with a handicapped person which helped to surmount fears, which was in some way compelling and which called to change. 'When you enter into a relationship with someone, washing the dishes is different,' one assistant would claim who had come to l'Arche having 'discovered herself' when faced with the suffering caused by the 1982 Israeli invasion of Lebanon. She had previously been used to having a maid and a secretary. 'When you are doing the cooking you think of each one and his likes and dislikes, when you make his bed it is specially for him. My mother couldn't believe it – me making beds!'

What was it that wrought such a change? What was it that made Maria Conchita continue to give her time and her services to l'Arche in Honduras? The first time she had gone to cook at the Casa Isabella, Brenda had given her a black eye and bruises. Instead of cooking she had spent her time cleaning up the mess after Brenda had defecated on the floor, yet there was something so strong between them. She did not know quite what.

Chris Peloquin who co-ordinates the different houses in the region at Trosly-Breuil would refer specifically to her relationship with Edith at 'La Forestière'. Edith has touched the lives of so many who have had contact with her, not least of them Jacques, one of the men with a handicap at La Petite Source, who has a history of violence but who as her godfather values and fosters the relationship between them with regular visits and invitations to meals, and extraordinary delicacy and protective kindness. Edith came to l'Arche at the age of sixteen, having spent all her previous life in institutions. Severely handicapped, she had been given away at birth and,

deprived of affection and attention other than for her most
basic needs, she had resorted to vomiting up her food, tearing
things or trying to poke her eyes out with a spoon. When she
came to 'La Forestière' she used to beat her head. At times
it had to be bandaged and her hands restrained even while
she slept.

Edith is a very affective person, a very calling person. She
awoke all the violence there was in me. She would yell and
scream with such anguish. It took two of us to look after
her and I remember once I had been away for a week or
so and when I returned I was supposed to be taking care
of her, but all she did was resist and yell. She just wouldn't
help herself and I got really mad with her. Then suddenly
I stopped, realising what I was doing, and started to speak
to her properly. I took my time with her whereas before I
had just been pulling her around. She became calm and
she looked at me with a very deep serious look she has,
and we started again. I found myself asking her forgiveness
and she made the effort to help herself, and I had this
overwhelming feeling of love for her. Before I had been
living a kind of inner revolt. I enjoyed being in 'La Forestière' but there was this inner revolt: Why them? One of
them was only six days older than me. Why should he be
the way he was? Why not me? Why Edith? What was the
sense of their lives? To be successful you had to do things
well, you had to get married. At least in the workshop
people were doing something productive but not these
people. Why did God permit it? Then suddenly I found
myself loving Edith and with a love that was somehow very
pure. You never know why you love people but this was
pure in the sense that it wasn't because I was helping her
or because she needed me but just like that, and in this
very pure feeling for her I found that I could forget that
she was handicapped. We shared a sense of humour and I
would giggle with her. That changed my life. If I in all my
human weakness could love Edith then God must and, if
God loved people like that, he could love me too. That was
a very freeing feeling for me.

'For Edith', Chris Peloquin would conclude, 'it doesn't
matter whether you're the Queen of England or a tramp.
What she feels is how you are.' It is a gift which challenges

and disturbs and makes great demands upon those called to live with those who have it. In London, Paul too is highly sensitive and intuitive. For part of his life he had been completely out of touch with his family. By the time the l'Arche community brought him back into contact with the family about whom he had talked so much, his father was dead. His mother showed him pictures of her deceased husband in an attempt to make Paul realise that his father was no longer there and what that meant. One night during that period Paul came downstairs crying. 'I had never seen Paul cry,' Katharine Hall would remember,

> but he was crying his heart out. He came into the kitchen and said, 'I want my dad.' There were four assistants there at the time and I said, 'I can't give you your dad, Paul. You know he's dead.' Then he said, 'I want my mum,' and I said, 'There's no way you are going to see your mum at 11 o'clock at night. I can't give you your mum . . . or your brothers and sisters', because he went through the whole string. His next words were, 'I want a glass of water.' Paul is much better now but then if he could get you to do something for him rather than do it himself, he would. So I said, 'You get the glass and the water.' He proceeded to fill his own glass which shocked me immensely. His face was still streaming with tears and he stood there and said, 'Can you heal my dad?' 'Heal' is not a word Paul often uses. I replied, 'No, I can't heal your dad, Paul', wondering where on earth this conversation was going to lead but he then said, 'Well, I know who can . . . Jesus will heal my dad'. He turned to one of the assistants and said, 'It's all right, Mary', and he went round and gave the four of us the sign of peace. 'It's okay, I'm going to bed now.' We were all so shocked, firstly at him crying, then by the question and really by the existential nature of the question that we couldn't believe he was going to bed, but maybe we needed it and that's why it happened.

It was good to face Paul's loss. Good too, to recognise that it was all right to be powerless in front of Paul, that it was not necessary to know all the answers. It was a very gentle way of telling that part of them which wanted to solve problems and be in control that all Paul wanted was for someone to be there. It was an important discovery: 'I cannot heal your dad, Paul. I cannot heal you, Paul. All I can do is be in relationship with you and be Katharine beside you.' It was also an experience which touched upon the value of the wounded healer.

Fatigue is a major and pervasive problem among assistants in l'Arche. Much of it is all too understandably a product of the physical and particularly the emotional demands made by mentally handicapped people who have been rejected by or made to feel a disappointment to their families, who are not accepted by society, who suffer from a sense of having no value and who desperately need relationships because that is the level on which they function. Living with people whose behaviour reflects their loss in the form of anger, aggression, depression and a multitude of other ways takes its toll, as does an assistant's struggle with his or her own vulnerability. In addition to this they are subject to pressures at all kinds of levels. In some countries the ecumenical dimension produces stress, most obviously when two assistants are needed to see that the handicapped people in the household go to three different churches while they themselves would like to go to a fourth, but undoubtedly also in less tangible ways. Finding an appropriate space for personal prayer or intellectual nourishment can require a strength and maturity of which not all are possessed when the requirements to do other practical community work are almost constant.

There are tensions which arise because many assistants live and work in the same place. The lack of privacy in cultures where life in general is less gregarious can be a source of strain. Even though an assistant may have his or her own room, the opportunities to be in it alone may be limited. Heads appear round doors with small requests, anecdotes that must be urgently recounted, handiwork to be shown, beaming smiles or simply the need to re-establish the warmth of relationship and so fend off the anguish of thwarted desires and ingrown loneliness. Acceptance in such moments may be a matter of salvation. It would be inappropriate and difficult to close the door, however much one's own need might be crying out for solitude. The door must be open wide to others too: to the visitors who come to the communities for a variety of reasons and not always with great understanding of what is going on around them. It cannot always be easy to muster one or more extra places at table, an additional bed and a welcoming smile.

One Saturday night at Daybreak springs particularly to mind. Brad Colby, the young houseleader was left alone in the house with half a dozen of the handicapped people, some of whom had decided they would like to watch a video. The video recorder would not work. Another had to be fetched from one of the other community houses. Popcorn and beer were an integral part of Saturday viewing. Brad set about making popcorn in the kitchen. A Japanese priest arrived from the airport for a few days' stay in the community. He was one of a group hoping to start a community similar to l'Arche in Japan and had come to see how things were done, but he spoke only half a dozen words of English. He was settled in front of the video while Brad went off to find him some refreshments. In between making popcorn and a visitor's tray at the end of a long day, he was trying to make a stranger evidently confused by a very North American style video and a totally unfamiliar environment, welcome. It was at this point that one of the 'folks' decided to remove her clothes and carry them, naked but for her slippers, through the assembled company to the washing machine. Brad began tactful attempts at explanation to the newcomer, and all this under the watchful eye of someone who was there to write a book about life in l'Arche. I could feel only admiration for the way in which at eleven o'clock at night, over the washing up, he was still prepared to talk about what it was that kept him there.

There are pressures from professionals. In the Erie community the people with handicaps are required to have 'goal plans' which set objectives for them and monitor their progress. Assistants have to complete paperwork for each handicapped person every evening. They try to do it when the 'folks' themselves are not present, but this often means waiting until after they have gone to bed. Elsewhere there are inevitably tensions between the perspective of the psychiatrist or psychologist and those who are living a family life with the subjects of professional analysis in the houses. Many assistants feel that relationships should be natural. The professional who starts to look closely at and label these affective relationships and at how the team of assistants are relating to each other can be seen as a disturbance and a threat. Most assistants recognise the value of professional care but not all have great confidence in their own intellectual ability, and talk in terms of professional formulae can cause them to feel crushed. If the involvement of professionals is constructive in that they compel communities not to turn in on themselves and forget that other sources of inspiration exist, if they challenge communities in their support because they have other reference points and draw on other experiences, it is in the nature of challenges to be taxing.

Demanding too, are the very structures designed to ensure the input and information of members of the community not only in relation to what is happening in their own household but at the level of the International Federation. The development of the common consciousness of a house, then of a community, a region, a zone and so of the extended international communities takes considerable energy and effort. For some communities the awareness of the international family is not yet really a factor. For Felipe in Honduras who has never travelled beyond the nearest town of Choluteca, to grasp that he has 'cousins' in the community in Tegucigalpa is in itself a large step. For others in cultures more used to world travel the grasping of the concept of an international community does not present such problems. The time and energy consumed by meetings which take place on all the different levels can also be a source of pressure. Meetings are valued as opportunities to share and to nourish, as times when each one has an opportunity to speak, as times of listening, support, evaluation and of reviewing each other's authority. They are also another demand on heavily taxed resources.

Authority in itself can be a source of stress which some integrate more easily than others. In the early days of l'Arche in Trosly-Breuil when new houses were being so rapidly acquired, and in other young communities, it was possible for people barely in their twenties to find themselves in charge of a household within months of their arrival. That meant not only being responsible for the welfare of the handicapped people, budgetting for and ensuring the smooth running of the house, but also exercising authority over the other assistants, some of whom might be considerably older or have been in l'Arche much longer than the houseleader. Authority in such circumstances, with the added dimension that the usual levers of kudos or financial incentive were absent, could be an illusive and complex issue. The relinquishing of it, both for people who had held positions of authority in the 'outside world' and for those who had held authority in l'Arche, could be equally difficult.

Over the years l'Arche has developed a system of 'discernment' to appoint the director for a given community. At Trosly-Breuil a discernment team is nominated compiled of the president of the board of directors, the regional co-ordinator and three assistants elected by the community. As founders, Jean Vanier and Père Thomas are also included in the team. This discernment team then consults the whole community not necessarily individually but a representative group from all sections of the community – handicapped people, short-term assistants and more permanent assistants – firstly as to what they feel the current needs of the community are and secondly for nominations. One nominee is then finally confirmed by the board of directors who appoint the director for a mandate of three years. At Trosly-Breuil the local bishop is also consulted as to whether he can see any difficulties in relation to the appointment of a particular nominee and invited to endorse it.

With this triple endorsement appointment as director can be, as Alain Saint-Macary would put it,

> a beautiful experience . . . You don't get the feeling that you've been chosen simply because somebody's got to do the job and they think you might be capable. It's something much stronger, something reassuring. What reassured me greatly the first time I was appointed was that the discernment team told me all my weaknesses. I felt they knew what they were doing when they told me to be careful of certain things.

One more critically inclined would view it as a cumbersome and sometimes painful procedure which was the necessary consequence of the inability to ground authority either in the will of God or in more worldly bases such as finance or the power and justification of the State:

> Discernment is a word that has come into vogue where there is no authority. As a Jesuit you are told what to do and it's called doing God's will. If a policeman shoots you

he does it in the name of the State, but what do you do when you can't ground authority in religious justification because you're not exclusively a religious community and you can't ground it in money because you pay people so little?

Certainly, discernment can be an exceedingly painful experience. Discussion of people, their gifts and their weaknesses, even when it is done in the Holy Spirit, can feel at times more like proceedings in Maoist China. Furthermore, once his or her mandate has been fulfilled, a person who has carried considerable responsibility can find himself suddenly with none whatsoever. Like the servant who has been ploughing or looking after sheep, he is then required not to expect appreciation or rest but to feel only that he has done his duty (Luke 17:7–10). It can be hard in human terms: the children of fathers who no longer hold positions of authority can be cruelly uncomprehending. It is not easy to accept the direction of one who appears to be less competent than oneself, even harder to accept that he is more competent. As one outgoing director would put it: 'It will be difficult down the road there when it hits me in terms of moving out of my office or of when people stop asking my advice. And the real crunch will come when people start doing things better than I did.'

Hardest of all, no doubt, is the relinquishing of the role of community leader on the part of founders, those people who have felt called in a special way to people and places of need, who have struggled and made sacrifices to initiate tiny communities, who have been through all the birth pangs, led the way through the trying early years during which wounds of rejection and anguish have to be healed before trust is born, and who are then called upon to die a little to their own project. Yet it is recognised that the cycle of change is important to any community. Each person has their particular style and gifts, and at different moments in the life of the community different requirements come to the fore. An outgoing director may still be young and far from ready to retire but, were he to remain director for the next twenty-five years, it would stunt the growth of other people.

Underlying the cycle of change is the message that an individual's value to the community consists of who he or she is as a person and is not assessed on the basis of the role fulfilled or the position occupied. It is, however, a difficult dynamic. On the one hand there is a challenge to nurture human growth and individual gifts which is necessary if young assistants are to feel that l'Arche is something to which they can give their lives, and on the other there is the spiritual message that fundamentally l'Arche is about faithfulness to the relationships with the handicapped people that are at its heart. Ultimately in l'Arche it is the poor who are the 'elders', in the sense of the word as it was used in the early days of the Church. That is why, based on the vision of Père Thomas and Jean Vanier of their own roles, there are no 'fathers' or 'mothers' in l'Arche, only 'brothers' and 'sisters'. The leader is a servant. It is the poor who confirm, and everything is done by reference to them. The litmus test for l'Arche is the relationships with the handicapped people, and so it is that conventional lines of reasoning are frequently turned upside down. Ostensibly more capable is not better, city rather than country or vice versa is not necessarily better, nor is bigger automatically better.

It is a message which is not always easily conveyed to people outside the community, even to boards of directors. In a country like Honduras, where the poverty is so great and where there are so many mentally handicapped people, it is understandably difficult to justify to people who are often themselves wealthy and who would willingly exert their far from negligible influence to raise funds to help many more people in a way which in conventional terms would be more efficient, the need to remain small and in some ways 'inefficient'. It is not always easy to convince people profoundly touched by the magnitude of the need of the importance of not sacrificing the quality of the relationships with the few in order to help the many, especially when many assistants themselves experience difficulty in sustaining a sense of the value and relevance of such tiny, fragile symbols of an alternative way of living.

The value of boards of directors as pools of expertise to be tapped has come to be increasingly recognised and appreciated. Recently in Toronto, when an institution for severely handicapped children was due for closure, Daybreak was among the places approached to take the children concerned. Authority was given by the government to purchase what is now the 'Corner House' in Richmond Hill but, having bought the house, Daybreak was subsequently told by the government that it was too expensive. L'Arche had purchased a house which would provide accommodation for both the handicapped children and the assistants who were to live with them, but the government allocated funds per handicapped person. From their point of view it was not necessary for all the assistants to live in. The cost of the house in relation to the number of children it would take was thus too expensive. The possibility of selling it was raised. Nevertheless the principle of 'living with' was not one on which l'Arche was prepared to compromise. An emergency meeting of the board of directors was called and it was they who were able to convey this message in effective terms to the government official invited to attend.

This was an issue which was uncontentious. Others might be less so: that of the money spent on assistants travelling to international meetings of the Federation, for example. There are board members who, not recognising the importance of fostering the spirit of l'Arche in this way, of the reciprocal support and nourishment the exchange of ideas and perspectives bring, would contend that the money could be better used in ways which the poor themselves would more readily understand. In the 'sixties there was often friction between young assistants in scruffy jeans, who tended to be disinclined to cut their hair and shave and inclined to anti-authoritarianism, and board members of an older and very different generation. Assistants now are rather different. Even those who came in the 'sixties disclaiming the value of their degrees and skills have tended in time to rediscover the value of their qualifications in the context of community. Nevertheless tensions do still exist. Boards of directors again represent the challenge of a different perspective. They are made up of valued, creative people who often have a very real understanding of the community and who, Jean Vanier feels, should be more honoured in l'Arche. They can also at times be a source of pressure.

If there are conflicts they have a way of resolving themselves through that same relationship with the people with handicaps. Time has shown that the closer board members are drawn to the handicapped people themselves, the more their lives have been transformed. Professional people who have at first been worried by such considerations as the appropriate way to dress when invited for a meal in l'Arche and quite unable to relate to individuals in the community have found themselves welcoming handicapped people into their own homes and lives. Committee members will sit through intolerably long meetings because they are eager to hear news of very basic personal relationships in the houses. Talented, capable people have given their services on committees for many years, because in some way even those sometimes laborious encounters offer a little vision which they carry with them into other corners of their lives.

For over ten years Père André de Jaer has been bringing a group of from five to seven Jesuits from different countries to spend six months of their tertianship at Trosly-Breuil. They come, Père André would explain, 'to become more simple . . . They come with their degrees in philosophy, theology and mathematics and they can just leave them on the doorstep. Really we have to be ourselves and nothing more, we have to accept not having any social standing and the feeling that we are "wasting time".' Such acceptance did not come easily to all the young Jesuits who came to l'Arche. A Swiss graduate in theology about to start as chaplain to the university in Basel was convinced, after two weeks of working in the garden, that he was achieving nothing and would do better to go straight to the students awaiting him. Père André advised him to suspend his decision for two or three weeks. At the end of that time he had completely changed his mind. As a Swiss person he was used to being well organised and efficient. He was also an intellectual. L'Arche helped him to the discovery of what it meant not to organise but just to be with people and let them touch his heart and discover there a richness.

For Jesuits, Père André would point out, because they did extensive studies and because they often moved amongst the rich, there was a very real danger of becoming rich and of only grasping with their highly developed minds the importance of the poor. Among the handicapped people at l'Arche they were called upon to drop the barriers that their cassocks and their status could create and acknowledge their own fragility. He could cite numerous examples of gifted young priests being touched in a special way by the time they spent, sometimes initially reluctantly, among the handicapped. There was the Englishman who had read Greats at Oxford, a highly cultured man with an extraordinary appreciation of music and history, for whom communication was of great importance, but verbal communication. There was even doubt in his mind as to whether the severely handicapped could really be considered people. The first months of living with them were very hard for him but they brought a real discovery of another kind of communication, of deep communion through touch and through being more completely present. It also brought a new sense of the cross, of the actuality of the passion and resurrection of Jesus in the contemporary world.

Another member of the Society of Jesus from Zaïre was moved by all the young people he saw living a kind of poverty with the handicapped to examine his own conscience. He was a teacher in a high school who knew nothing of the poor in a country where the poverty was so great. His time at Trosly-Breuil was particularly difficult because he was the first black person to come there and some of the handicapped people were slow to accept him. One woman would not even get in the same car with him to go to work, but he accepted to go through the experience and after three months they were good friends. When he left he felt called to 'accompany' prisoners who had been condemned to death.

Recently five Jesuits came to Trosly-Breuil from Central America, from Salvador, Nicaragua, Panama, places where the poor were struggling for justice. They too were deeply involved in the struggle and drawn in their desperation to violence as a political solution. For them l'Arche, Père André would explain, involved the discovery that the struggle should not be only for a just society but should take into account the fact that every individual was important. In working for structures there was a danger of forgetting the person. Some people remained poor even when structures were completely changed, and the new rich too were liable to oppress other people. Even for those with the best of intentions there was a danger of 'working for' the poor and forgetting the value of 'being with'. Some were afraid that an acceptance of the values of l'Arche would demobilise them. Père André would maintain that this was not the case, that it enabled them rather to go back to the struggle with a new vision which was not violent, even though there were times when violence might appear more effective, but which was founded instead upon a deep love, primarily for the poor but also for the rich. The value of the tiny communities in Honduras, ostensibly nonsensical in a world of violence, must be upheld. In many Central American countries contemplative communities were not allowed by governments which found the Church acceptable only when it was manifestly useful. L'Arche communities could combine the contemplative with the 'useful' in a very significant way.

If the assistants in l'Arche have a common denominator it is the desire to live an alternative culture in which the weak are not rejected but given dignity, combined with the desire to see this culture integrated into society. In other respects they are as diverse as the handicapped people themselves. Nor would it be true to suggest that all who go to l'Arche experience life with handicapped people as a benediction; but perhaps it is true to say that those who remain in l'Arche must in some way at some time. The real question in relation to l'Arche, Jean Vanier has said, is 'Who is going to live with handicapped people?' What do assistants need to be confirmed and deepened in their choice? It would be arguably impossible to take on all that life in l'Arche involves were it not for the fact that, in sharing the lives of handicapped people, assistants come to witness the quality of soul which shines through the wounds of their bodies and the wealth of love which a poverty-stricken spirit cannot hide. Perhaps it is that the assistants too are craving communion, that in each one of them also the poor person is crying out his thirst, his pain and his depression. In some mysterious way a reciprocal healing takes place and at its most profound level it is possibly that healing which confirms people in l'Arche. If assistants as part of our broken world are of necessity also wounded, then the question, as Jean Vanier would point out, really amounts to, 'What is going to heal the wound in you and me?' It could be healed by a warm community, but even that is not sufficient: 'Somewhere the wound can only really be healed or accepted in its reality through an experience of God.' People grow in the consciousness that they are loved by God and begin to accept the broken body.

In the experience of l'Arche, in the West at least, today's

generation of assistants are those whose parents questioned, who had no certainties and who subscribed very largely to the conviction that each individual should find his own truth. They tend not to be very formed in their ideals and attitudes and have often experienced problems in the home: 'In one way it gives a great openness. They are ready to discover the handicapped person and Jesus very quickly because they don't have all the obstacles of formation. It is also the first time they are making such a discovery, and so it happens with all the enthusiasm of a child.' At the same time however, unlike the generation of the 'sixties, they are looking for security. They belong to an era of unemployment and broken relationships and have often experienced great hurt. They tend to want to identify with strong, visible things and to be reluctant to make long-term commitments.

Over the years communities have evolved different levels and forms of commitment in recognition of the changing needs of individuals in relation both to the community and to society as a whole. Married couples, for example, no longer have to face the problems which Steve and Ann Newroth doubtless did in seeking space to develop their own family relationships. Some people may live independently of the community but have a commitment to a role in a particular *foyer*. It is possible in some instances to carry on a full professional life and still be very much part of the community. Some may prefer the tendency towards monastic separation from the outside world and, in one sense, the impersonality of a large community like Trosly-Breuil where the community still dominates the village; others are happier in smaller communities where they feel very much a part of the surrounding metropolis or neighbourhood. Their natural preferences can be accommodated.

There is now a greater awareness of specific areas in which conditions for assistants could be improved in concrete ways: the elimination of some of the avoidable fatigue, for example, and the need to develop intellectually. Jean Vanier's appreciation of the value of his own doctorate has not failed to make him aware that one of the poverties of l'Arche is the lack of intellectual formation:

There is a high note of affectivity, a high note of spirituality, but the whole element of rooting through the intelligence is often lacking. It is so different when people are not just spiritually on the right track but are intellectually grounded. There is a great fear today, as if the intelligence can tell us nothing, but the energies which could come from an integration of the intelligence are not being called forth.

The need to prepare retreats and talks had meant that Jean Vanier himself had had to create the space in which to keep up his reading and reflection. He was always moving forward in his retreats. He never just repeated ones he had previously given. He wasn't certain whether his weekly commentary in Trosly on the Gospel of St Luke was important for anyone else, but it was important for him because it meant that he set aside two hours a week just to reflect upon two or three verses. More time and opportunity could be made for others who did not have the same specific incentives, to read and study. There remains the feeling, however, that whilst it is undoubtedly important to raise such questions and to act upon them, ultimately commitment to l'Arche does not rest upon them.

For assistants to be able to put down their roots in l'Arche, Jean Vanier would maintain, there needs to be a call from God, a call that gives them the energy to make the 'passage' from a society built upon values of power and status and riches, in which the weak and the powerless are put to one side as useless and disturbing, to a society, a community, in which the values are those of love and total acceptance of others, and the weak and the broken are welcomed as friends. The challenge for assistants, having once discovered that they are called by Jesus to do his work of love in communion with him, was to retain the sense of that call and the mission given them and not to become too engrossed in the many things they had to do, not to become caught up in their own project or in the need to prove themselves. Their challenge was to *remember* in a way which could transform the ordinary actions of the every day, through the process of taking, offering, breaking and giving, into something extraordinary: to remember their call, to remember that in the activity and pain and the breakages they could turn anew to the Father, to remember that they were part of a plan of communion, to remember the truth of the Eucharist – 'Do this in remembrance of me.' The challenge to l'Arche was also to remember: to remember the actuality of being a eucharistic community and to help its assistants remember, to give them the space in which to be still and listen to the call which was renewed each day. When people touched their limits, Jean Vanier would insist, then the opportunity was there to discover prayer, to cry out to God, 'Come', and to return to the plan of communion. The alternative was anger and depression and compromise. 'But to turn to the Father when we are broken and hurt,' he would acknowledge, 'calls for a certain maturity of faith . . . Did l'Arche nourish this?' He posed the question himself, for it was one with which he was manifestly 'still walking'.

Over the years l'Arche had come to recognise the vital importance of renewals and retreats, and of 'interludes' – namely ten weeks of prayer, talks and shared reflection on such themes as the cry of the poor, on human growth, family and community life, signs of hope and peace in the world, and the vision and calling of l'Arche – for those assistants who had lived in community for five years. The dangers of not giving assistants the space in which to discover anew that they were loved by God, that their lives had meaning and that the Father was with them, were dangers of which Jean Vanier was fully aware: 'If the call is crushed by our work and by tensions, then the very energy which gives assistants power to befriend the poor and to see them in the light and presence of God will be lost, and they will no longer be able to live the mystery and the gift of l'Arche.'

The question of how to articulate the commitment to living that mystery and gift, the deep commitment to a relationship of reciprocity with the poor entrusted to l'Arche, arose out of a letter written from Haiti in March 1977 by Robert Larouche. The letter was born of the need he felt to put into words what his commitment to l'Arche really was, and to discover the response and support of others to his expression of how and why he wanted to commit himself. He had reached a point where he felt the need to say to Yveline, Joliboa, Bernadette, Raoul and Jean Robert with whom he shared his life in Kay Sin Josef that he wanted to live his commitment to them more fully, where he wanted to respond to his call to the poor at a fixed moment in time: 'I would almost say a solemn moment when I can realise the depth of the commitment, seize it in all its fullness and then say "Yes" to it.' To answer the call of Yveline and Joliboa, and indeed of the poor people who lived around them who were so hungry for the Good News was to answer the call of Jesus. Robert went on to acknowledge his need for Jesus in his attempt to answer the call of the poor with ever increasing fidelity and at the same time to intimate his need, in the relative isolation of Haiti, for a sense of unity with others who were answering the same call:

> Through meetings and visits I feel closer to many of you who make a similar choice each day: the choice of a radical sharing and gift to the poor within the heart of l'Arche. I feel more and more dependent on you, and at the same time I need to associate myself more and more with that which each of you is receiving and living wherever you may be. I feel the need to be very close to you, not only as part of a spiritual community (created through our mutual desire to live the spirit of the Beatitudes in l'Arche) but also a part of a tangible community which gives strength to each person and which makes us trust each other more and trust Jesus who is guiding us.

Assistants from different communities were touched and challenged by what Robert Larouche had written about his call to live with the poor and his enquiry whether there were others growing in the same direction. At the end of a retreat led by Père Thomas's brother, Père Marie-Dominique o.p. (prior to the international meeting of l'Arche in 1978) about thirty of these assistants expressed aloud the links which they felt Jesus had created between them and the poor and their desire to remain faithful to them. It was not, it was stressed, a question of taking vows, of forming a group amongst themselves as in a religious order. It was simply announcing publicly a deep call to give themselves to Jesus and the poor in their different communities and their 'yes' to this call. It was a recognition of a certain spirituality, that for them the poor were a privileged way to enter into the heart of Jesus, the heart of the Gospel and so into the heart of the Church.

The word which Jean Vanier felt best reflected his relationship with Raphael and Philippe was that of a 'covenant'. Exodus (2:23–4) described how 'the children of Israel sighed by reason of the bondage, and they cried, and their cry came up unto God by reason of their bondage. And God heard their groaning, and God remembered his covenant.' Then Yahweh revealed himself to Moses (Exodus 3:7–8) and said,

I have surely seen the affliction of my people which are in Egypt and have heard their cry by reason of their task masters, for I know their sorrows. And I am come down to deliver them out of the hand of the Egyptians, and to bring them up out of that land unto a good land and a large, unto a land flowing with milk and honey.

The covenant between God and the poor remained, Jean Vanier would insist in *Community and Growth*. Communities continuing the work of Jesus, in that they were sent to be a presence to the poor living in darkness and despair, were entering into a covenant with Jesus and the poor. Furthermore,

When we know our people, we also realise that we need them, that they and we are interdependent. We are not better than they are – we are there together, for each other. We are united in the covenant which flows from the covenant between God and his people, God and the poorest.

So it was that after Père Marie-Dominique had given his endorsement as a theologian to the idea, those who wanted to give expression to the relationship which they felt existed between themselves and Jesus and the poor he had entrusted to them, were invited to answer 'Yes' to the question ' . . . [name], you are invited to live a covenant in l'Arche with Jesus and with all your brothers and sisters, especially the poorest and the weakest. Do you want this?'

There were those who were not present on that initial occasion of 'announcing the covenant' who felt excluded and hurt by the fact that others came away with the feeling that something wonderful had been given and a sense of deepened union. Sue Mosteller, who was still international co-ordinator at the time and who had a prominent role to play in the Federation meeting that followed immediately afterwards, found the pain of not having been a part of what had happened almost intolerable. In time, however, she would see that personal pain as linked to grace. Time and grace and pain would turn the covenant into the gift of her life. Jean Vanier had been humble in his response to her reproaches. He had not tried to compel her to accept it, but rather said only: 'We've hurt people but I believe that it's right for us. It was given and I ask you to try and keep going with it.' In 1982 she herself announced the covenant as have many other long-term assistants in l'Arche:

> For me it's a way of thinking and expressing and knowing about my life in l'Arche. It gives a language in which to be able to speak about what it is that we are living but it is also bigger than l'Arche. I don't just feel united with the handicapped people here but with all of the world's poor. I feel close to people, I pray for them and carry those who are suffering in my heart. Somehow the covenant is growing deeper and deeper in me.

Bill Clarke, a Jesuit priest who spent a period in l'Arche and who has remained close to it, sometimes conducts covenant retreats in preparation for the announcing of the covenant: 'There comes a point in a friendship when you and I recognise the relationship and determine to be faithful to it,' he would explain. 'By articulating this something happens to our relationship.' Until 1986 covenant retreats in Europe took place in France or Belgium and in the context of a daily Roman Catholic Eucharist. When ecumenical covenant retreats began, during which Anglican and Roman Catholic Eucharists were celebrated on alternate days, inevitably the question arose as to at what point the covenant, which had been recognised as closely linked to the Eucharist, should actually be announced. A solution seemed to lie in St John's account of how before he died Jesus washed the feet of his disciples. In the ecumenical retreats the covenant is announced on the last day during a paraliturgy of the Washing of Feet. There are those who remain in l'Arche for many years without announcing the covenant. It is in no way a condition of commitment but it is one expression of it which many find helpful.

The shortage of assistants, in particular of those prepared to make long-term commitments, remains a problem worldwide. Even Trosly-Breuil, which appears to be a rich community in terms of assistants, is dependent to a large degree on people coming from outside France, frequently from Eastern-block countries. Assistants are not coming from France or Canada as once they did. The tendency is also to come for a year or two and then move on to other things. The result is a rate of change in the lives of the handicapped people which is very demanding. Young assistants come, form deep relationships with them for a year or so, and then move on and are replaced by others before people have really had time to grieve the loss of their predecessors.

A certain amount of flow is healthy and normal in most people's lives: families change, friendships change, people move on, and on the whole the handicapped people cope with the frequent changes extraordinarily well. Their maturity and understanding manifests itself in a multitude of ways, and because of it l'Arche is moving towards giving the handicapped people a more active say in the running of the community. Daybreak has formation groups to prepare some of the handicapped people to vote for the community council. In 1988 they had their first opportunity to take part in an election, and the questions they asked the candidates astounded the director for their relevance and intuition. They rise to the changes of role on the part of different members of the community, often better than the persons concerned, and it is part of the pain and the gift that they carry that they continue, despite the many departures, to welcome new people into their lives. There are nevertheless those who cope by cutting themselves off from entering too deeply into relationships too quickly, for each time an assistant leaves them it triggers off the pain of a multitude of other departures.

There has always been a shortage of assistants in l'Arche. From the early years of the all-too-swift acquisition of the honey-coloured houses in Trosly-Breuil it has rarely been possible to be certain that when the handicapped people arrived there would be the necessary assistants to look after them. Miraculously, divine providence has always provided in a way which encourages trust that it will continue to do so, and the human uncertainty is something which can be viewed in a positive light as a form of poverty at a time when l'Arche in other respects is not as poor as it once was. There is also the knowledge that young people who may have spent what represents but a brief interlude in their lives in a l'Arche

community will still have been touched in some way by it
and carry away with them into other corners of a broken
world the vision that it offers. It remains a fundamental
challenge of l'Arche to show people, particularly in Western
countries, that among the many choices open to them giving
their lives to l'Arche is a viable option. The problem for most
communities is, as one director would put it, 'combatting the
feeling of "How can I commit myself to l'Arche when I
haven't sniffed all the other flowers?"' In others, such as
Erie, there is no shortage of long-term assistants, but their
challenge as the original members of the community grow
older is to remain open to new blood. 'For me', Jean Vanier
would reflect:

> the whole question is how to keep open. Because we are
> wounded we close up. Individuals close up. Communities
> close up. The only way that a human being or a community
> can keep open and moving is through the experience of
> God, the knowledge that we are loved with all our littleness
> and brokenness.

11

Opening the Door to Lazarus

It was after one of those long and leisurely lunches at the Val
Fleuri. The conversation at the tables in the three spacious
reception rooms had ranged haltingly but with animation
from Madonna and her music and proposed costumes for a
forthcoming fancy dress party to the progress of the crops in
the vegetable garden and a healthy grumbling about a hard
morning's work. Jean Vanier had outraged his fellow diners
by pinching the last grape. The washing up had been done
amidst much jostling and jollity and we had gathered to relax
over coffee and a visitor's gift of a box of chocolates.

What did the men of the Val Fleuri feel should be said in
a book about l'Arche? enquired Jean Vanier. 'Tell about our
anguish,' responded Girard, 'About the suffering that is in
my heart. About how hard it is when I can't sleep.' 'I've been
in l'Arche for twenty-five years at the Val Fleuri,' interjected
Jean-Claude, 'I came with my mother who thought I would
be happier here. L'Arche is my real family.' There was a
general chorus of agreement: 'L'Arche is my place. The Val
is my home.'

'Write about Josiane's death' – the reference was to an
assistant who had not long since been tragically killed in a
car accident. 'I'm afraid of death,' commented Girard. 'For
me it's hard,' said Dédé with a deep sigh, 'but the greatest
joy of my life is my godchild.' 'Write about our anguish,'
directed Marc, a talented artist, having reflected long and
solemnly over his pipe, 'but also about our hopes.' 'About
celebrations,' another voice appended eagerly, 'We have a lot
of celebrations and birthdays.'

There were those who chose not to talk in front of the more
than thirty others present, but over the next few days they
sought me out and spoke of what was important to them,
their families whom they visited or did not see, the mobiles

they made in the workshop, holidays past or yet to come, the assistant who had moved to another house but whom they telephoned every day . . . and all, it seemed to me, not so much in a spirit of wanting to unburden themselves but of support and giving. Lulu's need to do something for others was the same as everyone else's. People who had known what it was to be constantly on the receiving end of attention not always gladly given, were happy to be supportive. 'It must be hard to write a book about us,' were recurring words of sympathy.

I learned to value the repeated requests for progress reports and the spirit with which people struggled with evident difficulty but enormous good will to articulate their thoughts into my tape recorder. It was good to hear Pete in Toronto talk of his activities in the local church choir or bowling club; to be part of Ann's constant word games and to become her 'Kattee', to have breakfast in Erie with Andy who, prior to coming to l'Arche, had been one of numerous children adopted by a woman interested only in the government cheques they brought with them and who had consistently deprived him of food; to fold the laundry with my room-mate, Mary, and listen to her admonishing the community dog in the night; to hold Adam's head in my lap in the car to Orangeville because the journey had caused him to have a seizure. I found myself wordlessly appreciative as I was shown people's paintings, their knitting, their trophies for horse-riding or bowling, the pictures of them with the Pope or in Disneyworld, the photographs of past assistants or their much loved young nephews and nieces, and I discovered something of the vital importance of presence in communion.

It was hard to believe that the Val Fleuri had once been a place of violence, just as it was hard to believe that Lita in Honduras who took such evident pride in her appearance and whose fingernails I had carefully to paint had once been left to play with her own excreta, or that Claudia who in her blindness found her way so calmly about the Casa Nazaret, emitting the occasional two-noted sound that smacked rather of contentment than of disturbance, had at one time screamed and screamed incessantly. It was not that there were not days when Marcia took to her bed and refused to get up, when Santos struck another member of the household and would not apologise, when Sam shut himself in the bathroom in a

tantrum, swiftly followed by loud appeals to the Lord to
help him cool down, or when people simply withdrew into
themselves unable for a while to laugh or share; but most of
the handicapped people had found a certain peace, a home,
a maturity.

Each one of the l'Arche communities has experienced the
evolution of men and women who were physically broken and
spiritually dead into people of peace and light. They have
seen the dead rise in a very tangible way. There have been a
few who have had to leave l'Arche over the years. In the early
days the community had taken in people who it transpired
were too mentally sick to live in community. It was usually
a question of violence with which the community could not
cope. One of the more recent instances was of a man who
simply could not live with the structures in l'Arche. 'We tried
for ten years,' Chris, the co-ordinator at Trosly-Breuil would
acknowledge:

> I think there is always something in us which says it isn't
> possible to send people back to hospital, but then things
> became very difficult. He'd feel guilty about not going to
> work. He suffered from back-ache and became scared of
> people. He could be very violent. Now he's been back in
> hospital 'for about a year and a half and he's fine. He
> needed a hospital structure in which he could say he was
> sick and did not have to make choices.

There have been other instances of people preferring even the
conditions of the asylum in Tegucigalpa, to the challenge of
a much less impersonal and more demanding life in l'Arche.
Their choice is respected as are, wherever possible, the wishes
of individuals to move to smaller or larger *foyers*, or to communities in more urban or more rural areas.

Neither Raphael nor Philippe, the two men with whom
Jean Vanier began l'Arche, have remained at Trosly-Breuil.
As the community grew larger Raphael in his advancing years
found it hard to cope with the influx of new people. He was
given the opportunity to go and spend weekends in other
communities. In the smaller rural community of 'La Rose des
Vents' in Verpillières, half an hour's journey from Trosly-
Breuil, Raphael seemed to be more peaceful and so he was
given the option of living there and chose to do so. It was a
choice which was not accepted without a certain sadness on

the part of those who from the beginning had felt so specially bonded to him, but it was accepted nonetheless. As for Philippe, he too had been happy initially to be in Trosly-Breuil because it represented such a change from the asylum where he had been, but he was a city man at heart. He loved to walk in congested streets, window-shop or go to the cinema and he found the lack of city activity in Trosly hard to take. When therefore the community began in the nearby city of Compiègne he too was given the opportunity initially to try it for weekends and then to choose. He elected to leave and is happy in the busier atmosphere of Compiègne.

Looking back over the twenty-five years of its history, Jean Vanier could see that l'Arche had much to celebrate, for the evolution of l'Arche was the story of men and women and an increasing number of children who had come from asylums, psychiatric institutions and other situations of rejection and abandonment and had 'made the passage from death to resurrection, from anguish to trust, from loneliness to community, from despair to hope, and had been able to do so because many extraordinary assistants were there to accompany them'. It was also the story of many assistants and friends who had found new life through their covenant with very wounded and weak people.

Jean Vanier's own life and heart had been transformed. There had been naivety on his part and on the part of others, a lack of wisdom, setbacks, crises and shortcomings, but in all these potential for learning and those graces which only frailty can allow. Faith and Light was held together by such fragile people. Each one of the l'Arche communities had at some stage come close to closure. There had been communities in French-speaking Canada born under the direction of people with undoubted charisms but situated like small islands far apart from each other, and without very much support, in a vast country where there was much anger against religion. There the basic human securities no longer prevailed and young people wanted security rather than to hear about the problems of the Third World. There had been communities near Ottawa, in Montana and in Norway, originally formed independently of l'Arche. They had joined the Federation but subsequently left. At the time of joining they had not fully appreciated the requirements of belonging to l'Arche. Their leaving brought the recognition of the need for founding-directors and founding teams to spend several years in an existing community in order to create bonds of shared understanding before giving birth to a new community.

Other communities, apart from the one in Kotagiri, India, had closed. The community in Bouaké had been founded on the Ivory Coast in 1975. Shortly afterwards l'Arche had been encouraged by the Bishop of Man to open another foundation nearby, but the newly founded community in Bouaké had not been strong enough to take responsibility for another foundation so soon. The community in Man closed in 1978. Eight years later the community in Milton, Australia, also closed. The parish priest who had encouraged its opening as a parish project had been transferred elsewhere. His successor's lack of interest created too many problems. Elsewhere, communities had dwindled for lack of good direction. Assistants had also been welcomed whose vocation was obviously not really to l'Arche. Power struggles and open conflict had ensued in a way which had made it all too clear that l'Arche must be wiser and clearer in the way it welcomed assistants: it must learn how to discern better and set up a system of trial periods and evaluation. The circumstances of some incidents and departures had caused pain and suffering, but then l'Arche was founded upon suffering, and pain was a necessary part of growth.

There is scope for criticism of l'Arche. Those more concerned with the struggle to change social structures have at times viewed it as personalist and in general inclining towards conservative reactionary positions based on the idea that social structures are in some way out of reach, cannot be changed, and the only thing that matters is this person. Those who, through relationship with the handicapped people, become more sympathetic in their criticism could still hold on with some justification to the idea that not all communities are sufficiently concerned with the social reality that encompasses them. In the larger communities l'Arche life, like any organisational or institutional life, tends to become the total universe and there are those who see this fact as a grave short-coming. There are criticisms also associated with the inbuilt dilemma between the essential focus on the handicapped people on the one hand and the care for the life of the assistants on the other. As one priest at Trosly-Breuil would put it, 'The insight about the handicapped has been tried and tested and is clearly of the spirit and solidly in place. The same cannot be said of the assistants.'

Ultimately perhaps it is a problem of structure. To a Jesuit coming from an order which, according to its own criteria, is well structured and has been so for a long time, l'Arche in its desire not to reproduce tired structures from the past had put together a system which was unnecessarily cumbersome and in which responsibilities were not well defined and clearly located:

> It betrays its youthfulness and its nervousness about the more tried and true forms of communal organisation which are basically contained in the structures of religious life. I understand its nervousness about not becoming a religious order, but the fact remains that its structures take an enormous amount of time and energy and are not necessarily more sensitive to people's needs, nor more flexible or charismatic.

Where responsibilities are not well defined and mandates clear, painful decisions tend to fall between the cracks. When it came to the question of an individual's leaving, for example, there could be an understandable but lamentable confusion between the good of the community and the good of the individual, particularly when in the initial, though not the final, analysis it was almost invariably better for the person to stay because the community needed assistants. 'But the community needs to have more self-confidence and trust in its structures in order to be able to make the distinction between its own survival and the needs of John or Joan who should be helped to tackle the question of staying or leaving in freedom.'

To some professional carers there was scope for envy of the conditions in which people in l'Arche could encourage the growth and development of handicapped people, of the fact, for instance, that an assistant might have the opportunity to spend the greater part of his day with one handicapped person. In one respect, l'Arche had a flying start in relation to health authorities and social service departments. In terms of the idea of shared life and handicapped people being brought out of hospitals and institutions, l'Arche, when it began in 1964, had been somewhat in advance of its time. Its convictions about professional practice or the appropriate circumstances for mentally handicapped people within and not outside the wider community had subsequently proved to be in the forefront of a widespread movement which has been gaining momentum ever since. On the other hand, l'Arche's strong emphasis on living a family life, with all the mutual support which that entailed, did not always meet with the approval of those who believed in promoting maximum independence. L'Arche encouraged those who had the wish to go into complete independence to do so, but on the whole the people who came there were those who were seeking a supportive family life, epitomised perhaps by the sizeable dining table round which quite a number could be seated with space for one or two newcomers. There were some professionals who would say that not many people in the West were in fact now living in this way and that the quest for 'normalisation' should not mean the creation of conditions for handicapped people which were different from the lifestyle of the majority of the remainder of the population. L'Arche on the other hand would like to show that 'normalisation' does not mean exclusively conforming to what is the 'norm', that human beings are not necessarily fulfilled in independence and loneliness. It believes that human fulfilment comes through bonds of love, of family and of city, and that it is from this source of love, this network of relationships, that each one can grow in his or her capacity to serve, work, accomplish works of art and discover communion with God.

There were all too obvious areas for potential questioning associated with the very idea of untrained people living with the handicapped and linked also to the whole issue of the space and distance between the carer and the cared for, the detachment which most professionals would consider necessary for them to operate efficiently. One of the aspects of work in the hospice world which particularly interested Thérèse Vanier was the fact that there it had been possible to marry commitment and involvement to a highly professional approach. In her view this had been achieved by putting a tremendous accent on working as a team instead of working in isolation. Such a solution, it might be thought, should be obvious to l'Arche as a body which sets out to be a community, but it remains as yet an unresolved tension. The question of how members of the community, as opposed to professionals who come in from outside to help, can marry what is labelled a 'professional' approach to commitment to another person in the spirit of l'Arche, has yet to be satisfactorily answered.

There is a tension associated with the issue of the sexuality of handicapped people. L'Arche has at times found itself firmly out of step with the school of thought which subscribes to sterilisation and the equation of the right to sexual pleasure with happiness. It has also been attacked for allegedly driving vulnerable people into religion: 'There has been a feeling that we push people into religion, that we make handicapped people feel like Jesus when they don't want to be Jesus. It is easy to attack on those grounds. It is easy to deform religious language.' Other criticisms arise in connection with the spiritual and ecumenical life of the communities. From l'Arche's own point of view the question arises as to what constitutes an appropriate shared spiritual life in the houses. Quite a spectrum exists in the various l'Arche communities in terms of the lived religious life, ranging from the spiritual intensity of the 'Farm' at Trosly-Breuil to something very far removed from it. 'It would be madness to try and reproduce the "Farm" everywhere, but the question does arise as to whether you are living l'Arche if you don't have a shared religious life within the houses.'

Outside the community l'Arche has undoubtedly disturbed and challenged, inevitably perhaps for, in the vision of Jean Vanier, its folly reflects the folly of the plan of God. The folly of God's plan was 'Jesus dragged through the streets of Jerusalem, a political prisoner breaching national and religious security. For this he was tortured and put to death. Yet it is he the healer – the broken and wounded healer – the lamb who is our shepherd.' The folly continues in that it is he who is hidden in the poor, the weak, the broken, the useless, the marginal, those who are sick, naked, imprisoned or strangers. Jesus disturbed the quiet order that so many wanted, the power and privilege of the rich and of the 'religiously straight'. And so today, Jean Vanier maintains, the poor and the weak continue to be condemned to death, sometimes even in their mother's womb, or are shut away – because they disturb the quiet order. Nor is this true only of the poor with handicaps but of all those who cry out their pain and loneliness, of the people with Aids, of unwelcome immigrants, of the lost and angry young, of the lonely old, of the hungry of the Third World. People want solutions to the problem but not to be disturbed by the cry for communion. As a community seeking to listen and respond to that cry, l'Arche too disturbs. Its history is an illustration of what happens when the door is opened and Lazarus, the poor man calling for change and disrupting the quiet order, is invited to come in.

Since its inception l'Arche has been a sign of contradiction. It has failed to conform to the usual prescribed definitions of either State-recognised institution or Christian community. Yet it wants to be both a centre accepted according to the norms of the State and a Christian community firmly anchored in the values of the Gospel. Furthermore, even whilst finding unity in communion with God and communion with the poorest and the weakest, it has recognised that its communities are non-homogeneous and must take into account the great diversity of its members, their vocation and way of expressing their faith. It is small wonder then that these ambiguities have at times disconcerted both State and Church. As it was pointed out at Daybreak, 'You're never efficient when at the heart of everything is the growth of people. Government representatives do not always fully appreciate that.' They do not necessarily understand, for example, that Daybreak needs so many vehicles because the ten houses there, though geographically some distance apart, are connected, and that their occupants need to come together for meetings and celebrations. Other organisations with ten houses similarly situated tend not to live that sort of bonding. In France, the social security representatives reacted strongly to the policy of assistants not receiving normal salaries. There was no provision in French law for centres to have volunteer workers or assistants with lower salaries. It took several years for l'Arche to negotiate an agreement with government officials by which an assistant could be considered under training for the first two years, and so receive simply a stipend and social security benefits. Only after two years would he or she receive the minimum legal wage.

Jean Vanier is fully appreciative of the number of men and women in administration who do recognise the values of l'Arche in relation to the real needs of people with a handicap. One head of the Department of Social Welfare in Beauvais, France, in particular had understood and summarised most clearly the position, questions and concerns of people in government authority with regard to l'Arche. When Jean Vanier explained to her in 1977 the aims and life in l'Arche, she had responded: 'I admire what you are doing. It is surely the best thing for people with a handicap, but if something goes wrong . . . If, for example, assistants accepting small salaries and your lifestyle no longer come, what can I do to help you? If I give you subsidies, what guarantee do I have that l'Arche will be able to continue?' She was, Jean Vanier would acknowledge, pointing out the folly of l'Arche.

Similarly there have been difficulties associated with the question of specific religious identity, with the role of the priest within l'Arche and with the question of the relationship of a lay community to the Church. The relationship of l'Arche to the Church is based on a very deep need on the part of l'Arche as much as on desire. The importance of the role of priests in the spiritual and mystical growth of community members has been increasingly recognised, as has the value of having bishops to accompany communities. In a number of countries now an accompanying bishop provides a link with the episcopate. In France, once a year, the Bishop of Beauvais calls together the priests who accompany l'Arche communities. In Belgium the auxiliary bishop of Brussels does the same. In England, apart from Bishop Stephen Verney, the Archbishop of Canterbury has appointed another Anglican bishop, Richard Third, to accompany the United Kingdom communities in conjunction with Bishop John Rawsthorne, the Roman Catholic auxiliary bishop of Liverpool. All three meet regularly with the communities' regional co-ordinators and every now and then with priests and pastors close to the various communities. Such links reflect a move to grow in deeper communion.

The relationship between the priest and the lay person, Jean Vanier has said, should be one of communion. At the heart of l'Arche, it may be suggested, is the communion between Père Thomas and Jean Vanier. Where there is such a relationship between the priest and the lay person, the history of l'Arche has shown that communities flourish. Where there is opposition between the two, where unconsciously the lay person locks the priest up in the sacristy or the priest treads constantly on the toes of the director, the community suffers. The same, Jean Vanier intimates, is true of the wider community that is the Church. Conscious that l'Arche is only one of a number of new communities in the West, he believes nonetheless that because of the particular gift of people with handicaps it has a significant role to play in the rediscovery of the mystery of what community is all about.

The discovery of the way in which the spirit of Jesus was guiding all Christians had in no way diminished Jean Vanier's love for Roman Catholicism. Rather, as his heart had grown to new dimensions so too his love for the Church of Rome and for the Pope as the shepherd of shepherds had grown. John Paul II, he was quick to affirm, was a man with a deep sense of communion, a man who listened and who knew the value of celebration. The Church, however, had allowed itself to be too influenced by culture. It had espoused a hierarchy too often based on power and riches and lost sight at times of the 'upside downness' of the world that Jesus revealed, a world in which it was by going down the ladder rather than by scrambling up it, 'by meeting people who had been excluded and set aside that we are healed'.

Jean Vanier had identified a need in the Roman Catholic Church to find again a sense of the Church as a Body in which the members who were the weakest and the most fragile were fully recognised as necessary and honoured: 'In the Roman Catholic Church there is very much a sense of hierarchy. There is value in that but a breakage in the sense of the body.' Few priests had undergone training for community life, for relationships of vulnerability, for working in real communion with lay people. Essential to the refinding of communion and the sense of the body in the Church, was the right relationship between the priest and the lay person and a recognition of the poor not as objects of charity but as a treasure of the Church. This was where handicapped people had a special value:

> People with handicaps are incredible, because communion is their immediate need. They are not there to be taught or to do things or to evangelise. They are there to live communion. They offer a vision of the whole mystery of the Trinity: not doing things but being in communion with. They are also really at the heart of community and the Church, because their unique need is communion and that

is what the Church is in the vision of Jesus: being in communion.

With hindsight it is very clear to Jean Vanier that the priesthood was not what God wanted for him. The fact that l'Arche was founded upon two vocations, that of a priest and that of a layman was undoubtedly significant. Furthermore as a layman he has trodden paths outside the community of l'Arche which would not have been open to him and spoken out in a way which might not have been possible as a priest. Jean Vanier has a very easy entrée to Church leaders throughout the world. He has had sustained contact with people such as Dom Helder Camara and Mother Teresa of Calcutta, and has worked hard to promote understanding within the Vatican of what l'Arche is. At the same time he has not been afraid to speak out on the dangers of ecumenism falling into the ways of collaboration rather than of a communion which takes into account the intimate relationship between the broken body of Christ and the bodies of broken people:

> We have to learn what it means to wash each other's feet, to discover what it means to eat with the poor because for me that will always be a package deal. The two poles of the Church are the broken body of Christ in the Eucharist and the broken body of people but there can be an ecumenism around the Eucharist which does not pay enough attention to the broken body of people. There would be something terrible about Churches being united in their power and glory and cult if they haven't really discovered the fundamental meaning of the incarnation: the presence of Christ in the poor.

Having lived twenty-five years in a mixed community with the experience of working with both men and women leaders, Jean Vanier has also been in a strong position to call upon the Church to look more closely at how women can take their place more fully in it. He is convinced of the amazing wealth in the complementarity between the sexes: 'We can help each other so much to grow and advance, as long as we can listen to one another.'

As a lay member of a lay community he has also strongly endorsed the spirit of the Second Vatican Council in relation to the vocation and mission of lay people within the Church.

In October 1987, Pope John Paul II invited him to take part in a Synod at which that vocation and mission was the central theme. It was an opportunity for which Jean Vanier was deeply grateful. He felt that the Pope's invitation to lay people to be present and address the assembly, even though they did not have a vote, was a prophetic gesture. His reflections on the Synod, which he afterwards committed to paper, were full of words of welcome and appreciation for many aspects of it and for the fundamental message:

> We are all called to be holy as is the Father in heaven, according to our particular vocation. In our times, the thirst for holiness grows more and more in the hearts of the faithful, when they accept the call of God inviting them to live with Christ and to change the world.

They also included criticisms of the methodology of the wording and writing of proposals to be given to the Pope which, he felt, allowed little space for the prophetic, the expressed regret that so little had been said about ecumenism, and a strong, characteristic call to see the people who are poor and fragile and who often cannot assume responsibility or participate in decisions as being at the very heart of the Church. In insisting on active participation and speaking of the place of lay people in terms of collaboration and co-responsibility, the Synod was, he considered, overlooking the specific mystery of the gift of the poor to the Church, of those whose intangible contributions were those of giving life and awakening love.

In his covenant with Père Thomas and by his baptism Jean Vanier felt himself linked to the Church, born and reborn in it. In the Church he had been nourished by the flesh of Jesus and the Word of God: 'It is my life. All that is good and holy in me flows from the covenant with Jesus in the Church.' And yet to him the Church, the Churches, seemed so caught up in the ways of the world, so frightened of the prophetic, subject to that terrible tension between considering the institution and living the prophetic, and nervous of seeing Jesus hidden in the poor who disturbed and healed. And l'Arche was there, not a new Church, not rejecting the Church as obsolete and irrelevant but in terrible need of the Word and the Body of Jesus which alone could give meaning to the lives of its people. L'Arche did not want to feel better, superior to

others. It wanted only to be part of the Body of Christ and
to live silently the ways of Nazareth, to be a community of
peace. 'I must learn,' Jean Vanier would recognise, 'to
become like a child, laughing and trusting, playing and dancing, asking forgiveness and forgiving, learning to die each
day, hidden in the womb of God.' Yet at the same time there
was a call to be a sign, to the Church and to the world, to
cry out a way, a path to healing. If l'Arche did not enter the
political struggle *per se*, it was by no means oblivious to the
struggle for justice. The role of l'Arche on the political scene,
as Jean Vanier saw it, was to create a model to show that
people could live with each other despite, even because of,
their differences. It was there to be a constant reminder of
the value of weakened people. There was also a vision, a
message that

> We don't have to be heroes. We don't have to be in l'Arche.
> We don't have to do big things, but to live each day in
> love, doing little things, learning to welcome one another,
> particularly the weak and those in pain, the heart-broken,
> creating a milieu where each one can be him or herself and
> grow in safety and in peace, a milieu where God is present
> and can lead each one gently into the good news of love,
> creating a milieu and a network of relationships, a place of
> covenant and communion, where the Trinity can make
> their drinking place, and where we can celebrate our
> humanity and give thanks.

The fundamental insight that handicapped people not only
deserve an equal amount of dignity but in fact have something
special to contribute, and linked to it the criticism of power,
competition, consumerism and individualism, is one which
Jean Vanier and other l'Arche members with him are carrying
into the world at large at a time when medicine has produced
the means to identify the handicapped prior to birth, and
when the pressures to abort those who will always be
especially vulnerable and, in this world's terms, unable to
compete, are strong. Every science, Jean Vanier was fully
aware, brought with it its opposite. As a consequence of
looking more closely at birth and death, at the immediate
reality after birth and the preparation for death, the issues of
abortion, genetic manipulation and euthanasia had become
powerful realities. He had been deeply touched by a recent

television film entitled 'The Baby is a Person', which had depicted the birth of a premature child:

> The mother was holding the child and the paediatrician was calling the child forth. Then the child opened its eyes and looked into the eyes of the mother. That child's eyes almost popped out of their sockets and the film ended with the words, 'And now he knows he's loved'.

There was still, however, a long way to go before the world stopped seeing the weak and the 'abnormal' either as objects of pity and charity or rejecting them.

If people are to come to an appreciation of their brothers and sisters with handicaps as a gift rather than a liability, if they are even dimly to perceive the truth of the paradox of the Beatitudes, there is much explaining to be done, for in this world's terms the truth of l'Arche is ridiculous. If government authorities are to support l'Arche by modifying certain laws or permitting certain exceptions, they have somehow to be brought to an understanding of what l'Arche has been shown by its own history – namely that, in the words of the psalmist, 'The stone which the builders refused is become the headstone of the corner' (Psalm 118:22).

This is not an easy season for l'Arche politically and economically. Whereas at one time in certain parts of the world the deinstitutionalisation, decentralisation and reintegration of mentally handicapped people were high on the list of social and government priorities, now, in the struggle to provide places and care for Aids victims and battered wives and children, handicapped people are becoming more marginal amongst the marginals. L'Arche occasionally has trouble with finance. Consultation with financiers in France has revealed that, whereas at one time if funds were needed it was best to ask for money for India or Africa, now one must ask for France. The same attitude of looking after one's own people first before looking elsewhere is prevalent in many other countries. People are closing in on themselves. Nor is it easy in a world where the threats range from Aids to the atomic bomb to attract people in the materialistic West to communities which appear insecure. 'People are too fragile to come to us. They are looking for more institutionalisation and more security and probably need it before they can go onto the next stage, because they may not be able to accept the insecurity of the Gospels without some human security.'

The shortage of assistants has brought home to l'Arche in a very specific way the importance of something which is of undoubted relevance to the world at large, namely 'announcing the vision'. It is something which Jean Vanier has been doing since the very beginning of l'Arche. Even those who might be inclined to criticise l'Arche for not expressing the meaning of the Gospel in terms of social structures would concede that Jean Vanier has pursued his insights on a large scale. For years he has been called upon to address religious retreats and conferences for professionals in the human services field. His movements have attracted the attention of the press, his books are widely reviewed and read, and he appears not infrequently on television in connection with ethical issues. The man who gravitates most naturally to the poor has carried that vision from the marginals of New Zealand to President Jean Claude Duvalier of Haiti. Not so long ago the community in Trosly-Breuil was thrown into frenzied activity to find him suitable clothes to wear for lunch with Queen Elizabeth II at Buckingham Palace. His scant regard for clothes meant that he did not possess a suit and one of his father's had to be altered for the occasion.

In England, because of her own professional reputation and familiarity with the professional world, Thérèse Vanier has done much to bring the vision of l'Arche to the attention of professional carers. The impact of l'Arche in such circles is difficult to measure but it is, Thérèse Vanier herself would concede, probably greater than l'Arche imagines. In its awareness of its own shortcomings, in the lack of time to reflect, in the fatigue from which many of its assistants suffer, there is a tendency to underestimate its value. In Choluteca, Honduras, Pilar has been speaking on local radio together with mothers of handicapped children in an attempt to bring about that 'inner transformation' which enables parents to see their handicapped children as a gift. Many others in l'Arche have long been announcing the vision in their different ways, but the time, it is felt, has come to do more of it. In recent years it has been found that no one does this more effectively than the handicapped people themselves. Henri Nouwen, and others invited to talk to university and other gatherings, have taken to taking some of the handicapped people with them. Philip in his spotted bowtie explaining gently the progress of his life from birth to institution to l'Arche, illustrated with his own very appealing drawings on a cardboard television screen, touches people in a way that even Jean Vanier cannot, for if the message is that the poor are a source of life, the medium is unmistakably the message.

It is not that l'Arche is unaware that there are 'lots of good things happening elsewhere'. The importance is consistently stressed not only of announcing but of listening.

Ecumenically we must look at what others are living, at groups like Focolare. We must be really open to what the human sciences are saying, open to the knowledge that psychiatry has to offer, and open to what theology can teach us, for theology is rooted in the Word of God and the work of the Holy Spirit. It calls all people from all times to conversion and to the discovery of the way of humility and love.

Nor is it most important to have all the answers: 'L'Arche is wonderful because it is bringing up more questions than answers. What is important is walking with the right questions and having more and more people conscious of the questions and knowing that only God can answer them.'

Jean Vanier has a gift for transforming limitations and criticisms and blockages into challenges to be viewed with excitement and with a certain peace: 'It is peace giving when we discover that we don't have to succeed but just to let Jesus work in us and through us.' There was confidence, though not complacency, to be derived from the fact that if security and unity within the communities had not always led quite as it should to an outward movement into the wider community, then John who waited at the garden gate in Norwood and chatted to anyone who happened to pass his way would, in his own unique fashion, promote 'integration' and good will. The poor man had his own way of making his voice heard. There was confidence to be drawn too from the evident evolution of the people with handicaps and from the evolution of 'community wisdom': 'I think we now have wise systems of support. We have seen clearly that communities cannot live without a good support system and there has been great progress.' One of the challenges to which l'Arche must now rise was that of enabling its people to grow old with dignity.

Another was that of how best to support those assistants who had chosen a way of celibacy in that choice: 'Do you leave it, as we tend to at the moment, to one individual accompanying another or do we move into something else?' In the next few years the communities must make sure that they did not fall into being places of collaboration more linked to the word and the doing than to presence and the body and silence. They must try to find the space of silence, of recognition, the space where people were recognised as themselves at a much deeper level than mere collaboration.

As to the longer-term future, Jean Vanier could see two tendencies in tension with one another: one tendency would be for some assistants in l'Arche to form a religious order which would provide them with a certain security but which would separate them from the handicapped people. The other tendency would be to become a group home, in which the religious values were subsumed under the pressure of the need for professionalism. In either case the central idea of living as a family with people with handicaps would be lost. History suggested that the attempt to balance the two was in danger of failing. The struggle was an ongoing one, but one of l'Arche's strengths was that it was supple enough to accept that some elements of its life must die in order that the notion of family might be maintained.

In his sixties and as full of energy as ever, when I last met him in the early summer of 1989 Jean Vanier had just returned from giving a number of talks in Russia. The international vice-coordinator of Faith and Light was Polish, and Jean Vanier had always harboured the heartfelt desire to move into Eastern-bloc countries: 'Between him and me it could not happen.' The guest of the Canadian Ambassador in Moscow, he had been able to meet not only leading Soviet people concerned with the care of the handicapped but also Christians from the Orthodox Church, the Roman Catholic Church, Pentecostals and Baptists. It had left him with the conviction that something very important and special was going to be given from Soviet Russia: 'There is a thirst in the Russian people and something very deep coming up from the groundswell of their unconscious. Human nature is so beautiful. You can't keep it down. You can persecute it but it will always rise up again.' It had left him also with the conviction that there must be a lot of prejudices inside him:

'I found as I was going through the beautiful Moscow subway that I was amazed that I was actually there.' It had been a great liberation for him really to fall in love with the Russian people and he had come away with the resolve to look more closely at the Orthodox tradition and at the works of Dostoevsky and Stravinsky to discover there the vision of people who were considered mad, but who were in fact prophetic, saying things that others might know but did not dare to say.

In June he was due to give a retreat in Budapest, then he was returning to Canada before snatching two weeks of quietness. The greatest therapy for him was still the prayerful silence of a Trappist monastery. In December he would be in England and he was starting to think about China: 'We have a very special Asian co-ordinator in Faith and Light who has already helped to start two tiny Faith and Light communities in Taiwan. She can't wait to move into China.' It was a take-over bid for the world and yet, he was quick to interject, so small. Communion was such a little thing, like a very small flower, and it must never be forgotten that the spirituality of l'Arche was a spirituality, not quite of failure but of 'no-success'. When you lived with severely handicapped people there was no success. In hospital people were healed, in a school people attained certificates and diplomas, but in l'Arche often it was a question of just discovering through the day-to-day living of humility and littleness the wealth of communion, with no particular achievement in a world orientated towards success.

The naval officer who, by his own account, had been quick to subservience and quick to command but ill-schooled in the art of working in harmony with people, had journeyed a long way to the commitment to the living of communion. He was conscious that had he stayed on alone the whole thing would have foundered, more conscious now than in the early days of there being many 'founders'. Nor would he have said so clearly then as now that the poor were prophetic in their littleness. The prime danger he now foresaw was the consequence of some people beginning to see l'Arche as important: 'When you become important it is easy to fall from a true prophecy into a false one. One has continually to come back to the crucifixion and the immense tensions inside oneself between littleness and bigness.'

Fidelity is central to l'Arche: fidelity to communion with

the Father through prayer and fidelity to communion with
the poor person who reveals a hidden presence of God.
Beyond the activity and the daily fatigue of those who had
so little time to pause and reflect, it was possible for an
outsider to sense the power of prayer in hidden operation.
One of the great beauties of l'Arche, Jean Vanier would point
out, was the fact that some fifty men had left for the priesthood
and eighty women for contemplative orders which had
brought the l'Arche communities into contact with many
different groups and built up enduring links of prayer. One
'socially conscious' young woman, who is now a Benedictine
nun, recalls during her first visit to l'Arche meeting, in the
company of Jean Vanier, a Canadian who had just spent two
weeks in the forest praying: 'I started to say how awful I felt
that was, escaping away to pray. Prayer was action! I think
I was shocked to think that someone as involved with suffering
as Jean Vanier could sanction such desertion. He looked at
me and said, "What about Martha and Mary?" and that was
the beginning of my journey.'

In the early days of l'Arche Odile Ceyrac had brought Jean
Vanier into touch with Marthe Robin. He had visited her
and, physically handicapped as she herself was, she had been
moved in a special way to pray for l'Arche. The community
in Tegucigalpa was carried in a very particular way by the
prayers of the Jesuits. In the asylum in the Honduran capital
where once Marcia had been kept I would meet a friend of
hers, too physically handicapped even to alter the position of
her limbs in bed. Her frail life was given up to praying for
Marcia and her 'family' in Casa Nazaret. There were numerous other examples. As to fidelity to the poor, I was only one
among many to be touched by the fact that on returning to
a community I was remembered and greeted by the handicapped people, who picked up the relationship where it was
left and who held a visitor in their hearts and in their prayers
in a way in which I, for a multitude of inconsequential
reasons, could not hold them. In their fidelity they illuminate
the way. Just as ultimately the well-being of the handicapped
people, whose faces full of light and love and laughter contrast
so sharply with the closed, sad, angry faces of so many on
our city streets, is the measure of l'Arche, so fidelity to them
is the safeguard for the future. As Jean Vanier would confide:

The greatest seduction is power, whatever type of power: speaking on television, writing books, having books written about one, even being powerful to do good, the seduction of leaving the poor to talk about them. The only real answer is to be powerless, so that the power of God can go through us. We must keep always in our mind that to be with the poor is our greatest strength. It seems so little just to be with them yet it's through the littleness that the power of God is manifest. So truth comes daily as we discover the holiness of our people.

Books by Jean Vanier

In Weakness Strength (biography of Georges Vanier). Toronto, Griffin House, 1969. French edition: *Ma Faiblesse c'est ma Force*. Montreal, Bellarmin, 1972.

Tears of Silence. Toronto, Griffin House, 1971.

La Communauté: Lieu du Pardon et de la Fête. Paris, Les Editions Fleurus, and Montreal, Bellarmin, 1978. Translated into English by Ann Shearer and published as *Community and Growth*. London, Darton, Longman and Todd, 1979; revised and extended edition 1989.

Homme et Femme Il Les Fit. Paris, Les Editions Fleurus, and Montreal, Bellarmin, 1984. Translated into English by Elizabeth Buckley and published as *Man and Woman He Made Them*. London, Darton, Longman and Todd, 1985.

The Broken Body: Journey to Wholeness. London, Darton, Longman and Todd, 1988.

Treasures of the Heart: Daily Readings with Jean Vanier, edited by Sister Benedict Gaughan OSB, with an introduction by Sheila Cassidy. London, Darton, Longman and Todd, 1989.

A Hope That We Can Grow and *Our Inner Journey* are pamphlets published by l'Arche.

Addresses of l'Arche Communities

Telephone numbers given here are those used with the international call number for that country. For internal dialling, it is necessary to follow the national dialling system, e.g. in the United Kingdom to dial '0' before the relevant numbers.

AUSTRALIA

L'Arche Sydney
306 Burwood Road
Burwood 2134, NSW
Tel: (2) 747 53 16

Beni Abbes
40 Pirie Street
New Town 7008
Tasmania
Tel: (002) 28 31 68

Genesaret
PO Box 1326
Woden, ACT 2606
Tel: 81 26 30 (H)
    82 27 27 (O)

BELGIUM

Aquero
14 rue St Pierre
B-1301 Bièrges
Tel: (10) 41 43 86

Ark Antwerpen
Madona
12 Janssenlei
B-2530 Boechout
Tel: (3) 455 4532

L'Arche Bruxelles
35 rue des Bataves
B-1040 Bruxelles
Tel: (2) 734 3623

Le Murmure
49 rue du Châlet
4070 Aywaille
Tel: 41 84 64 84

L'Arche Namur
Chaussée de Waterloo 118
B-5002 St Servais
Tel: 81 73 02 83 (Cascatelle)
    81 21 41 60 (Bartrès)

BRAZIL

L'Arche
Rua Manuel Aquilino dos
Santos 151
CEP 02873
Jardin Elisa Maria
Sao Paolo CP
Tel: 11 858 5622

BURKINA FASO

Nongr Maasem
BP 1492
Ouagadougou
Burkina Faso
Tel: 226 31 04 35

CANADA

L'Arche Agapé
19 rue Front
Hull, Quebec
J8Y 3M4
Tel: (819) 663 5735 (H)

Alleluia House
9 Melrose Avenue
Ottawa, Ontario
K1Y 1T8
Tel: (613) 729 1601

L'Arche Antigonish
69 St Ninian Street
Antigonish, Nova Scotia
B2G 1Y7
Tel: (902) 863 5945

Arc-en-Ciel
1570 30e Rue
St Prosper
Beauce, Quebec G0M 1Y0
Tel: (418) 594 5604

L'Arche Calgary
429 54th Avenue S.W.
Calgary, Alberta
T2V 0C6
Tel: (403) 255 3909 (O)
     (403) 255 4728 (H)

La Caravane
R.R. 2
Green Valley, Ontario
K0C 1L0
Tel: (613) 525 1921 (O)

L'Arche Cape Breton
R.R. 1
Orangedale, Nova Scotia
B0E 2K0
Tel: (902) 756 2976

Daybreak
11339 Yonge Street
Richmond Hill, Ontario
L4C 4X7
Tel: (416) 884 3454

Emmaus House
1241 Parisien Street
Sudbury, Ontario
P3A 3B5
Tel: (705) 560 1966

L'Etable
2663 Fernwood Avenue
Victoria, British Colombia
V8T 3A1
Tel: (604) 595 1014

L'Etoile
617 Franklin
Quebec
G1N 2I7
Tel: (418) 648 9588 (O)

Fleurs de Soleil
221 Bernard Pilon
Beloeil P.Q.
J3G 1V2
Tel: (514) 467 9655

L'Arche Arnprior
23 Lake Street
Arnprior, Ontario
K7S 1Z9
Tel: (613) 623 7323 (O)
      (613) 623 0129 (H)

L'Arche Hamilton
78 Sherman Avenue S.
Hamilton, Ontario
L8M 2P7
Tel: (416) 544 5401

Homefires
PO Box 1296
Wolfville, Nova Scotia
B0P 1X0
Tel: (902) 542 3520

Kara Foyer
102 First Avenue East
North Bay, Ontario
P1B 1J6
Tel: (705) 474 0168

La Maison de l'Amitié
239 Des Erables
Cap de la Madeleine
Quebec
G8T 5G9
Tel: (819) 375 2790

Le Printemps
100 route Frampton
St Malachie, Quebec
G0R 3N0
Tel: (418) 642 5785 (O)
      (418) 642 5000
      (maison Gaston)

Le Saule Fragile
191 2nd Avenue West
Amos, Quebec
J9T 1S4
Tel: (819) 732 5036

Maranatha
82 Huron Street
Stratford, Ontario
N5A 5S6
Tel: (519) 271 9751

Shalom
7708–83 Street
Edmonton, Alberta
T6C 2Y8
Tel: (403) 465 0618

Shiloah
7401 Sussex Avenue
Burnaby, British Colombia
V5J 3V6
Tel: (604) 434 1933 (O)
      (604) 435 9544 (H)

The Skiff
1030 3e Avenue
Verdun, P.Q.
H4G 2X8
Tel: (514) 761 7270

L'Arche Winnipeg
128 Victoria Avenue West
Winnipeg, Manitoba
R2C 1S5
Tel: (204) 224 2692
      (204) 224 2626

DENMARK

Niels Steensens Hus
Nygade 6
3000 Helsingor
Tel: (2) 21 21 39

DOMINICAN REPUBLIC

Comunidad del Arca
Apdo. 1104
Santo Domingo
Tel: (809) 547 3543

FRANCE

Aigrefoin
78470 St Rémy les Chevreuses
Tel: (1) 30 52 21 07

L'Arc-en-ciel
11 rue François Mouthon
75015 Paris
Tel: (1) 45 32 83 91 (H)
      (1) 42 50 06 48 (O)

L'Arche
BP 35
Trosly-Breuil
60350 Cuise-la-Motte
Tel: (1) 44 85 61 02

L'Atre
21 rue Obert
59118 Wambrechies
Tel: 20 78 81 52

Communauté de l'Arche
Ecorcheboeuf
76590 Anneville-sur-Scie
Tel: 35 04 40 31

Le Caillou Blanc
La Fabrique
Clohars Fouesnant
29118 Bénodet
Tel: 98 54 60 05

Le Levain
1 Place St Clément
60200 Compiègne
Tel: 44 86 25 03

La Merci
Courbillac
16200 Jarnac
Tel: 45 21 74 16

Moita
St Germain
26390 Hauterives
Tel: 75 68 81 84

Le Moulin de l'Auro
Route de Murs
84220 Gordes
Tel: 90 72 04 55

La Rebellerie
49560 Nueil-sur-Layon
Tel: 41 59 58 79

La Rose des Vents
Verpillières
80700 Roye
Tel: 22 87 10 83 (H)
      22 87 22 57 (O)

Les Sapins
Les Abels
Lignières-Sonneville
16130 Segonzac
Tel: 45 80 50 66

Le Sénevé
21 rue l'Abbé Larose
44190 Gorges
Tel: 40 06 96 23

Les Trois Fontaines
62164 Ambleteuse
Tel: 21 32 61 83

GERMANY

Arche Regenbogen
Apfelallee 23
4542 Tecklenburg
Tel: (49) 54 82 77 00

Arche Volksdorf
Farmsener Landstr. 198
D-2000 Hamburg 67
Tel: 040 603 71 22

HAITI

L'Arche de Carrefour
BP 11075
Carrefour
Port-au-Prince
Tel: 509 14 42 55

L'Arche Chantal
Zone des Cayes
CP 63 Cayes

HONDURAS

El Arca de Honduras
Apartado 1273
Tegucigalpa DF
Tel: 504 32 77 92

Comunidad del Arca
Casa san José
Apartado 241
Choluteca

INDIA

Asha Niketan
53/7 Bannerghatta Rd.
Bangalore 560029
Tel: (81) 64 03 49

Asha Niketan
308 Acharya P.C. Road
Calcutta 700009
Tel: (33) 35 6299

Asha Niketan
Nandi Bazaar P.O.
Katalur
Calicut DT
Kerala 673531

Asha Niketan
Kottivakkam
Tiruvanmiyur P.O.
Madras 600041
Tel: (44) 41 6298

IRELAND

L'Arche Cork
Green Park, Wilton Lawn
Wilton, Cork
Tel: 353 (21) 34 26 16

Moorfield House
Kilmoganny
Co. Kilkenny
Tel: 353 (56) 256 28

ITALY

Il Chicco
Via Ancona 1
00043 Ciampino
Roma
Tel: (39) 6 617 11 34 (H)
     (39) 6 727 21 04 (O)

IVORY COAST

L'Arche de Bouaké
04 BP 373
Bouaké 04
Tel: 225 63 44 53

MEXICO

Comunidad del Arca
Apartado Postale 55–232
Mexico DF 09000
Tel: (52) 855 64 57

PHILIPPINES

Ang Arko 'Punla'
307 D. Valencia Street
Nagtahan Sampaloc
Metro Manila
Tel: (63) 2 609 435

SPAIN

El Rusc
Lista de Correos
Tordera
Barcelona 008399
Tel: (93) 764 0150 (El Rusc)
       (93) 83 00 301 (Moia)

SWITZERLAND

La Corolle
26 Chemin d'Ecogia
1290 Versoix
Geneva
Tel: 41 (22) 55 5189

UNITED STATES

The Arch
402 South 4th Street
Clinton
Iowa 52732
Tel: (319) 243 3980 (H)
       (314) 243 9035 (O)

L'Arche Syracuse
1701 James Street
Syracuse, NY 13206
Tel: (315) 437 9337 (O)
       (315) 471 5862 (H)

Community of the Ark
2474 Ontario Road N.W.
Washington, DC 20009
Tel: (202) 462 3924

The Hearth
523 West 8th Street
Erie, Pa. 16502
Tel: (814) 459 4850 (H)
       (814) 452 2065 (O)

Hope
151 S. Ann Street
Mobile, Alabama 36604
Tel: (205) 438 6738 (H)
       438 2094(O)

Irenicon
73 Lamoille Avenue
Havenhill, Ma. 01830
Tel: (508) 374 6928 (O)
       374 9162 (H)

Lamb of God
1730 E. 70th Street
Cleveland, Ohio 44103
Tel: (216) 881 0682 (H)
       (216) 881 7015 (O)

L'Arche
9187 West 85th Street
Overland Park
Kansas, Missouri 66212
Tel: (913) 642 6070

Noah Sealth
816 15th Avenue East
Seattle, Wa. 98112
Tel: (206) 325 8912

Spokane Nazareth
E 3403 Farwell Road
Mead, Wa. 99021
Tel: (509) 466 9713

Tahoma Hope
The Farmhouse
11716 Vickery Road East
Tacoma, Wa. 98446
Tel: (206) 535 3171 (H)
       535 3178 (O)

UNITED KINGDOM

The Anchorage
127 Prescot Road
Liverpool L7 0LB
England
Tel: (51) 260 0422
     (51) 228 4247

L'Arche Bognor Regis
Emmaus
123 Longford Road
Bognor Regis
West Sussex PO21 1AE
England
Tel: (243) 86 3426 (O)

L'Arche Inverness
Braerannoch
13 Drummond Crescent
Inverness
Scotland
Tel: (463) 23 9615 (O)
     (463) 23 8921 (H)

L'Arche Kent
Little Ewell
Barfrestone, Dover
Kent CT15 7JJ
England
Tel: (304) 83 0930 (O)
     (304) 83 1090 (H)

Lambeth l'Arche
15 Norwood High Street
West Norwood
London SE27
England
Tel: (1) 670 6714 (O)

0181 - 670 - 9294

WEST BANK

Beit-al-Rafiq
B.P. 51214
Jerusalem
Israel

0181 :
Office - 670 6714